Wavelength

Intermediate • Teacher's Resource Book

Kathy
Burke

Ben
Rowdon

with

Lynne
Rushton

Contents

Skills	Wavelength pages
Speaking and writing: talking about and describing people Reading and listening: self-help books Listening and writing: television advertisement Listening: conversations	*Writing for work and pleasure 1* **Keep in touch!** Formal and informal language
Listening, speaking and writing: describing a city Listening: interview about living in a city and a description of a disastrous weekend Reading: extracts from modern books about cities Speaking and writing: inventing a short story	*Conversations* **Well, hello!** Greetings and starting conversations Showing interest, asking for clarification and checking Echo questions and statements
Listening, speaking and writing: describing a club / bar Listening and speaking: describing dilemmas and making decisions / offering advice Reading: theme restaurant web pages Writing: designing a theme restaurant	*Day to day English* **How about . . . ?** Making / talking about arrangements Making suggestions and talking about preferences Present Continuous for fixed arrangements *Reading for pleasure 1* **Heat wave** Exercises on *Heat wave* from *Heat wave and other stories*
Reading: *Do great minds think alike?* Listening and speaking: describing jobs and abilities Speaking: job interviews Reading and listening: an actor tells his story Writing: a "rags to riches" success story	*Writing for work and pleasure 2* **I am writing to apply . . .** A CV and a job application letter
Listening: conversations in various venues Listening: conversations about art Speaking: presenting ideas for a community art project Reading: Andy Warhol Writing: describing the achievements of a famous person	*Conversations* **I'm not sure . . .** Language of doubt *Look / look like / look as if* Hesitation phrases Pron: stress and intonation
Listening, speaking and writing: describing clothes and talking about fashions Speaking: talking about the advantages / disadvantages of being rich and famous Listening: imagining a different life Writing: reporting the results of *My fantastic life* questionnaire Reading: *The History of Beauty*	*Day to day English* **If I were you . . .** Suggestions and advice *Reading for pleasure 2* **"Oh, really!"** Exercises on *"Oh, really!"* from *Heat wave and other stories*

Units	Grammar	Vocabulary / Pronunciation
(7) **Can we talk?** *page T58*	Past Perfect Simple Reported speech: *say, tell, ask*	Talking about means of communication Phrasal verbs and expressions for telephoning Pron: sentence stress
(8) **Life, death and the universe** *page T66*	*Will / going to* + infinitive for predicting Third Conditional	*Otherwise* and *in case* Pron: weak forms and linking in Third Conditional sentences
(9) **It's a family affair** *page T74*	*Should / shouldn't have done* *Wish / If only* + Past Perfect Simple Language of criticism Giving reasons and contrasting	Talking about family celebrations
Do you remember? **Units 7–9**	1 *Tell me more* 2 A sorry tale 3 *It's all your fault!* 4 Max's diary	
(10) **What's going on?** *page T84*	The Passive The Passive with *get* and indirect objects Negative questions Modal verbs for laws, rules and social behaviour Verb + *-ing* and verb + infinitive	Talking about news stories and crime Describing behaviour
(11) **The silver screen** *page T92*	*All, whole* and *every* Verb tenses for telling stories and jokes Reporting verbs	Talking about films and the cinema Describing film scenes
(12) **Taking off** *page T100*	Modal verbs of present and past deduction	Describing travel and holidays Pron: stress in modal verbs of deduction
Do you remember? **Units 10–12**	1 Disgrace! 2 *You could be telling the truth . . .* 3 A letter to the editor	

Photocopiable activities   *page T110*   **Progress tests**   *page T136*

Skills	Wavelength pages
Reading and speaking: *The funniest thing happened ...* Speaking: victims of a conman role-play Listening and speaking: leaving and taking telephone messages Speaking: narrating stories Reading and speaking: a phone maze role-play	*Writing for work and pleasure 3* **Guess what!** Telling a story
Reading: articles on predicting the future Listening: discussing predictions Speaking: predicting outcomes Reading and writing: a website about regrets	*Conversations* **Points of view** Persuading, refusing persuasion, giving opinions, agreeing / disagreeing, interrupting Pronunciation: stress and intonation for emphasis
Speaking and listening: family celebrations Reading: *American Beauty* film script and extract from *Bridget Jones's diary* Speaking: talking about parent / child relationships Listening: cross-cultural wedding Reading: wedding websites Speaking: criticising actions and expressing regret	*Day to day English* **Isn't it?** Question tags for checking information and asking for agreement Pron: intonation in question tags *Reading for pleasure 3* **Dear Sue** Exercises on *Dear Sue* from *Heat wave and other stories*
Reading: newspaper extracts Listening and speaking: news broadcast Reading and listening: *The end of a career?* Speaking: discussing illegal and anti-social behaviour Writing: expressing an opinion on a law or rule	*Writing for work and pleasure 4* **On the other hand ...** Writing a report
Listening: conversations Reading: memorable film moments Listening and speaking: describing a plot Listening, reading and writing: *The Lost House* film script Writing: a film review	*Conversations* **Well, actually I ...** Asking for permission and making / refusing requests politely Pron: stress and intonation to sound polite
Speaking: describing different types of travel Reading: *The art of travel* Listening and speaking: describing holidays from hell Speaking and listening: making deductions Speaking: holiday advice	*Day to day English* **Was it worth it?** Phrases / expressions for giving opinions and recommending, adding emphasis and giving contrasting opinions *Reading for pleasure 4* **Merry Christmas** Exercises on *Merry Christmas* from *Heat wave and other stories*

Introduction

Wavelength Intermediate

Wavelength Intermediate is the third level of a course for adult and young adult learners who have completed *Wavelength Elementary* and *Pre-Intermediate* or similar courses at these levels.

Course structure

Core material
- Approximately 96 hours: 12 units of 7–8 hours each.

Extra material
- **Photocopiable activities:** one for each unit and a song for Unit 9 onwards (in the Teacher's Resource Book).
- **Progress tests:** a test of 1½ hours after every 3 units (photocopiable in the Teacher's Resource Book).
- **Reader:** *Heat wave and other stories* (at the back of the Coursebook) and the **Reading for pleasure** pages after every 3 units (in the Coursebook).
- **Grammar reference** and **Grammar and vocabulary puzzles** (in the Coursebook).

Units
- There are 12 units of 8 pages each. The course is divided into 4 sections of 3 units each. The first 6 pages of each unit (the core unit) cover the main grammatical and vocabulary aims. The final pages in each unit are the *Wavelength* pages: **Writing for work and pleasure** (writing skills), **Conversations** (conversational strategies and expressions), **Day to day English** (functional and situational language). The *Wavelength* pages (which take approximately 1–1½ hours) are loosely linked by topic or language to the main unit but can be done separately without disrupting learning. After every 3 units there is a **Reading for pleasure** page (an extract from *Heat wave and other stories* with accompanying exercises) and 2 *Do you remember?* pages (classroom revision activities).

The course

Grammar
- The selection of grammar and related language is based on what students most frequently need for communication.
- Grammar is always presented in context using texts, recorded material and visuals.
- Forms and tenses are contrasted, e.g. Unit 1 contrasts *used to* and *would*.
- Students are encouraged to think about language use and work out rules by answering questions and filling in the Language Boxes.
- Controlled checking exercises as well as freer speaking and writing activities practise grammar in every unit.

Vocabulary
- All units have a specific lexical and topic area, e.g. people and relationships (Unit 1).
- The emphasis is on enriching students' vocabulary through the presentation of grammatical devices and frequently used vocabulary, phrases, expressions and phrasal verbs related to a broad topic area.
- Word building and collocation are focused on.
- There are **Word lists** for each unit on Coursebook page 122.

Pronunciation
- *Wavelength Intermediate* continues the work of *Wavelength*'s earlier levels on stress, intonation, weak forms and linking to encourage natural-sounding speech and develop effective listening skills. Importance is given to practice and recognition.

Skills

Speaking
- *Wavelength Intermediate* constantly provides students with the opportunity to speak in pair and group work. In addition to the speaking activities in the core units, **Conversations**, **Day to day English** and the *Do you remember?* pages contain speaking practice to increase students' communicative effectiveness and confidence.

Listening
- Listening activities linked to the unit topic in every unit include authentic, extensive and intensive listenings.
- Listening skills are developed by tasks where students anticipate context and listen only for important information.

Reading
- Every unit contains reading activities linked to the unit topic. A variety of authentic text types develops students' reading skills and increases their reading speed.
- The **Reader** *Heat wave and other stories* gives further reading practice and encourages students to read extensively. A CD of the **Reader** is available.
- The **Reading for pleasure** pages in the Coursebook and the recorded extracts on the Class cassette / CD introduce each story and provide exercise material to exploit them.

Writing
- Every unit contains a writing activity to consolidate the language covered.
- The **Writing for work and pleasure** pages develop writing skills related to formal / informal letters, CVs, letters of application, narratives and reports, e.g. organisation, format, typical formal and informal expressions and linkers.

Teacher's Resource Book
- The Teacher's Resource Book contains clear and concise teaching notes, keys, language notes and alternative procedures for different-sized classes. There are also Optional extra teaching ideas to extend the Coursebook.
- **Make Your Life Easier!** pages of ideas and suggestions for the teacher are included.
- 13 **Photocopiable activities** with instructions provide practice and revision of skills, grammar and vocabulary.
- There are 4 photocopiable **Progress tests** with instructions and keys.

Workbook
- There are 12 units corresponding to the Coursebook units which reinforce and give further practice of the structures and language the students have studied.
- A Workbook cassette / CD accompanies the Workbook.
- There are also 8 **Extend your reading** pages, 4 **Extend your grammar** pages and 4 **Extend your writing** pages. These optional pages offer students more challenging practice in reading and writing skills and structures.

We hope your students enjoy using *Wavelength Intermediate*!

Make Your Life Easier!

Ideas and teaching tips on getting the most out of *Wavelength Intermediate*. See also *Wavelength Elementary* and *Wavelength Pre-Intermediate* Make your Life Easier! pages.

Exploiting your Coursebook

Your Coursebook is a rich source of materials and ideas which you can use to interest and motivate your students.

Pictures and photos
Use the pictures and photos to activate known language and / or teach new lexis.

➤ Encourage students to focus on a picture by making sure that they've got a piece of card or paper to cover the surrounding text. Then ask students to **describe the picture** in as much detail as possible.

➤ In pairs / teams. Students **brainstorm all the familiar words in the picture** as a competition. Give them 3 minutes, for example, to write down all the words. The winners are the pair / team with the most correct words.

➤ Ask students to **build up profiles of the people pictured**, e.g. *She looks very intelligent.*

➤ Students **match a list of words / phrases to the picture**. The lexis can be both known and new. This activity is often part of an exercise in the Coursebook, but you can also use it with other pictures.

➤ Ask students to **compare the situation in the picture with their own reality**.

➤ In pairs. Students **guess what happened before or what will happen after** the scene illustrated.

➤ Use the pictures for a memory game. In AB pairs. Ask Student A to look at a picture for one minute and then give the Coursebook to Student B. Tell Student A to describe the picture from memory. Student B listens and checks.

Reading and listening texts
➤ Before asking students to read or listen, do as much as you can to **activate their knowledge of the topic**. This will make understanding of the text much easier and build their confidence.

➤ Ask students to **predict what they're going to read or listen to**. For example, brainstorm and write on the board things that students are sure of / things they aren't sure of / things they would like to know.

Or give students key words and phrases from the text on the board / OHT to predict what the text is about. They then listen / read to check.

➤ Vary the way you approach texts. For example:
- **Cut up the text into paragraphs** or small blocks of text and ask students to put it in order.
- **Remove the first sentence of each paragraph**. Give students the sentences. Students then match the sentences to the paragraphs.
- **Write the first sentence of the text on the board / OHT**. Ask students to read the sentence and to predict what the text is about. You can also do this with individual paragraphs.
- Ask **students** to **write comprehension questions** for each other.
- Read the text aloud, stop at a word with a common collocation and ask **students** to **guess the next word or phrase**.
- **Blank out language in the text**. Students can guess what the language is, or you can write the language on the board or on an OHT for them to match to the gaps. With listening texts, they can listen to find the missing words / phrases.
- Ask **students** to **choose 3 or 4 words / phrases they don't know**, look them up and teach them to each other.

➤ Use **texts as models for writing and speaking tasks**. Analyse the organisation of the original and note any useful language / phrases. Students then produce their own piece of writing or dialogue, which can be put up in the class for everyone to read or act out.

➤ **Analyse listening texts** for sentence stress, intonation and connected speech. Initially recognition is more important than production. Let the students control the tape recorder / CD player sometimes to replay parts of a recording as many times as they need.

➤ Use the **Reading for pleasure** pages to whet students' appetites for the stories in the Reader. Encourage students to read other graded readers from levels 3 and 4 of the *Penguin Readers* series.

Energising and bonding activities

Energising activities which get students out of their seats are useful to get students "in the mood" when they first arrive or to change the pace at different stages in the lesson. Use a variety of interaction patterns in these activities, e.g. pairs, groups or large teams. Bonding activities where students work collaboratively create good relationships within the group. If students find their lessons enjoyable and feel close to their colleagues, their motivation will also increase.

Several of the following activities are for recycling vocabulary. You can simply make lists of lexis to practise or you can use a "vocabulary bag". This is a collection of vocabulary items, compiled by the students. For how to organise one, see "Encouraging student independence" on page x.

➤ *Change places if . . .*
This is good for practising tenses. Students sit on chairs in a circle with bags and books put away and no spare chairs. You can demonstrate first. Stand in the middle of the circle and say, for example, *Change places if you have had lunch today / have been to the cinema this week / have ever flown in a plane.* All students who have done the thing mentioned have to get up and run to sit in a different place, including you. (You can then join in or sit out to monitor, as preferred.) The student left in the middle must ask the next question. The activity can continue until all students have had a turn or they're starting to get tired of it. Other tenses can be used, e.g. the Present Simple: *Change places if you like chocolate / play football / go the cinema once a week;* the Past Simple: *. . . if you went to the cinema last weekend / played football yesterday;* going to: *. . . you're going to play football this weekend / see your friends,* etc.

➤ Running dictation
Number each sentence of the text and write it on a piece of paper. Put the sentences in different places round the room and make sure the students can't read them from their seats. Tell the students how many sentences there are and explain that they have to copy them perfectly. In pairs: a writer and a runner. Writers stay in their seats. Runners go and read one sentence, then come back and tell the writer what to write. The runners can look at the sentences as many times as they want. The first pair with the correct sentences wins.

➤ Reading race
Display short reading texts round the class. In AB pairs. Give Student A a worksheet with questions about the texts. Student A reads out the first question and Student B goes round the class and reads each of the texts quickly to find the answer. Student B tells Student A the answer. Student A then writes the answer on the worksheet and reads out the next question. When Student B has found the answers to half the questions, they swap. The first pair to answer the questions correctly wins.

➤ Alphabet brainstorm
Use this activity to lead into a topic area. For example, if the topic is sports, students have to shout out a sport beginning with each letter of the alphabet from *A* to *Z.*

➤ Back to the board
For this vocabulary activity, divide students into teams of 4–5 and give them (or let them choose) names or letters: Team A, B, etc. Then number the students 1, 2, 3. Number 1 from Team A sits in a chair with their back to the board. Then you write a word / phrase on the board (either from the bag or just from a list you have made). Team A must then help Student 1 to guess it. They should first consult and then can give definitions or examples, do a mime, etc. For example, *You can use it to eat soup.* Answer: *spoon.* If the student guesses the word / phrase correctly, the team gets a point. The team with the highest number of points wins.

➤ Shout
This and the following activity, "Jump", may appeal to younger students. You can use this activity in any question-and-answer stage of a lesson, for example, for checking answers to an exercise or for a warmer when students exchange personal news about their weekend, holiday, etc. Put students into pairs, with the 2 partners, A and B, sitting as far away as possible from each other. Ask students to shout their questions and answers across the room to their partners. Give instructions so that sometimes the As have to ask the question and sometimes the Bs. This activity is noisy but fun and can help restless, energetic students to let off steam. Obviously it may not be suitable in some situations where it may disturb other classes.

Energising and bonding activities continued

➤ Jump

This activity checks students' comprehension of many areas of language. Ask students to stand in a line or lines and to jump to the left or right in response to *Yes / No* questions about, for example, opinions, likes and dislikes. They can do the same to show if statements are true or false or to distinguish between 2 alternatives. For example, you can check students' knowledge of countable and uncountable nouns by reading out examples. Students have to jump to the left if the word is countable and to the right if it's uncountable. You could check their understanding of word classes, tenses, collocations and even features of pronunciation in this way.

➤ Standing discussion

For a short discussion activity, stick up controversial statements about a topic round the classroom. For example, if the topic is education, you could put up statements like *All schools should be single sex* or *Exams should be abolished.* Ask students to walk round reading all the statements and decide which one they want to discuss most. Then tell them to go and stand next to that statement and discuss it with other interested students. Set a time limit for the discussion.

➤ Questionnaire

Writing questionnaires is a very useful activity for monolingual classes as it stimulates students to produce something together in English. You may have an obvious topic for the questionnaire or you can brainstorm possible topics. You can also create a class questionnaire by brainstorming some questions and then asking students to contribute more. Each student has to devise at least one question. Then students ask each other all the questions and report back on their findings. You could ask them to write a short report on the results and / or they could interview other classes.

You can do a shorter version of this activity by using a questionnaire which you've already prepared. Cut the questionnaire up into individual questions and give one to each student. Then tell each student to ask the others in the class for their opinions and to note down the results. When all the questions have been asked, students pool their results. They can then summarise them in writing.

➤ Noughts and crosses

Draw a noughts and crosses grid on the board. In 2 teams. Toss a coin to see who starts. You read out a word / phrase. The team consults to decide on the meaning or on a sentence which includes the word / phrase. If students can't give the meaning or a sentence, the other team tries. When students give a correct answer they, or you, can add a nought or cross to where they want it on the grid. The team that gets a line of noughts or crosses first wins.

➤ Word search

Write words you want to revise in a square, horizontally, vertically and diagonally, on a piece of paper. Then fill in the gaps with other letters. Individually or in pairs, students find the words within a time limit. The winner is the one with the most words. Students can also make their own word search boxes to test each other.

➤ Dictagloss

You read a short extract from a text at natural speed only twice. The first time, students just listen. The second time, they can make notes and write key words. In groups: they pool ideas, rewriting the text as closely as possible to the original. They then check their version with the original (perhaps on an OHT) and you say which differences are acceptable or not.

➤ Mini-tests

In groups of 3–4. Students select a few words / phrases which they think are important. (3–4 are usually enough.) They then write one question for each word / phrase to ask the other groups, e.g. a sentence with a gap, a definition of a word. Monitor students. Students then pass the questions to the other groups to answer. Feedback with the class. The winning group is the one with the most right answers.

➤ Storytelling

Give, or let the students pick out, 5–6 random words from the vocabulary bag (see page x) or their general knowledge. They then work in groups and have a time limit within which to write a story incorporating all the words. The story is read out to the class, who have to shout out when they hear a word from the bag. Students could also write dialogues using the words, rehearse them and act them out for the class.

Encouraging student independence

If students feel at least partly responsible for their own learning they're more likely to be motivated to continue. To build a sense of involvement and responsibility you can raise their awareness of what they're learning and show them ways to develop their language learning outside the classroom.

Understanding learning

➤ **State your aims**, both short and long term, for the lesson and for the next month / course.

➤ Ask **students** to **reflect on what they've learnt** at the end of every lesson or series of lessons. They can summarise to you verbally or write it in their learner diaries (diaries they keep to record their experiences as a learner). You can collect the diaries every week and write in them, too.

➤ To help students to use a wider range of learning strategies, give them a **list of ways we study and learn** outside the classroom as well as inside. For example, sticking post-its with new lexis round their bedrooms, watching films in English, listening to music, surfing the Internet or keeping vocabulary books. They can discuss ways they use and choose a new way to try out.

➤ Whenever possible, explain your methodology to **help students understand the strategies you use**. For example, for reading and listening, encourage them not to try to understand every word but to get the general idea or gist. Looking up every unknown word in a dictionary is often very discouraging for students and they get bored.

Using dictionaries

➤ If possible, teach students to use a **monolingual dictionary** which is suitable for their level. For intermediate students an ideal dictionary is the *Longman WordWise Dictionary*. Show students that dictionaries don't only explain the meanings of words, they also give information about pronunciation, grammar, collocations and register. Make sure that students understand the abbreviations and phonetic symbols used.

Developing vocabulary

➤ Show students how to organise their vocabulary in **vocabulary notebooks**, either alphabetically, in topic groups or in word maps. Students can include example sentences with new words. They can write the vocabulary into their notebooks in class or make notes in class and write the vocabulary up at home.

➤ Use **word maps** to highlight areas of vocabulary that go together, e.g. lexical sets, word families or common collocations.

➤ Encourage students to do **a few minutes of vocabulary revision every day** as this is much more valuable than an hour every week or just before a test.

➤ Students can make **vocabulary posters** which can be left on the walls for peripheral learning.

➤ **Vocabulary bags / boxes** are extremely useful for helping students to take more responsibility for learning new lexis. Students take it in turns to choose 5–6 vocabulary items from each lesson and at home they write them on slips of paper or cards that you provide. They should include the word, its meaning, phonemic transcription, part of speech and an example of the way it is used in a sentence, e.g. *shy /ʃaɪ/ adjective. Nervous about talking to other people, especially people you don't know. He was so shy that he didn't say anything.* Encourage them to select words they like or think are particularly useful.

The student brings the slips of paper or card back the following lesson, you check them and pass them round for everybody to see. Then put them in a box, large envelope or plastic bag, which can be kept permanently in the classroom. Students are usually very motivated by this, not least because they're usually surprised by how little they remember!

➤ Encourage students to do **personal reviews of vocabulary** by taking the cards or bags home.

Developing reading and writing skills

➤ Encourage students to read graded readers from *Penguin Readers* levels 3 and 4.

➤ Give students an individual research project which involves reading and writing in English. You can give them complete freedom of choice of topic, but stipulate that at least some of their sources are in English. Ask them to bring in their work at intervals for you to see. For example, at the planning stage, first draft, second draft, etc.

➤ Encourage students to write reviews of films, books, CDs and websites. Display students' reviews in the classroom.

➤ Students can write regularly to other students as pen friends or "mouse-pals" (e-mail correspondents). If they've got access to the Internet, they can communicate in writing with other students in discussion areas such as those offered on the Longman website at www.longman-elt.com.

Feedback and error correction

The amount of feedback and the way you give it can build students' confidence and maintain their motivation. If students also have an opportunity to give you feedback on the course, they feel involved in it in a more active way.

➤ Ask **students to correct themselves and each other** in a supportive atmosphere. They can compare their answers in pairs or small groups before you feedback with the whole class.

➤ Write answers on the board / OHT so **students can check their own, or even each other's, work**. As students often have very different problems, they can help each other with wrong answers. You can also monitor and give help to those who don't understand why an answer is wrong. You will also be able to see how generalised the problem is before you feedback with the class.

➤ If a student makes a mistake while speaking during a class activity with an accuracy focus, **prompt the student to self-correct** or ask other students to help rather than correcting the mistake yourself. Prompting techniques include things like repeating the sentence up to the mistake, facial or hand gestures, repeating the mistake with a quizzical intonation or using terminology like "tense?", "preposition?".

➤ During a freer speaking activity, **note down examples of good language and any recurring or important errors**. You can focus on these afterwards or in the next lesson. You could write the errors on the board / OHT or make a worksheet. Students correct the errors in pairs before the class feedback.

➤ A motivating way of doing error correction is through an **auction** activity. Prepare a worksheet with some correct sentences and others containing errors. Individually, students select the correct sentences they want to buy. Each student gets a sum of money, e.g. £1,000. Students then bid against each other for the sentence. The winner is the student with the most correct sentences or the most money left over, if there is a tie.

➤ **Mark extended written work with a code**, e.g. *G* for grammar mistake, *Sp* for spelling, *WO* for word order, *P* for punctuation, *V* for vocabulary.

➤ **Spend class time on students correcting mistakes made in written homework.** Without this there is a tendency for students to look at their mark, put the paper in a file and never look at it again. Often students are able to correct their own mistakes, which is very motivating. They can consult you if they've got problems, or better still, their colleagues.

Assessing progress

At intermediate level students can often feel that progress is slow which is very demotivating. Reviewing their progress with them and encouraging them to do so themselves can be very helpful.

➤ Have **regular review slots**, perhaps as individual tutorials, while the rest of the class is working on something else.

➤ Provide **continuous assessment** by setting a fixed number of compulsory homework tasks. Distinguish these from optional ones which students can do if they like. Marks for continuous assessment can be recorded with test marks to give students a more realistic picture of their progress.

➤ **Assessment of class work** can also be done periodically on speaking, listening and reading skills, as well as via informal vocabulary tests.

➤ Give students an **"Assessing progress / planning future work"** sheet on which they note at the end of each unit, for example, some things that they found easy and others that were difficult. These might be reading or listening, a grammar point or an aspect of pronunciation. They then write on the sheet how they can improve in this area in the next 2 or 3 weeks. For example, they could borrow a reader from the self-access centre or library, listen to English on the radio or do some extra exercises on the grammar point. They then tick off the problem areas when they feel they've improved.

➤ Give students a **retrospective timetable** to remind them of what's been covered and how much they've learnt. They can also refer to these in relation to their "Assessing progress / planning future work" sheets.

① *It takes all sorts*

Grammar / structures	Present Perfect Simple (general past experience and with *for* and *since*); Past Simple (details about past experience and with time expressions); *used to / would* + infinitive (past finished habits / states)
Topic / vocabulary	Describing mood, character and appearance
Pronunciation	Stress and intonation in questions
Wavelength pages	**Writing for work and pleasure 1** *Keep in touch!*: writing formal and informal letters

Coursebook page 6

Is this seat free?

1 a) Warmer
- Keep this introduction to descriptions of mood and character light-hearted and brief.
- In the class feedback elicit reasons why students chose to sit next to a particular passenger.

Optional extras
Before 1b) Pronunciation: word stress
- With books closed, write the words in the Word Box for Exercise 1b) on the board without the stress marks. In pairs. Students write down the words and underline the stressed syllable in each word.
- Students open their books and check their answers using the stress marks. You could point out that the second syllable in *interesting* /ˈɪntrɪstɪŋ/ isn't pronounced.
- Practise the pronunciation of all the words with the class.

b) Speaking: practice
- Elicit one or two sentences about the people with the whole class using *He / She looks* + adjective, e.g. *She looks strange.* Remind students of the structures *look* + adjective and *look like* + noun.
- Tell students not to say which person they're describing when they work in groups.
- In the feedback encourage students to use other adjectives not in the Word Box to describe the different people.

2 a) 🎧 1 (Recording script Coursebook page 147)
Listening: to check
- Set the scene by telling students about a particularly interesting, nice or irritating person you sat next to on a journey.

- In pairs. Encourage students to speculate in detail about the situation.
- Before playing the recording ask *Do you think they know each other? Why? / Why not? How does the man feel? What makes you say that?*, etc. Write summaries of students' ideas and predictions on the board.
- Play the recording. Then feedback and compare students' answers with their predictions.

> **Key** The 2 people at the back of the bus don't know each other. The man feels uncomfortable because he doesn't want to talk to the woman. The woman is trying to find out if she's met the man before.

b) 🎧 1 (Recording script Coursebook page 147)
Listening: gap fill
- Play the recording twice if necessary.
- Feedback with the class.

> **Key** **1 Have** you **ever been** to India? **2 Have** you **travelled** much? **3** Where **have** you **been**? **4** When **did** you **go** there? **5 Did** you **go** on safari?

Pronunciation: stress and intonation in questions

3 a) Pronunciation: revision
- Remind students of the importance of stress and intonation in both speaking and listening. Do the example with the class:
  Have we <u>met</u> be<u>fore</u>? ↗
- In pairs. Students underline the stressed words / syllables and mark the intonation with arrows.
- In the feedback, write the questions on the board. Ask individuals to underline the stressed words / syllables and to mark the direction of the intonation. Ask the class if they agree but don't feedback or you'll pre-empt Exercise 3b).

b) ⟨oo⟩2 **Listening: to check**
- After the class feedback drill the sentences but keep the pace fast and the atmosphere light.
- Before students read the Language Box try to elicit which words are usually stressed and which words aren't usually stressed in spoken English. Remind them that stressing the information words is common to all sentences in English, not only questions.
- Tell students they mustn't expect to hear all the unstressed words. Play the recording again and focus on the unstressed words.

> **Recording script / Key**
>
> 1 Have you ever been to India? ↗ 2 Have you travelled much? ↗ 3 Where have you been? ↘
> 4 When did you go there? ↘ 5 Did you go on safari? ↗

> **Coursebook page 7**

Present Perfect Simple and Past Simple
4 a) Presentation
- Feedback and ask students to name the tenses of the verbs used in the questions in Exercise 2b). Remind students of the form of some irregular Present Perfect Simple and Past Simple verbs, e.g. *He **took** all the money from my account* and *He's **taken** all my money.*
- Point out that we can't use the Present Perfect Simple with finished past times (*yesterday,* etc.) but we can use it with unfinished times (*today,* etc.). Check students understand that the Present Perfect Simple is used for experience where the time is unfinished or isn't specified; the Past Simple is used when the time in the past is mentioned or when we give details of a specific past event. Elicit sentences to illustrate this, e.g. *Mark's broken his leg* (which focuses on the experience) and *He broke it when he went skiing in Austria* (which gives details about the particular experience).
- You could reassure students that the choice between the Present Perfect Simple and the Past Simple can be difficult even for expert speakers of English!

> **Key**   1 = questions 1, 2, 3 (Present Perfect Simple)   2 = questions 4 and 5 (Past Simple)

b) Grammar: practice
- Feedback on the full form of the sentences.
- **Language note:** highlight the tendency in spoken English to use short answers or to give only the necessary information in short incomplete sentences when answering questions.

> **Key**   1 No, I haven't ever been to India.   2 Well, yes, I've travelled a bit.   3 Well . . . I've been to Europe . . . Africa.   4 I went there 2 years ago.
> 5 Yes, I went on safari.

c) Grammar: practice
- Ask students to do this work individually and then compare their answers in pairs.
- Don't feedback or you'll pre-empt Exercise 4d).

d) ⟨oo⟩3 **Listening: to check**
- Play the recording. In the feedback draw attention to the example. Point out that *I've travelled* (Present Perfect Simple) is correct because the woman is only mentioning the experience, not when it happened. Ask students to explain why they chose the Present Perfect Simple or the Past Simple in answers 1–6.

> **Key**   1 I've been   2 I first visited   3 I've been
> 4 I've never been   5 I wanted   6 I didn't have

I know I know you!
5 a) Speaking: practice
- If your students are from very different parts of the world and haven't travelled much, adapt the exercise so that they try to find a place they've both been to in the area where they're studying, e.g. a museum, club, department store, etc.
- Go through the example questions with the whole class and elicit alternative questions, e.g. *Have you ever visited . . . ? How long were you there? What did you buy?* Encourage students to have conversations which sound as natural as possible and remind them to use polite intonation.
- Remind students to keep their conversations to details of places they've been to.

b) Speaking: practice
- After working in groups, ask students to feedback with interesting or unusual examples.
- Refer students to the Grammar reference on pages 111 and 112 for information on the Past Simple and the Present Perfect Simple.

Coursebook page 8

Friends and family

6 a) ●●4 (Recording script Coursebook page 147)
Listening: for gist

- Pre-teach / check that students understand *acquaintance, colleague, member (of a family)*.
- Explain to students that they're going to hear 5 telephone conversations but that they'll only hear one of the 2 speakers, Beth.
- Ask students to listen once and compare answers in pairs. Then play the conversations again for students to confirm their answers. Feedback.

> **Key** **b)** = 5   **c)** = 4   **d)** = 3   **e)** = 2

b) Reading: matching

- Students work individually. Tell them to use the categories a–e (an acquaintance, etc.) from Exercise 6a).
- Students compare answers in pairs. Don't feedback or you'll pre-empt Exercise 6c).

c) ●●4 (Recording script Coursebook page 147)
Listening: to check

- Play the recording again so students can check their answers from Exercise 6b). Feedback.
- Students work in pairs to explain the sentences in Exercise 6b) in their own words. Play the recording again if necessary.
- In the feedback let the students give their own explanations to show they understand the sentences. Encourage them to refer to the context in which the sentences are used.

> **Key** **1** her best friend   **2** a member of her family   **3** her boyfriend   **4** a colleague   **5** an acquaintance   **6** a member of her family   **7** her best friend   **8** a colleague   **9** an acquaintance   **10** her boyfriend

After 6c) Writing: practice

- Ask students to choose one of Beth's conversations from Recording script 4 on page 147. Tell students to complete the conversation by writing what the other speaker says. Ask students to write out the whole conversation for homework.

Present Perfect Simple with *for* and *since*

7 a) ●●5 Listening: gap fill

- Feedback with the whole class. Leave discussion of *for* and *since* until Exercise 7b).

> **Key** **2** been like this   **3** known each other   **4** been together

b) Presentation

- Use the sentences and the questions about the sentences to highlight the use of the Present Perfect Simple for a situation or state which began in the past and still continues / is still true in the present.
- **Language note:** highlight that many languages express the same idea using a present tense. Point out or elicit possible problems / typical errors, e.g. *I've known her for five years* **NOT** *~~I know~~ her for five years.*
- Give other examples with *for* and *since*, e.g. *I've lived in my flat for four years / since 1998.*
- Refer students to the Grammar reference on page 112 for information on the Present Perfect Simple with *for* and *since*.

> **Key** **2** Yes, she is.   **3** Yes, she does.   **4** Yes, they are.
> **Language Box:** We use **for** with a period of time. We use **since** with a point in time (when the period began).

c) Writing: practice

- **Language note:** before students write the sentences point out that ***get** married = the act of getting married* and ***be** married = the state of being married.*
- Use the example to focus on the change of verb to the Present Perfect Simple and the use of *for* or *since*. Elicit the past participles of the verbs in the Word Box and do sentence 1 with the class if you feel students need more help. Point out that students must use all the verbs in the Word Box.
- Feedback with the whole class.

> **Key** **1** They've been Buddhists for a year.
> **2** He's worked here since he left university.
> **3** He's had his car for a few months.   **4** They've been married since 1997.   **5** He's lived in Rome since his wife died.

8 a) Writing: practice

- As students write, check they're using the Present Perfect Simple to describe states or situations which began in the past and still continue / are still true in the present.
- **Language note:** if students ask about the difference between *live* and *work* in the Present Perfect Simple or Present Perfect Continuous form, explain briefly that the 2 verbs can be used in either tense without a big difference in meaning. However the use of a Continuous tense can give a more temporary feel, i.e. *I've been living in a hotel since I arrived here. It doesn't feel that long to me. I don't plan to stay forever.* The use of the Present Perfect Continuous is covered in Unit 5 but you could refer students to the Grammar reference on page 113.

b) Speaking: practice

- Encourage students to ask as many questions as possible about the sentences.
- Make a note of errors and correct them in the feedback after the group activity.

Nice or *nasty?*

9 a) Vocabulary: practice

- Students work individually. Draw attention to the example in sentence 1 and point out that Sue is self-confident because she seems to feel so good about herself.
- In the whole class feedback ask students to justify their answers.

> **Key   2** unsociable   **3** two-faced   **4** out-going
> **5** insensitive   **6** generous   **7** hard-working
> **8** impatient

b) Vocabulary: practice

- Students work individually and fill in the table in their notebooks. When they finish, ask students to discuss any differences and agree on a final table in groups of 4.
- Feedback and discuss any differences between groups' tables. Point out that *sensitive* (= *aware of other people's needs and feelings*) is usually considered a positive trait unless you're oversensitive, and highlight that *shy* (= *modest and unassertive*) can be considered positive in certain people / situations.

- At the end of the activity, emphasise the importance of keeping organised vocabulary notes. Encourage students to categorise words by theme / meaning and grammar (verb, noun, etc.).

> **Key**
>
> | | Positive | Negative |
> |---|---|---|
> | 2 | sociable | unsociable |
> | 3 | sincere | two-faced |
> | 4 | out-going | shy |
> | 5 | sensitive | insensitive |
> | 6 | generous | mean |
> | 7 | hard-working | lazy |
> | 8 | patient | impatient |

I know so many people . . .

10 a) Speaking: preparation

- Tell students that they're going to find out information about each other's lives.
- In pairs: Student A and Student B. Students read their information. Remind them not to look at each other's page.
- Draw 4 boxes on the board. Write the name of the place where you were born in box 1 and the number of years you've been a teacher in box 2.
- Tell the students to ask you questions to find out what the name of the place and the number represent. Encourage the students to ask you questions to find out more about the information in each box.
- Tell students to choose people / places / things they can easily talk about. Monitor as students fill in their boxes individually.

b) Speaking: practice

- Go through the example with the class.
- In pairs. Encourage students to ask questions to find out as much as they can. As students work, make notes of common errors.
- Ask a number of students to feedback to the class on the information they found out.
- Feedback on some of the linguistic errors and elicit corrections.

c) Writing: practice

- Remind students of the adjectives / structures presented in this unit. Elicit a short example description from students. Write it on the board.
- Ask students to write a description for homework. When students bring their work to class, ask them to swap with a partner and proofread each other's description before giving it in.

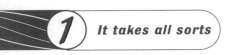

You can do it!

11 a) Warmer

- Tell students to read the titles of the books. Help with vocabulary as necessary.
- Elicit the kind of book. If students don't know the phrase *self-help books*, accept reasonable definitions, e.g. *books to help you as a person* and then teach the term *self-help*.
- Ask students if they've read, heard about or like any of these books but don't discuss the books in detail or you'll pre-empt later exercises.

b) Reading: matching

- Teach *blurb*. Students work individually.
- Feedback. Students justify their answers.

> **Key** 1 = c) 2 = d) 3 = b) 4 = a)

c) Vocabulary: matching

- Students work individually. They then check their answers in groups. Feedback.

> **Key** 1 deal with 2 improve 3 assertive
> 4 exhausted 5 wind down 6 keep calm
> 7 crisis 8 expert 9 proven 10 techniques

After 11c) Writing: practice

- Write on the board:
  One-Minute Stress Management
  It's for people who're always stressed and can't sleep. They want to learn how to relax and feel stronger emotionally and calmer.
- In pairs. Ask students to write 2 sentences for books 2–4 explaining the target audience and the aspect of the readers' lives the book aims to improve.
- When pairs finish, ask them to compare sentences with another pair. Then feedback.

---

d) 🎧6 (Recording script Coursebook page 147)
Listening: for gist

- Tell students that these are ordinary people talking. Play the recording twice.
- After the feedback play the second recording again. Elicit / point out *keep my head straight* (= *stay calm and organised*) and *if I let the stress get to me* (= *if I let the stress affect me*).

> **Key** 1 *How To Make Anyone Fall In Love With You:* he doesn't think anybody needs this kind of book because you can't make other people fall in love with you. 2 *One-Minute Stress Management:* she thinks that she would find this book useful. 3 *Don't Say 'Yes' When You Want To Say 'No':* she thinks this book would make her life so much simpler as it would give her the confidence to know what to say and how to deal with situations when she says yes when she wants to say no.

e) Speaking: practice

- Feedback after the group discussions. Do students know any funny or inspiring stories about books which have changed their or other people's lives?

Another satisfied customer
Used to / would + infinitive

12 a) 🎧7 (Recording script Coursebook page 147)
Listening: for gist

- Focus on the picture. Explain that American infomercials are extended commercials in which the developer of a product (the author of a book, a famous film star, etc.) talks to several "users" who say how the product has changed their lives.
- Build up students' interest in the topic. Ask *Do advertisers in your country use infomercials or similar techniques to try to sell their products?*
- Students read the titles. Elicit / give the meaning of *slow lane, respect* and *get rid of*.
- Play the recording twice if necessary. Feedback.

> **Key** The ad is about 4 *Queen of the House.*

b) 🎧8 (Recording script Coursebook page 147)
Listening: for detail

- Play the recording twice. After the first listening students compare answers in pairs. Feedback with the class after the second listening.

> **Key** 1 Her husband and kids. 2 She used to cook supper, wash the dishes and clean the house. 3 The little voice used to say "Say no! Don't do it!" 4 Everything is different. They're all much happier together and love each other.

c) 🔘 8 (Recording script Coursebook page 147)

Listening: gap fill

* Pre-teach *slave*. Ask students to try to fill in the gaps before they listen to the recording.
* Play the recording. Students check answers.
* If students ask about the difference between the use of *used to* and *would* during feedback, explain that this point will be covered in Exercise 12d).

> **Key** 1 would / 'd, wouldn't, used to 2 used to, would / 'd 3 used to, would / 'd 4 used to, didn't use to 5 used to 6 used to

d) Presentation: *used to / would* + infinitive

* Feedback. Then use the sentences in Exercise 12c) to explain that we use *used to* + infinitive to talk about past habits and states that aren't true anymore. We use *would* ('d) to avoid repeating *used to* again and again. Point out that we can't use *would* for states, e.g. **I used to** *have a lot of problems* NOT ~~I would~~ *have a lot of problems*.
* Focus on the form / use of *not . . . anymore* and *not . . . any longer* and on how the phrases can be shortened.
* Refer students to the Grammar reference on page 111 for information on *used to / would* + infinitive.

> **Key** not anymore not any longer

After 12d) Grammar: practice

* Ask students to write 3 true sentences about how they've improved as they've got older and 3 true sentences about how they've got worse as they've got older. Tell them to use *used to* + infinitive and *not . . . anymore* or *not . . . any longer*, e.g. *I used to get up early when I was young but I don't anymore. I used to be insecure when I was a child but I'm not any longer.*
* In groups. Students take it in turns to read their sentences.
* In the feedback ask a student from each group to report what one student in his / her group said without giving the person's name. The rest of the class guesses which student said each sentence.

After 12d) Photocopiable activities

* See 1 *Who is the real Lord Slimey?*, page T110.

---

13 a) Speaking: preparation

* Give students an overview of the eventual task: they're going to write a TV ad for their book.
* Monitor as students work in pairs. Help with ideas and vocabulary as necessary.

b) Speaking: preparation / Writing: practice

* Tell the students to divide their ad into 2 parts. In part 1 the author introduces the satisfied reader. The satisfied reader says how wonderful the author's book is and gives one or two examples. In part 2 the author interviews the reader. The reader says how horrible their past life was and how his / her life has changed because of the author's book.
* Remind students to use *used to / would* + infinitive and *not anymore / any longer* in their ad.
* Emphasise that the ads should be persuasive and the authors blatant about promoting their book and controlling or prompting readers. Help students write their scripts and include author's obvious and biased prompt questions, e.g. *So how has this book changed your life? Why did your life use to be so awful? Tell us, why is your life so wonderful now?* Focus on the reader's enthusiastic praise of the book and their descriptions of how wonderful their life is now after reading it, e.g. *This book has helped me so much. Life is much better since I read your book. When I read your book, I learned how to solve my problem.* Tell the students to read Recording scripts 7 and 8 for more ideas.
* Monitor pairs and help them to write their script by prompting them with specific questions, e.g. *What kind of problems does the book try to solve? What problems did this reader use to have?* Check students are using the target language (*used to, would, not anymore / any longer*).

c) Speaking: practice

* Pairs practise their ads. Tell them they can read their scripts and pretend that they're autocues (machines which display TV scripts). Reassure students that infomercials can be artificial and tell them not to worry if their ad doesn't sound realistic or true-to-life.
* With smaller classes, pairs act out their ads for the class. With larger classes, divide the class into groups of about 10 and ask pairs to act out their ads for the group. Make notes of errors.
* Ask students to choose the most persuasive ad. Feedback on important errors but don't let this detract from the enjoyment of the activity.

Writing for work and pleasure

① Keep in touch!

Topic / vocabulary	Keeping in touch with people
Writing skills	Organisation of paragraphs; punctuation and spelling; formal and informal letters and messages

Coursebook page 12

Making the message clear

1 a) Reading: for detail
- Before students open their Coursebooks, ask them to discuss briefly in pairs some situations and events which would cause a boss to ask the police to investigate an employee. When students finish, feedback with the whole class and listen to a selection of students' ideas.
- Focus students on the situation and the instructions. Ask students to read Harvey's e-mail to Pete and to answer the 4 questions.
- Feedback with the class.
- Elicit / check *house-warming party* (a party to celebrate moving into a new home) and the expression *one thing led to another*.

> **Key** 1 In Hong Kong. Harvey borrowed some money from his company. His boss threatened to call the police if he didn't give it back. Harvey panicked and decided to leave London quickly.
> **2** Pete is probably a friend of Harvey's. Susie is probably Harvey's wife / partner / girlfriend.
> **3** To sell Harvey's computer, hi-fi and car and to send the money to Harvey. **4** Informal.

b) Reading: for detail
- Briefly review with the class the main points about the use of basic punctuation: capital letters, full stops, commas, apostrophes and question marks.
- Ask students to work individually to find, underline and correct as many of the 15 mistakes as they can. Then tell students to compare their answers in pairs.
- Feedback with the whole class.
- Help with any vocabulary as necessary or ask students to use their dictionaries.

> **Key**
> Dear <u>Pete</u>
> Just a quick note. I'm really sorry I couldn't make it to your house-warming <u>party.</u> I hope it went well and you <u>aren't</u> too annoyed with me for not coming. The thing is, <u>I've</u> had a bit of a problem. A few weeks ago I borrowed a lot of money from the company <u>account.</u> I was going to return it, but one thing led to another and <u>I</u> lost the money. My boss found out and he threatened <u>to</u> call the police if I didn't give it back <u>immediately.</u> I really panicked and decided to get out of <u>London</u> fast. Susie and I flew to Hong Kong on <u>Wednesday</u> and <u>we're</u> staying in her <u>brother's</u> flat at the moment. I think we're going to be here for a while. Can I possibly ask you a <u>favour?</u> We're getting desperate for money and I need you to sell my <u>computer,</u> hi-fi and car for me. I'll write again soon and let you know <u>where</u> to send the money. Thanks for your help.
> Harvey
> 1 Pete 2 party. 3 aren't 4 I've
> 5 account 6 I 7 to 8 immediately 9 London
> 10 Wednesday 11 we're 12 brother's
> 13 favour? 14 computer, 15 where

c) Reading: for detail
- Remind students that a new paragraph shows that we're writing about something new. Ask students to mark the beginning of each paragraph with a square bracket. Students work individually and then compare their answers in pairs.
- Feedback with the whole class.

> **Key** 1 [Just a quick note. 2 [The thing is, . . .
> **3** [I really panicked . . . **4** [Can I possibly . . .
> **5** [I'll write again . . .

Formal or informal?

2 a) Reading: matching

- Check *employment agency* and *estate agency*.
- Encourage students to skim the parts of e-mails and letters.
- Feedback with the class.

> **Key** **2** = c)   **3** = e)   **4** = b)   **5** = d)

Coursebook page 13

b) Writing: analysis

- Students could work in pairs to identify which messages are formal and which are informal. Feedback with the class before students read the Writing Box.
- Go through the formal and informal features in the Writing Box with the class and give further examples if necessary.
- Ask students to work individually. Tell them to read the e-mails / parts of letters (1–5) again. Then ask them to underline formal features and circle informal features.
- Ask students to compare their answers in pairs. Go round the class and monitor and give help to students as necessary.
- Feedback with the whole class and ask students to justify their answers by referring to the information in the Writing Box.

> **Key**   **1** = informal   **2** = formal   **3** = informal
> **4** = informal   **5** = formal
> **Formal features:**   NO CONTRACTIONS 2 I am writing, I would be; 5 I would like, he will be
> THE PASSIVE 5 has been left
> FORMAL LANGUAGE 2 I am writing in response to, I would be grateful if; 5 I am writing to inform you, in the near future
> **Informal features:**   CONTRACTIONS 1 can't, We're, can't; 3 I'll, we've, we've; 4 didn't, I'm, we'll, I'll
> ACTIVE TENSES 3 we've given the keys to the estate agents; 4 I'll explain everything one day
> INFORMAL LANGUAGE 1 dying to, can't make it; 3 just a quick note, moving about; 4 took off, taking it easy
> SHORTER SENTENCES 1 Really sorry, really upset; 4 all a bit last minute, Hope Dad . . .

3 a) Reading: for gist

- Students read the e-mail Harvey sent a friend individually and decide if he's telling the truth.
- Feedback. Elicit / check *hectic*, *catch up* and the expressions *at such short notice*, *it's been ages*.

> **Key**   No, he's lying.

b) Matching

- Ask students to do the matching in pairs without using dictionaries.
- Then ask students to make new pairs and to compare their answers. Tell them to use their dictionaries to help with vocabulary if necessary.
- Feedback with the class.

> **Key**   **2** = d)   **3** = b)   **4** = i)   **5** = h)   **6** = k)
> **7** = a)   **8** = f)   **9** = c)   **10** = e)   **11** = j)

4 Vocabulary: practice

- Ask students to read the letter. Help with vocabulary as necessary. Students could work in pairs to fill in the gaps with the formal expressions (a–k) from Exercise 3b).
- Feedback. Draw students' attention to the similar content but different style used in Harvey's e-mail in Exercise 3a) and his letter in Exercise 4.
- You could point out that when we begin a letter with *Dear Mr / Mrs / Ms* + name we end the letter with *Yours sincerely*.

> **Key**   **2** = d)   **3** = b)   **4** = i)   **5** = a)   **6** = h)
> **7** = k)   **8** = f)   **9** = c)   **10** = e)   **11** = j)

5 Writing: practice

- Check students understand the scenario and the instructions.
- Encourage students to read the Writing Box in Exercise 2b) again and to use the informal expressions in Exercise 3b).
- Students could work in pairs to plan Harvey's letter to Jack in class. Monitor as necessary.
- Ask students to write the letter for homework.
- When students bring their work back to class, ask them to swap letters with another student and to help each other with corrections.
- Display the letters in the classroom.

② In the city

Grammar / structures	Countable and uncountable nouns; Present Simple and Present Continuous; state verbs; question formation; Past Simple and Past Continuous in narrative
Topic / vocabulary	Describing cities; British English and American English city words
Pronunciation	Strong and weak forms of auxiliary verbs
Wavelength pages	**Conversations** *Well, hello!*: starting and keeping conversations going; echo questions

Coursebook page 14

City scenes

1 a) Warmer
- Students discuss the photos and decide which photo shows which city.
- After the feedback with the class, ask students which aspects of the photo helped them to match a city to each photo, e.g. architecture.

> **Key a)** = 3 **b)** = 5 **c)** = 4 **d)** = 1 **e)** = 2

b) Speaking: practice
- Students discuss the questions in groups.
- In the whole class feedback after the discussion ask students to name the films if they can. Ask them to give brief details of any famous films which have been set in their city, town or the capital of their country.

> **Key 1** *Notting Hill* **2** *Buena Vista Social Club*
> **3** *A View to a Kill* **4** *Two Weeks in Another Town*
> **5** *Godzilla*

Optional extras
After 1b) Speaking: practice
- Elicit the names of 6 famous films and write them on the board.
- In groups of 4. Ask each group to choose a film. Tell them to write a short dialogue recreating a scene from the film with lines for each person in the group. Give groups time to write and practise their dialogue.
- Groups take it in turns to act out their dialogue for the class. The class listens and guesses which film the group chose.
- In the feedback ask the class to vote for the best dialogue.

2 Vocabulary: presentation
- Feedback and check that students have found the words in the photos. Then practise the word stress of the vocabulary presented in the Word Box. Point out that in compound nouns the stress is often on the first word, e.g. **road** *sign*, **post**box.
- **Language note:** explain that there is no fixed rule for whether a compound noun is written as one word (*postbox*), 2 words (*road sign*) or is hyphenated (*lamp-post*). Encourage students to check the spelling of words in the *Longman WordWise Dictionary*.

> **Key 1** building, pavement, postbox, traffic lights, phone box, corner **2** building, pavement, road sign, balcony, corner **3** building, monument, statue, lamp-post, rooftop **4** monument, lamp-post, cathedral, steps **5** building, pavement, skyscraper, lamp-post, taxi, railing

After 2 Vocabulary: practice
- With books closed. Ask individual students to come to the front of the class. Show them your book and tell them to choose a word from the Word Box in Exercise 2. Ask them to draw a picture of the word on the board. The first student to guess each word correctly writes the word on the board and chooses the next word to illustrate.

British English or American English?
3 Vocabulary: matching
- In the class feedback write the American English words (a–h) on the board and elicit the British English equivalents.

> **Key 2** = g) **3** = f) **4** = h)
> **5** = d) **6** = c) **7** = a) **8** = b)

Coursebook page 15

<table>
<tbody>
<tr><td colspan="2">

After 3 Vocabulary: presentation
- If students are interested in the difference between British English and American English, add to their list of city words.
</td></tr>
<tr><td>**British English**</td><td>**American English**</td></tr>
<tr><td>chemist's</td><td>drugstore</td></tr>
<tr><td>dustbin</td><td>trash can</td></tr>
<tr><td>garden</td><td>yard</td></tr>
<tr><td>off-licence</td><td>liquor store</td></tr>
<tr><td>rubbish</td><td>garbage</td></tr>
<tr><td>subway</td><td>underpass</td></tr>
</tbody>
</table>

- You could also point out that British English *kerb* is spelt *curb* in American English and that the word *pavement* in American English refers to the road surface.

Countable and uncountable nouns

4 Grammar: presentation
- Before students look at the Word Box and the Language Box, elicit from the class what students know about countable and uncountable nouns.
- Students then write C, U or C / U after the words.
- Feedback on the first part of the activity.
- **Language note:** elicit or point out that *noise* can be both countable and uncountable. As a countable noun, it's a single sound that breaks the silence, e.g. *She woke up because she heard a noise.* As an uncountable noun it's general and usually unwanted sound all round you, e.g. *I can't stand the noise in this place!* You could also explain that *litter* is paper and other small things that people drop in the street whereas *rubbish* is a more general word for anything you want to throw away.
- After students have read the Language Box check understanding by asking *What's the difference between how we use **a lot of** and **many**?*
- Point out that you can use *lots of* or *a lot of* but *lots of* is more informal.

> **Key**   shopping centre = C   fountain = C
> noise = C / U   river = C   smog = U
> car park = C   pollution = U   square = C
> nightclub = C   traffic = U   neon sign = C

My kind of city

5 a) Reading: gap fill / for gist
- Students work individually and then compare their answers in pairs. Don't feedback on the gap fill or you'll pre-empt Exercise 5b).
- Ask the students to justify their choice of city. (Michael talks about the West and East Side and the Statue of Liberty.)

> **Key**   New York.

b) ⚪⚪⁹ Listening: to check
- Play the recording. Students check answers.
- **Language note:** point out that we use *there is / are* to say that something exists, e.g. *There's a really good bar near here.* We use *it* and *they* to refer to something we've already introduced, e.g. *There's a really good bar near here. **It's** only two streets away.* Highlight that *there is / are* can also mean the same as *it's got / it has*, e.g. *There's a really good bar near here. I like it a lot because **there's / it's got / it has** a very relaxed atmosphere.*
- **Pronunciation note:** you could point out and drill the slight difference in pronunciation between *there are* and *they're.*

> **Key**   **1** it   **2** There   **3** a lot of   **4** there   **5** It
> **6** much   **7** many   **8** They   **9** they   **10** It

6 a) Writing: practice
- Choose a city / part of a city students will be able to guess but don't make it too easy. Students ask you questions, e.g. *Have you got a favourite city / part of a city? What's it like?* Use your answers to build up a short description on the board. Students then name the city / part of the city.
- Tell pairs to prepare their description by asking each other questions. Remind pairs to use vocabulary from pages 14 and 15 and encourage them to personalise their description. Ask pairs to choose a city / part of a city the other students will be able to guess in Exercise 6b) without making it too easy!
- Tell the students in each pair to write their description individually, then swap descriptions and correct each other's errors.

b) Speaking: practice

- In groups of 4. Make sure pairs from Exercise 6a) aren't in the same group.
- Draw attention to the examples. Elicit other example questions from the students and write them on the board, e.g. *Is there a lot of traffic / pollution / smog? Is it friendly / dangerous / crowded / expensive? Are there any famous buildings / monuments / fountains / squares?*
- Monitor the groups and feedback with the class.

Coursebook page 16

In town

7 a) 📼 10 (Recording script Coursebook page 147)
Listening: for detail

- Read the 2 questions and then play the recording once. Ask students to compare answers before the whole class feedback.
- Ask students to explain the use of the Present Perfect Simple in the second question and answer. Elicit that the Present Perfect Simple is used to talk about a state or situation which began in the past and still continues / is still true in the present.
- In pairs. Students discuss what else they can remember about the interview but don't feedback or you'll pre-empt Exercise 7b).

> **Key** 1 Because it's overcrowded, expensive, noisy, dirty and there's a lot of crime.
> 2 For about a month.

b) 📼 10 (Recording script Coursebook page 147)
Listening: for detail

- Before you play the recording again, elicit as many of the adjectives that Ross and the journalist use as students can remember. List their suggestions on the board but don't confirm or correct them.
- Play the recording for students to note down the adjectives. In the feedback compare students' answers with the list on the board.

> **Key** fantastic, friendly, cosmopolitan, historic, awful, fashionable, popular, overcrowded, bad, important, American, good, exciting, atmospheric, expensive, noisy, dirty, suspicious, worse, lucky, low-rent

c) 📼 10 (Recording script Coursebook page 147)
Gap fill / Listening: to check

- Revise the use of the Present Simple and the use of the Present Continuous by asking students to fill the gaps and then compare their answers in pairs before they listen.
- **Language note:** if students ask about *think* (sentences 2 and 6), explain that you'll answer their questions after Exercise 10 (which deals with state verbs).

> **Key** 1 hate 2 'm thinking 3 get up 4 come, sit 5 'm working, 'm not getting 6 thinks 7 are [they] doing 8 'm watching

d) Grammar: presentation

- Before students look at the activity, elicit uses of the Present Simple and the Present Continuous and write them on the board. Don't comment on students' suggestions.
- Tell students to read the 4 uses. Check their understanding of *temporary, necessarily* and *permanent*. Then ask students to fill in the Language Box. Feedback and compare students' answers with their suggestions on the board.
- Check students understand that they have to say which use of the Present Simple or the Present Continuous each sentence in Exercise 7c) shows. If necessary elicit from the class the answers to the first 2 sentences.
- After the feedback elicit sentences to illustrate the 2 uses of the Present Simple (2 and 4) and the 2 uses of the Present Continuous (1 and 3).
- Refer students to the Grammar reference on page 110 for information on the Present Simple and the Present Continuous.

> **Key   Language Box** We use the Present Simple for 2 and 4.   We use the Present Continuous for 1 and 3.
> **1** = use 4   **2** = use 3   **3** = use 2   **4** = use 2
> **5** = use 3   **6** = use 4   **7** = use 1   **8** = use 1

8 Grammar: practice

- Students work individually and compare their answers in pairs. Have a whole class feedback only if students are still having difficulty.

> **Key** 1 I'm staying, is painting 2 I stay
> 3 They're building 4 is driving 5 close

After 8 Grammar: practice
- Remind students of the uses of the Present Simple (2 and 4) and of the Present Continuous (1 and 3) in Exercise 7d). Ask them to say which use of the Present Simple or Present Continuous each sentence in Exercise 8 shows.

> **Key** 1 = use 3 2 = use 2 3 = use 3
> 4 = use 1 5 = use 4

Pronunciation: auxiliary verbs (strong and weak forms)

9 a) Pronunciation: presentation
- Draw attention to the example. In pairs, students take it in turns to read the sentences aloud. Then ask students to fill in the boxes. Don't feedback or you'll pre-empt Exercise 9b).

Coursebook page 17

b) 〔◉◉〕11 Listening: to check
- Play the recording for students to check. Play sentences again if necessary. Feedback.
- Ask students to fill in the gaps in the Language Box. Feedback by relating the information in the Language Box to the sentences in Exercise 9a).
- **Pronunciation note:** ask students to read the sentences in Exercise 9a) aloud with the correct stress on the auxiliaries. Point out the weak pronunciation of the auxiliaries in the questions in sentences 1 and 4 and the positive sentences (sentences 2 and 5). Highlight the strong pronunciation of the auxiliaries in the negative sentences in sentences 1 and 3 and the short answers in sentences 3 and 4.

> **Key** 1 I haven't [S] seen her for weeks. Has [W] she moved? 2 Lots of tourists have [W] visited this monument. 3 People say cars aren't [S] damaging the environment, but they are [S] .
> 4 A: Does [W] everybody here use public transport? B: No, but most people do [S] .
> 5 I think those men are [W] watching us.
> **Language Box** We use the strong pronunciation in **negative sentences** and in **short answers**. We use the weak pronunciation in **positive sentences** and in **questions**.

State verbs

10 Grammar: presentation
- Students read the Language Box. Help with vocabulary as necessary.
- With books closed, ask students to define state verbs and to give examples of state verbs, e.g. *agree, be, believe,* etc. Elicit from students that some state verbs can be used in both Continuous and Simple tenses with a change in meaning. Students then fill in the gaps in the sentences 1–6.
- In the whole class feedback elicit that *have = experience* in sentence 2 and *think = mental activity now* in sentence 3.
- **Language note:** you could remind students that *have* = possession and *have got* can be used interchangeably but *have got* is more common in British English.

> **Key** 1 don't agree 2 'm having 3 are you thinking 4 don't understand, do you mean 5 comes from 6 don't know, 's / is behaving

I am a camera

11 a) Speaking: preparation
- Draw attention to the photo. Elicit the name of the building (The Sagrada Familia, Barcelona) and of the man behind the camera (the film director, Pedro Almodóvar). Ask students if they know or like any of his films.
- Make sure students understand that they're going to prepare ideas for a short 15-minute film. Elicit ideas for the kind of film, e.g. a positive documentary, a film encouraging people to visit, a personal biographical film about places in the city that are particularly important or meaningful to students or a short mystery film shot in atmospheric parts of the city. Elicit ideas on where the film could be set, e.g. tourist attractions, completely unknown places, an impressive view from a building, street cafés, markets, etc. Explain that students can choose famous narrators and their own background music.
- In pairs. Students prepare their ideas. Monitor and help with information, names, etc.

b) Speaking: practice
- In groups. Pairs take it in turns to present their film ideas. Students ask questions to find out more about the locations, why the pair chose them, why they chose their kind of film, etc.

Coursebook page 18

City lights

Before 12a) Warmer
- Students brainstorm as many different kinds of book as they can think of, e.g. *travel book, historical / detective / comic / fantasy novel, biography, thriller, love / ghost / adventure story, science fiction.*
- List students' suggestions on the board and elicit a brief definition of each kind of book.

12 a) Reading: for gist
- Students read the 3 extracts quickly to find the answers to the 2 questions. Tell them not to worry about unknown vocabulary.
- Feedback. Students justify their answers.

> **Key**   1 No. Extract a) is about London, extract b) is about Cairo and extract c) is about Glasgow.
> 2 detective novel = extract c), travel book = extract b), love story = extract a)

b) Reading: for detail
- Read the questions quickly with the class and check understanding.
- In the feedback individuals justify their answers. Students say if they agree or disagree and why.

> **Key**   1 Extract a): my last view of London
> 2 Extract a): I was sitting on the top [of the 73 bus]   3 Extract b): I really felt as if I was coming home   4 Extract a): the winter sky   5 Extract c): in the rain. A wind was blowing   6 Extract b): the blue fog of car exhaust fumes

c) Reading: for detail
- The aim of the activity is to develop students' ability to deduce meaning from context. Don't let students use dictionaries.
- Make sure students understand the words or phrases used to explain the meaning of the words in the extracts, e.g. *cloudy, waste gas, powder.*
- In the feedback check pronunciation.

> **Key**   1 properly   2 once   3 recognise   4 fog
> 5 exhaust fumes   6 dust   7 twice   8 queuing
> 9 got to

After 12c) Reading: for detail
- Divide the class into 4 or 5 groups. Each group writes 6 comprehension questions about the 3 extracts and writes the answers on a separate piece of paper. Encourage the students not to make their questions too easy. Monitor and give help as necessary.
- When the groups finish, ask groups to swap questions and answer them.
- Feedback with the whole class.

Coursebook page 19

Past Simple and Past Continuous
13 a) Grammar: preparation / practice
- Check students understand the task. Students could work in pairs.
- In the feedback on question 3 elicit that the second action happened immediately after the first. Remind students that there's a very short amount of time between 2 actions in sentences with 2 Past Simple verbs linked with *when.*

> **Key**   1 The 73 bus was moving slowly along the Euston Road. I [the narrrator] was sitting on the top [of the bus]. [The narrator was] looking out across the city.   2 Smoke was coming from an open window. The radio was playing.   3 He got to the police station first.

b) Grammar: presentation
- Check with students the form of Past Continuous verbs in all persons and in statements, negatives, questions and short answers.
- After the feedback to check students have correctly underlined the verbs, ask students to fill in the gaps in the Language Box.
- Make sure that students are clear about the different uses of the Past Continuous.

> **Key   Extract a):** was moving, was sitting, looking out   **Extract b):** was coming home
> **Extract c):** was blowing, was coming, was playing.   **Language Box**   We use the **Past Simple** to talk about finished past actions / states / situations.   We use the **Past Continuous** to describe an activity which was already in progress when other events happened, or at an exact moment in the past.

14 a) Listening: preparation

- Set the scene by eliciting possible problems connected with some of the words from Ellie's story, e.g. *delayed* could refer to trains, planes or people delayed at a meeting; *public holiday* usually means that shops and other services are closed.
- In pairs. Students guess the possible main events.
- Feedback with the whole class and list students' most interesting or most plausible guesses on the board.

b) ⊙⊙ 12 (Recording script Coursebook page 148)
Listening: for detail

- After students listen to the recording, feedback on the first 2 questions. Students then comment on differences and similarities between their predictions and the actual events of the story. You could point out that the story is true.

> **Key** **1** A romantic weekend in Amsterdam was Ellie's thirtieth birthday present from her boyfriend. **2** It turned out all right in the end.

c) ⊙⊙ 12 (Recording script Coursebook page 148)
Gap fill / Listening: to check

- Monitor students while they're filling in the gaps. If they're having difficulty, ask them to re-read the Language Box in Exercise 13b).
- Play the recording. Students check their answers.
- Refer students to the Grammar reference on pages 111 and 112 for information on the Past Simple and the Past Continuous.

> **Key** **1** were sitting, remembered **2** got, rang **3** was getting, started **4** were walking, saw **5** was ringing, were bringing **6** were, slept

After 14c) Speaking: practice

- Ask the students to look at Recording script 12. In pairs: Pair A and Pair B. Pair A make notes and prepare to tell the story from the point of view of Adam, Ellie's boyfriend. Pair B make notes and prepare to tell the story from the point of view of the police officer at the police station where Adam and Ellie spent the night. Monitor and give help.
- In AB pairs. Students take it in turns to tell their stories. Note errors for the feedback.
- Feedback with the class.

It happened one night . . .

15 Speaking: practice

- In pairs: Pair A and Pair B. Explain that each pair is going to make up a story about something that happened to them one night in a city. Tell students that the story can be full of disasters like Ellie's story about her weekend in Amsterdam, about a problem which was solved in the end or about something unusual or interesting that happened. Ask students to read their instructions and to look at their pictures and phrases.
- Before pairs prepare their stories check that students understand the instructions. Emphasise to students that they must use the exact words or phrases given in the table and use something connected with the pictures that they've chosen. Remind students to use the Past Simple and the Past Continuous.
- Ask pairs to prepare their stories. Monitor and help with vocabulary and ideas as necessary. Encourage pairs to write stories which aren't too complicated but which have a coherent narrative for other students to follow. Make sure students don't write down the whole story but make notes.
- Pairs make groups of 4. Before pairs tell their stories point out that if the listening pair doesn't tick 8 prompts during the first listening, the pair tells the story again until the listening pair has ticked 8 boxes. Ask the storytelling pairs to share the story with each partner telling half.
- Monitor groups but don't interrupt as pairs tell their stories. Note down errors for later feedback with the whole class.

After 15 Writing: practice

- Students work individually and use their notes and ideas to write their stories in full. Allow time in class or ask students to do this for homework.
- When students bring their work to class, ask them to swap stories in pairs. Tell them to proofread each other's work before students give in their stories.
- Correct difficult errors but underline other mistakes that you think students could correct themselves. Give the stories back and ask students to write a final corrected version for display.

After 15 Photocopiable activities

- See City sights, page T112.

② Conversations *Well, hello!*

Grammar / structures	Echo questions to show interest
Functions	Greeting and saying goodbye; conversation strategies to start conversations, to show interest, to check understanding and to keep conversations going
Pronunciation	Widening intonation to sound interested

Coursebook page 20

Starting and keeping conversations going

1 Speaking: preparation
- In the feedback point out that we can use *Pleased to meet you* and *Nice to meet you* when we meet someone or when we say goodbye as the phrases could be short for *I am / I was pleased to meet you* and *It is / It was nice to meet you.*
- **Language note:** draw attention to *See ya* which comes from *See you*, meaning *I'll see you (later)* and isn't a written form. Point out that *Cheers!* is usually associated with drinking but it can mean *Goodbye* or *Thank you.*

Key

Meeting someone	Saying goodbye
Hiya!	It was nice to meet you.
How are you?	Cheerio!
Pleased to meet you.	Goodbye.
Hi!	Bye!
Nice to meet you.	Pleased to meet you.
How are you doing?	See ya.
	Bye bye!
	Nice to meet you.
	Cheers!
	Nice meeting you.

Hiya! and *See ya* are probably the least formal. *Pleased to meet you* and *It was nice to meet you* are probably the most formal.

---

2 ◓◓ 13 (Recording script Coursebook page 148)
Listening: for gist
- Emphasise that these are joke dialogues.
- In the feedback on conversation 1 elicit or emphasise that the speakers have learnt to ask *And you?* every time they say *Fine, thanks* and are concentrating too much on the form.
- In the feedback on conversation 2, elicit or emphasise that the man takes the question *How are you?* literally, instead of recognising it as a formulaic question with the meaning *Hello*.

3 a) Reading / Speaking: practice
- Make sure students understand that they have to classify the opening lines into acceptable and unacceptable ways of starting a conversation. Although people are free to begin a conversation any way they wish it's important to know that some openers can be considered inappropriate for starting a conversation with a stranger.
- Feedback and ask students which opening line they think is the best idea. Ask them to justify their choice. Elicit / check that *What sign are you?* refers to the astrological signs *Aquarius*, etc.

Key Acceptable opening lines referring to something obvious: **2** Are you enjoying the book? **5** I like that author – Stephen King. **7** Is anyone reading that paper? **9** Oh, no! It's raining again. Acceptable opening lines asking a harmless question: **3** Can I sit here? **10** Have we met before? **12** Did I see you in here yesterday? **15** Excuse me, have you got the time? Unacceptable opening lines about anything too personal to do with you or the other person: **4** Are you married? **6** Have you got a tattoo? **11** I'm a vegetarian. **13** My father owns a big company. **14** You're very beautiful. Unacceptable opening lines about anything strange or esoteric: **1** Is there life after death? **8** What sign are you?

---

b) Speaking / Writing: practice
- Elicit / point out that *No, I don't think so* is a polite and natural response to opening lines 7, 10 or 12. Although the response is grammatically possible after other opening lines, it would sound strange.
- In the writing part of the activity students could write amusing follow-on lines to the unsuitable openers. However, it's important that students learn suitable short responses for the more appropriate opening lines, e.g. **A:** *Are you enjoying the book?* **B:** *Er, yes, thank you.* **A:** *Can I sit here?* **B:** *Sure, go ahead.*
- Feedback. Some pairs read out their exchanges.

Echo questions and statements

4 a) 〇〇14 (Recording script Coursebook page 148)
Listening: for gist
- After the feedback elicit that Clara sounds interested in Antonio's conversation.

> **Key** London. Antonio speaks more, Clara less.

b) 〇〇14 (Recording script Coursebook page 148)
Listening: for detail
- After the feedback, improvise a short dialogue in which you speak and the students use some of the words or expressions in the Word Box to encourage you to keep the conversation going.

> **Key** Clara uses all the expressions except *I see, Sure* and *Oh yeah?*. She uses them to show interest and to keep the conversation going.

c) Presentation
- Feedback with the class.

> **Key** Showing interest: I see. Really? Oh yeah?
> **Checking:** Do you mean . . . ? So . . . ?
> **Encouraging / Showing you're listening:** Hmm. Yeah. Uh-huh. Mm-hm.
> **Agreeing:** I know. Sure. Absolutely.

d) Reading: practice
- Feedback with the class.

> **Key** 1 Yeah . . . , you know . . . , I mean . . . , um . . . , well . . . 2 . . . you know?, Do you know what I mean?

5 Speaking: practice
- Monitor pairs. When students finish, feedback and practise intonation.

Coursebook page 21

6 a) 〇〇15 (Recording script Coursebook page 148)
Listening: for detail
- With classes that need support, write the key words on the board and point to them as they occur. Play the recording twice if necessary.

b) Gap fill
- Ask students to suggest answers but don't feedback or you'll pre-empt Exercise 6c).

c) 〇〇15 (Recording script Coursebook page 148)
Listening: to check
- After feedback on the gap fill, students read the Language Box. Point out that we can show interest or surprise by an echo question on its own; an echo question followed by a further question or statement; expressions such as *Really? No! Oh?* or repetition of key words of the first person's statement as a question.

> **Key** 1 Eleven times? 2 Your school?
> 3 Two months? That's impossible! 4 Gone?
> Did you go after him? 5 Did he? What an idiot!

d) Gap fill
- Students suggest answers before looking at Coursebook page 148.
- After the feedback ask the class and then pairs to read the sentences with interested intonation.

> **Key** 1 I know exactly **what you mean**.
> 2 That's **strange**. 3 I can **imagine**!
> 4 That's **terrible**. 5 No **way**! **Really**?

7 Reading / Speaking: practice
- Write example words / phrases to express interest or surprise on the board, e.g. *Really? Is that right?* Students practise saying them as a class. Encourage them to start high, move their voices up and down and to emphasise the stressed words / syllables.
- Monitor pairs. In the feedback make sure students realise that it doesn't matter if listeners react with an echo question or with key words.

8 Speaking: practice
- Emphasise that students take it in turns to be the speaker, listener and observer within each group.
- Monitor and make sure each group member stays in his / her role. Stop the observers from joining in and commenting and the listeners from telling their own stories or giving their own views.
- When each student has acted out the roles of observer, listener and speaker, get preliminary feedback from the class. Ask the students how they felt in each of the roles. Take an interest in what observers have noticed and ask students if the activity helped them to spot strong and weak points in their own oral work.
- If students are enjoying the exercise, tell them to continue the activity with a new group.

③ When Saturday comes

Grammar / structures	Defining / non-defining relative clauses; First Conditional: *if, unless*; *going to* + infinitive
Topic / vocabulary	Places of entertainment; adjectives / phrases describing places, people, decor and atmosphere; strong and base adjectives
***Wavelength* pages**	**Day to day English** *How about . . . ?*: making suggestions and arrangements and expressing preferences; Present Continuous for fixed arrangements
	Reading for pleasure 1: *Heat wave*
	Do you remember? Units 1–3
Take to class	Coloured pens and large pieces of paper / card for Exercise 12a)

Coursebook page 22

There's a place . . .

1 a) Warmer
- In pairs. Students identify the 3 places shown.
- Feedback and ask students which of the 3 places they would prefer to go to and why.

> **Key   a)** a restaurant   **b)** a bar   **c)** a club

Optional extras
After 1a) Speaking: practice
- Write questions about leisure activities on the board, e.g. *Do you usually go out in a large group or with one or two people? Are there certain days when you always go out? What kinds of place do you usually go to?*
- In groups of 4. Students discuss the questions.
- Feedback with the whole class and discuss similarities and differences.
- Alternatively you could ask groups of 4 to choose a local place of entertainment on a Saturday night for: a) an adult / a parent aged about 45, b) one of the group members, c) a younger brother or sister aged about 11.
- Feedback and compare and contrast answers.

b) 🔊 16 (Recording script Coursebook page 149)
Listening: for gist and detail
- Play the recording twice if necessary.
- In the feedback don't elicit details about why and how the friends disagree. Students just need to understand they've got different opinions.

> **Key**   Place b).   No, they don't feel the same way about it.   modern, cool, crowded, noisy, smoky, busy, spacious, relaxed, smart, casual

c) 🔊 16 (Recording script Coursebook page 149)
Listening: to check
- In pairs. Ask students to classify the adjectives they ticked before they listen to the recording again. Explain that *place* is more to do with the physical aspects of appearance and decor (observable qualities that people can agree on) while *atmosphere* is about the way the place feels to the people in it (and can therefore be more of a personal opinion).
- In the feedback check *busy* and *spacious*.

> **Key   Place:** modern, cool, crowded, noisy, smoky, busy, spacious   **Atmosphere:** relaxed   **People:** smart, casual

d) Vocabulary: practice
- Students could use dictionaries.
- **Language note:** point out that *cool* can be used for a place, atmosphere or for people. You could also highlight that *bright* can be used to describe an intelligent person.
- When students finish, ask them to compare their tables in pairs. Then feedback with the whole class. The Key is a guide. Be flexible when accepting or rejecting answers, especially if students can justify their answers.

> **Key   Possible answers: Place:** modern, cosy, dimly-lit, bright, packed, cool, simple, crowded, comfortable, colourful, smoky, quiet, strange-looking, busy, elegant, dark, spacious, posh, traditional, sweaty, smart, fashionable   **Atmosphere:** cosy, lively, bright, cool, friendly, comfortable, noisy, quiet, fun, posh, welcoming, relaxed, traditional   **People:** lively, cool, friendly, noisy, colourful, quiet, strange-looking, elegant, fun, posh, welcoming, relaxed, traditional, sweaty, smart, fashionable, casual

2 a) Writing: practice

- In pairs. Students choose photo a) or photo c). Encourage them to add adjectives of their own.
- Ask students to put the incorrect piece of information towards the end of the description rather than near the beginning so that students will listen to the whole description.
- Monitor and help as necessary.

b) Listening: for detail

- In groups of 6. Pairs take it in turns to read their description (with each partner reading half) while the other group members listen to identify the place and the false information.
- Then ask students to identify descriptions that were detailed and atmospheric. Ask those pairs to read their descriptions to the whole class.

Coursebook page 23

Relative clauses

3 Grammar: gap fill / presentation

- Briefly elicit or provide sentences (not questions) which contain *which, who, whose* or *where* to give students examples of the target language.
- Check students understand *media people*, then tell them to fill in the gaps. Elicit suggested answers but don't confirm or correct them at this point.
- Tell students to check their answers by reading Recording script 16 or by playing Recording 16 again. In the class feedback point out that the pronunciation of *whose* is the same as the pronunciation of *who's*. If students are confused about the spelling, give sentences to contrast the 2 words, e.g. *That's the teacher whose class is very noisy. That's the woman who's having trouble with her back.*
- Focus on the Language Box to revise the use of defining relative clauses and of *who, which, that, where* and *whose.*
- You could discuss typical errors with your students and elicit the correct forms.
- **Language note:** if students ask about *whom*, e.g. *The girl who I was speaking to . . .* compared to *The girl to whom I was speaking . . .* explain that the second example is quite formal and that *whom* is used less and less nowadays, especially in spoken English.

Key 1 whose 2 which 3 where 4 who

After 3 Grammar: practice

- Give students further practice of defining relative clauses by writing sentences 1–8 on the board or use an OHT.
  1 The guy . . . . . was sitting next to me at the bar went to school with my sister.
  2 That's the place . . . . . James and I first met.
  3 That couple . . . . . were behind us in the supermarket queue were really rude.
  4 The cocktails . . . . . they make there are wonderful.
  5 The man . . . . . was dancing on the table is my boss.
  6 We went to see the comedian . . . . . dog takes part in his act.
  7 We sat at that table . . . . . has the huge sculpture on it.
  8 She's the girl . . . . . I saw with your boyfriend on Saturday night.
- Students fill in the gaps with *which / that, who / that, whose* or *where.*
- In the feedback point out that the relative pronoun can be omitted in sentences 4 and 8.

Key 1 who / that 2 where 3 who / that 4 which / that 5 who / that 6 whose 7 which / that 8 who / that

4 a) Grammar: presentation

- Try to elicit that *which has enormous windows* is extra information in sentence 1 (i.e. *The upstairs part is really nice* makes sense without the relative clause) but it's essential information in sentence 2 (i.e. *We were sitting in the upstairs part* doesn't make sense without the relative clause.
- After students have read the Language Box, point out to the class that commas separate non-defining relative clauses from the rest of the sentence as the additional information is optional and not essential.
- Refer students to the Grammar reference on page 115 for information on defining and non-defining relative clauses.

Key In sentence 2 the clause *which has enormous windows* tells you which part of the restaurant.   In sentence 1 the clause *which has enormous windows* just adds extra description.

b) Speaking: practice

- Read the 5 sentences and the story with the class. Check *greasy apron* and *folder*.
- Use the example to illustrate the activity. In pairs. Students add the 5 extra sentences.
- Students make new pairs and compare answers.
- Feedback. Accept answers if they make sense in the context and show an understanding of the use and form of the clauses and pronouns.

> **Key   Possible answers:**   We went to a cheap little café, **which was near the station** (4). The waitress, **who was wearing a paper hat and a greasy apron** (5), came and gave us a menu. A woman, **who was wearing a fur coat** (1), came in and sat at the next table.   They were both wearing sunglasses, **which looked very expensive** (3).   She took out a folder, **which had the words "For your eyes only" on it** (2), and showed him some photographs.

c) Writing: practice

- Illustrate the activity by giving an example, e.g. *The waitress, who was wearing a paper hat and a greasy apron, came and gave us a menu,* **which was old and dirty.**
- Either in pairs in class or individually for homework. Students write out the story, adding the 5 sentences from Exercise 4b) and 2 more non-defining relative clauses of their own.
- Collect and correct the stories, focusing on the correction of the non-defining relative clauses.

I know a place . . .

5 Speaking: practice

- Start the class off with your own example.
- In groups. Encourage students to talk about real places that mean something to them and to use as many relative clauses as possible.
- Monitor descriptions and note down errors.
- Feedback with the class.

Coursebook page 24

Decisions . . . decisions . . .

6 a) Warmer

- In the class feedback elicit information about local facilities, e.g. the names of shopping malls in or near the place where students are studying.

b) 🔘 17 (Recording script Coursebook page 149)
Listening: for detail

- Ask students to note the answers while you play the recording. Then tell students to compare their answers in pairs. Play the recording again if they disagree. Feedback.

> **Key**   Stephanie wants Alison to do more shopping but Alison's worried that she'll spend all her money and she won't have enough for her holiday.   Stephanie wants Alison to go for a drink at the pub but Alison's worried that if she goes, she'll be there all night.

c) 🔘 17 (Recording script Coursebook page 149)
Gap fill / Listening: to check

- With books closed write the gapped sentences on the board but don't give students the prompts to help them fill in the gaps. Elicit suggestions from the students and write them in the gaps but don't correct or confirm them.
- Then ask students to open their books. Tell them to work individually and use the prompts to fill in the gaps in the sentences. Play the recording so that they can check their answers.
- In the class feedback compare the initial suggestions on the board with the correct answers and ask students to analyse any errors in grammar.

> **Key   1** I'll spend   **2** I won't have   **3** I'll spend   **4** I'll be   **5** I might get

7 Grammar: presentation

- Feedback with the class.
- Students then read the Language Box. Check students understand that First Conditional sentences refer to a possible future with a possible result by asking concept questions and eliciting the answers in brackets, e.g. *Has Alison got any money? (Yes.) Can she spend her money? (Yes.) Does she want to spend any more money? (No.) What will happen if she does? (She won't have enough money for her holiday.)* Point out that the sentence in the Language Box *If I spend more money, I won't have enough for my holiday* refers to the very near future.

> **Key   1** The future.   **2** A present tense, usually the Present Simple.

8 a) Grammar: matching

- With books closed write only parts 1–5 of the sentences on the board. Ask students to choose one of 1–5 and to make a First Conditional sentence by writing the second half. When students finish, ask individuals to read their second half and tell the other students to match it to one of 1–5 on the board.
- Check *broke* (= *having no money*) before students do the matching exercise in pairs.
- In the feedback point out that conditional sentences don't have a set order.

> **Key**   2 = e)   3 = a)   4 = d)   5 = c)

After 8a) Grammar: matching

- Write 1–6, a–f on the board or use an OHT.
  1 I'll pay for the coffees today
  2 I'll lend you the money
  3 If you drive me there,
  4 If you drink any more,
  5 I might look stupid
  6 Unless you stop causing trouble,

  a) I'll pay for the petrol.
  b) if I wear these false eyelashes.
  c) you'll be sick.
  d) if you pay for them tomorrow.
  e) I'll call security.
  f) if you want to buy those shoes.
- Students make 6 First Conditional sentences.
- Feedback with the class.

> **Key**   1 = d)   2 = f)   3 = a)
> 4 = c)   5 = b)   6 = e)

---

b) Matching

- Feedback with the class. Elicit other examples of First Conditional sentences which could be said in each place or situation.

> **Key**   **1 In a café or restaurant**: I won't leave a tip if he doesn't serve us soon!   **2 Getting ready to go out**: I'll pay for the taxi if you pay for us to get in.   **3 In a shop**: If you buy any more clothes, you'll be broke again!   **4 Organising a party**: She'll be angry if we don't invite her.
> **5 In a club**: If you're scared to ask her to dance, I'll ask her for you.

Coursebook page 25

c) Grammar: presentation

- Revise / check *prediction, offer, warning, threat, negotiation* before students read the Language Box.
- Feedback with the class.
- Refer students to the Grammar reference on page 116 for information on the First Conditional.

> **Key**   **Prediction**: She'll be angry if we don't invite her.   **Offer**: If you're scared to ask her to dance, I'll ask her for you.   **Warning**: If you buy any more clothes, you'll be broke again!   **Threat**: I won't leave a tip if he doesn't serve us soon!   **Negotiation**: I'll pay for the taxi if you pay for us to get in.

d) Writing / Speaking: practice

- Go through the example with the class.
- As students write in pairs, monitor their work, ensuring that the form of the sentence is correct.
- Pairs then read out their sentence to the class. In larger classes do the activity in large groups and ask pairs to report back to the class.

A bit of a dilemma

9 a) 🔁 18 (Recording script Coursebook page 149)
Listening: for gist

- Pre-teach *dilemma* and the expression *to be in a dilemma*.
- Monitor students as they listen to the recording and take notes. Play the recording again.
- Students compare notes before the class feedback.

> **Key**   **Conversation 1**: The people are parents / probably a husband and wife.   They're in a jazz club.   Their dilemma is whether to go home (they promised the babysitter they'd be home by one o'clock) or to stay and enjoy themselves. In the end they agree to stay but the woman is going to phone the babysitter to check that everything's OK and to say they'll be back by 2:30 at the latest.   **Conversation 2**: The people are 2 female friends.   They're in a café.   The dilemma is whether Abigail wants to try and get back together with her ex-boyfriend, Jason. They disagree about what to do. Abigail just decides to eat her cheesecake to try and forget about Jason. Her friend wants Abigail to phone Jason and talk through their problems.

b) 🔘🔘 18 (Recording script Coursebook page 149)

Gap fill / Listening: to check

- Students have already covered *going to* + infinitive for plans / intentions so they should be able to fill in the gaps correctly. When students finish, play the recording for students to check.
- After the feedback tell students to read the Language Box. Draw attention to the fact that the plans / intentions are thought about and arranged beforehand and that there's a decision to carry out the plan.
- Refer students to the Grammar reference on page 114 for information on the Future: plans (*going to* + infinitive).

> **Key** **1** going to phone **2** going to check
> **3** going to sit **4** going to do **5** going to eat

c) **Speaking: preparation**

- In pairs: Pair A, Pair B, Pair C, Pair D. Make sure each pair looks at the appropriate page. Remind them not to look at any other pages. Students read and discuss their dilemmas in pairs. When you're sure pairs are ready, move on to Exercise 9d).

d) **Speaking: practice**

- Stress that students must consider the possible results of each situation. This will give them a clear context for the natural use of the First Conditional. Also point out that they should use *going to* + infinitive when they talk about concrete plans to solve their problem.
- Go through the example. Organise students in groups of 4, made up of students from an A, B, C and D pair.
- When students are in their groups, give more details about the example situation to illustrate the activity further: *The new position will pay much better and you've got some debts. But if you accept this position you'll move to a different office and have a new supervisor who you know and don't like very much. You get on really well with the people in your present office.*
- A, B, C and D students in each group take it in turns to describe their dilemmas and to discuss possible solutions with the rest of the group.
- Monitor the groups as they work and make notes on errors, focusing on the First Conditional and the use of *going to* + infinitive. Feedback with the whole class and elicit the best possible solutions to the 4 different dilemmas.

Coursebook page 26

Enjoy your meal!

> **Before 10a) Vocabulary: warmer**
> - Write these adjectives on the board / an OHT:
>
> | | | |
> |---|---|---|
> | 1 black | 10 medium | 19 still |
> | 2 boiled | 11 mineral | 20 strong |
> | 3 decaffeinated | 12 rare | 21 sweet |
> | 4 dry | 13 raw | 22 tender |
> | 5 free-range | 14 red | 23 tough |
> | 6 freshly-baked | 15 roast | 24 weak |
> | 7 fried | 16 scrambled | 25 well-done |
> | 8 grilled | 17 sliced | 26 white |
> | 9 iced | 18 sparkling | 27 wholemeal |
>
> - Write *a) bread, b) chicken, c) coffee, d) eggs, e) steak, f) water, g) wine* on the board / an OHT.
> - In pairs. Students match the adjectives (1–27) to the food / drink (a–g). (Some adjectives can describe more than one food or drink.) Students could use dictionaries.
> - Feedback.

> **Key** **a)** = 6, 7, 17, 26, 27 **b)** = 2, 5, 7, 8, 13, 15, 22, 23 **c)** = 1, 3, 9, 20, 21, 24, 26
> **d)** 2, 5, 7, 13, 16 **e)** = 8, 10, 12, 13, 22, 23, 25
> **f)** 9, 11, 18, 19 **g)** = 4, 14, 18, 21

10 **a)** **Reading: for gist**

- Encourage students to skim the texts. Feedback.

> **Key** **a)** The rainforest. **b)** Professional wrestling. **c)** Murder mystery.

b) **Reading: matching**

- Encourage students to do the matching without trying to understand all the words. Feedback.

> **Key** **1** = c) **2** = b) **3** = a)

c) **Reading: for detail**

- Students could do this individually for homework or in pairs in class. Students face each other. Student As cover the questions but look at the texts. Student Bs cover the texts but look at the questions. Pairs then ask and answer the questions without looking at each other's book. Feedback.

> **Key** 1 At the Nitro Grill and the Mystery Café.
> 2 The Mystery Café. 3 At the Nitro Grill.
> 4 At the Nitro Grill. 5 At the Mystery Café. So
> that you don't miss the beginning of the show.
> 6 The Rainforest Café. 7 The Rainforest Café.

d) Speaking: practice

- Before students discuss the questions in pairs, if you've been, or someone you know has been, to a theme restaurant, describe it to the class.
- Feedback with the class. Elicit which of the 3 restaurants students prefer and details of any local theme restaurants or major chain restaurants students have been to.

Coursebook page 27

Strong adjectives

11 a) Vocabulary: presentation

- Point out to students that they're looking for words, not phrases. In the feedback ask students to suggest other adjectives with the same meaning, e.g. 1 *brilliant, amazing, terrific*; 2 *massive, monumental, gigantic*, etc. Point out that *brilliant* can mean *extremely intelligent* and *extremely good*.
- When discussing the Language Box, check that students have understood the idea of base adjectives (which give the basic concept of the word) and strong adjectives (which give a strong, more intense meaning of the base adjective).

> **Key** 1 Text a) = wonderful Text b) = fantastic
> Text 1 = excellent 2 Text a) = huge
> Text 2 = enormous 3 Text 3 = delicious
> 4 Text c) = hilarious

b) Vocabulary: gap fill

- Ask students to try to fill in the gaps without using a dictionary. Point out that there are more adjectives in the Word Box than students need for this exercise. When they finish, ask them to check their answers in pairs.
- Feedback with the whole class, checking meaning and pronunciation.

> **Key** 1 furious 2 awful / terrible
> 3 exhausted 4 boiling 5 starving

c) Vocabulary / Writing: practice

- Elicit the adjectives not used in Exercise 11b): *enormous / huge, terrified, delicious, fantastic / wonderful, tiny* and write them on the board.
- In pairs. Monitor and give help as students write their exchanges.

d) Vocabulary: gap fill

- Pairs make groups of 4. Pairs swap exchanges and fill in the gaps. Pairs then swap exchanges again and check each other's answers.
- Feedback with the whole class by asking some pairs to read out their gapped exchanges and elicit answers from the class.

> **After 11d) Photocopiable activities**
> - See 3 *Spot the difference!*, page T114.

Design a theme restaurant

12 a) Speaking / Writing: practice

- This activity provides integrated practice of all the language in the unit by giving students an opportunity to create a restaurant web page.
- Build up the atmosphere and enthusiasm for the activity by making the aim clear. Focus on the prompt questions and check that the students understand them.
- Elicit from the class examples of any unusual theme restaurants students know about or have been to, e.g. restaurants they've seen on TV, particularly in American programmes, restaurants where customers have to participate in games while they eat, medieval banquets, murder dinners, etc.
- Students work in pairs on their designs. Tell students to draw a picture and to write the advertising blurb to accompany the picture. Make it clear students don't have to be artists! Give students coloured pens and large pieces of paper or card. Remind them of the vocabulary and grammar from this unit that they can use. Encourage them to be bold and imaginative in their choice of ideas.
- Monitor students' work and help with ideas and vocabulary as necessary.

b) Reading / Speaking: practice

- In the class feedback elicit comments from the class on any particularly funny, imaginative, horrible or wonderful theme restaurants.

③ *Day to day English* *How about . . . ?*

Grammar / structures	Ways of making suggestions and expressing preferences; Present Continuous for definite future arrangements
Functions	Making suggestions; talking about preferences; future arrangements

---

Coursebook page 28

What do you want to do?

1 a) 🔊 19 (Recording script Coursebook page 149)
Listening: for gist

- Point out that Marty and Angie (diminutive of the Italian name, Angelo) are in a bar at 5 o'clock on a Saturday afternoon. Elicit possible answers to the question before students listen.
- Play the recording. Then feedback with the class.

> **Key** They're talking about what to do / whether to call up a girl they met about a month ago. The problem is they can't decide what to do / Marty didn't like the girl Angie wants to call.

b) Gap fill

- Before students try to fill in the gaps, check they remember how to form verb + *-ing*, infinitive with *to* and infinitive without *to*.
- Students compare their answers in pairs but don't feedback or you'll pre-empt Exercise 1c).

c) 🔊 19 (Recording script Coursebook page 149)
Listening: to check

- Play the recording straight through for students to check their answers. Play parts of the recording again if necessary.
- Students read the Language Box. Make sure they focus on and understand the other phrases in the Language Box which aren't in the recording.

> **Key** doing doing to go
> calling call calling

2 a) 🔊 20 (Recording script Coursebook page 150)
Listening: for gist

- After playing the recording and eliciting what Rae and Brett's problem is, ask some questions on detail, e.g. *Why can't Brett meet Rae on Tuesday?* to elicit *He's playing golf.*

> **Key** The problem is that Rae and Brett can't find a time when they can meet.

b) 🔊 20 (Recording script Coursebook page 150)
Gap fill / Listening: to check

- Ask students to identify the tense Rae and Brett use in the gaps. Discuss but don't confirm the choice of tense. Then ask students to do the gap fill individually and to compare answers in pairs.
- Play the recording. Students check. Students then read the Language Box. Emphasise the pre-planned nature of this use of the Present Continuous to talk about definite future arrangements.
- Refer students to the Grammar reference on page 114 for information on the Future: arrangements (Present Continuous).

> **Key** 'm flying are you doing
> is giving 'm not doing

3 Speaking: practice

- This activity can also be done in pairs or in groups of 5 or more (not groups of 3 or each student will have the same prompt every time).
- Write 3 headings on the board: *Previous arrangement, New suggestion, Don't feel like it.* Suggest an arrangement for next week. Point to *Previous arrangement* and then to a student. Elicit *I can't. I'm (taking my mother to the cinema).* Point to *New suggestion* and elicit a new suggestion from the same student. Then point to *Don't feel like it* and another student. Elicit *I don't feel like (going to . . .)* or *I don't want to (go to . . .).* Point at *New suggestion* and elicit a new suggestion from the same student. Continue until a few students have rejected ideas and suggested alternatives. Give them help with phrases as necessary.
- You could refer students to Exercise 1c) for ways of expressing suggestions and preferences and Exercise 2b) for ways of talking about arrangements that have already been made or ways of suggesting alternative arrangements.
- In groups. Students do the activity. Monitor the groups. Let the students continue until they run out of ideas (probably after going round in circles 2 or 3 times). Then swap students between groups and start again.

Reading for pleasure
① Heat wave

Vocabulary	*appreciate, attention, background, bark* (v), *below, button, clip* (n), *cover* (v), *credits, despair* (n), *dish* (n), *fan* (n / v), *fire escape, fix, fur, gaze* (v), *gently, growl, heat wave, hide, imitate, in case, king of hearts, kitty, knock off, lap* (n), *lean* (v), *leave (something) alone, ledge, lie down, meow* (v), *pant* (v), *paw* (n), *press* (v), *purr* (v), *reasonable, recipe, series, shadow, shoulder, sigh* (v), *siren, slam* (v), *slow motion, snatch up, sniff* (v), *spicy, straight* (= *immediately*), *stretch, stroke* (v), *supper, sweat* (n), *tail* (n), *tear* (n), *theme music, unconscious, wag* (v), *waist, wipe* (v)

Coursebook page 29

Before reading

1 Presentation
- Elicit / explain *heat wave*. In pairs. Students imagine what the people are doing to fight the heat.
- Feedback with the whole class.

2 ⓞⓞ 21 (Recording script Coursebook page 29)
Reading and listening: for detail
- Pre-teach vocabulary as necessary before students read and listen to the recording. Point out the American English spelling. They could work in pairs. Feedback. With question 1, elicit suggestions, e.g. *traffic, sirens, planes*.

> **Key** **1** Noises of the city. **2** He's drinking iced mineral water and he pours some of the water over his head. **3** She's eating ice cream and fanning herself with a magazine. **4** There's a heat wave in New York and it's going to be the hottest night in history.

3 Reading: for gist and detail
- Pre-teach vocabulary. Students read the story and answer the questions for homework.

> **Key** **1** They probably haven't got a very good relationship. **2** He's preparing supper and cutting up a chicken. **3** He's just had a cold shower. **4** He's talking to his dog, Paloma.
> **5** She's playing a game of cards. **6** She's got an electric fan which she turns so that it blows directly in her face. **7** She phones someone to find out if she's got any messages, probably someone in her office or an answering service. She also phones her father. **8** She makes herself a strong drink with a lot of ice.

> **9** At first we think he's Alice's boyfriend / partner / husband. At the end we learn he's her cat.
> **10** They're probably a married man and his girlfriend / lover. **11** The meat sauce she has cooked for her son. **12** The cat. **13** The cat knocks it off the ledge and it hits the man with the gun on the head, knocking him unconscious.
> **14** He's probably about to shoot someone, perhaps Adam. **15** He goes back to Alice.

After reading

4 Speaking: discussion / practice
- Feedback on the answers to Exercise 3. Students could describe the relationships between:
  1 Adam and his dog
  2 the elderly woman and her son
  3 Alison and her cat
  4 the married man and the young woman.
  Ask students to justify their answers.
- Students could act out or read the film script aloud.

5 Vocabulary: practice
- Students look through the story. Ask them to list words and phrases associated with heat and with keeping cool: *heat wave, wide open, iced, water, hot, thirsty, ice cream, fan, hottest, cold shower, pant, refrigerator, ice, be cool, sweat.*
- Students look through the story again. Ask them to list all the words and phrases associated with animals: *pant, wag, tail, kitty, growl, bark, paw, fur, meow, stroke, purr.*

6 Personalisation
- Discuss these questions with the class. What do you think is important in a successful relationship? Do you think relationships between humans and animals are important?

③ *Do you remember?* Units 1–3

Grammar / structures / vocabulary   1 Present Perfect Simple; Past Simple
2 *Used to / would*; Present Simple
3 *Going to* + infinitive; First Conditional
4 Grammar / structures / vocabulary from Units 1–3

Coursebook page 30

1 *Hey! I've done that, too!*

a) Warmer
- Start off with an example, perhaps an experience of your own, to help students with ideas about their past experiences.
- As students are writing their questions about each of their experiences, go round and make sure the questions they write / think of aren't too detailed or specific. Give help with ideas and vocabulary as necessary.

b) Speaking: practice
- Point out that the aim of the activity is for students to go round the class asking different students questions until they find someone who's had the same experience. They then find out more information.
- Give an example by referring back to your experience from Exercise 1a). Find a student who has got this experience in common with you. The rest of the class then asks that student Past Simple questions to find out more details about the experience.
- In the class feedback find out if there were any amazing coincidences.

2 *Not like now*

a) 〔oo〕22 (Recording script Coursebook page 150)
Listening: for gist
- As a warmer, elicit from students where they go, who they go with and what they do on a typical night out. Do most students do the same kind of thing when they go out or is there a lot of variation in the class?
- Feedback and ask which decade Mark is talking about to elicit that he's talking about the 1950s.

> **Key**   Mark describes what Saturday night was like for his parents when they were young.

b) 〔oo〕22 (Recording script Coursebook page 150)
Listening: for detail
- Write the table headings on the board. Play the recording. Elicit what students remember about marriage, make-up, going out and public transport when Mark's parents were young.
- Play the recording again and check that the class is making notes. Note-taking is an important skill and should be practised, even in this relatively easy context.
- In pairs. Ask the students to compare notes. In the class feedback write the answers under the appropriate headings on the board.

Key

	People used to . . .	Now they . . .
Marriage	get married much younger	get married when they're older
Make-up	really paint their faces	don't wear much
Going out	only go out on Saturday night go to a dance hall dance to a live band until midnight	go out any night they want go to clubs dance to records until later than midnight
Public transport	use the bus or walk, as there were no buses after about 11 at night	can use public transport until later than 11 at night or they've got cars

c) Speaking: preparation
- Help the students with prompt questions before they make their notes about the differences, e.g. *Did your parents go to the cinema / read / listen to the radio more or less than you do now? What music do you listen to? Did your parents listen to the same kind of music? What technology didn't exist when your parents were your age?*
- Ask students to put themselves in their parents' place 25 or 30 years ago as they prepare their notes. Monitor students as they work and help with ideas and vocabulary as necessary. Remind them to use *used to* + infinitive when describing their parents' generation.

d) Speaking: practice

- In groups of 4. Students use their notes to discuss differences between their generation and their parents' generation. You could appoint a secretary in each group to record the main points of each discussion ready for the whole class feedback.
- In the feedback in monolingual classes focus on similarities and differences between the 2 generations. In the feedback in multilingual classes focus on similarities and differences between different cultures.

3 *That's a terrible idea!*

a) Speaking: preparation

- Make the aim of the activity clear to the students. Explain that they're going to make an unusual life choice and then defend their choice when their partner tries to talk them out of it. The prompts themselves should give the idea that the choices are unusual but don't highlight this aspect too much in case you offend someone's feelings!
- Read the instructions with students and make sure they understand the 5 life choices. You could encourage students to come up with an idea of their own.
- Have an example discussion with a student to illustrate the activity, e.g. give the advantages of your decision to become a celebrity cook. (Don't use one of the 5 decisions or you'll take away one of the possibilities from the students.) Tell students to try to predict the criticisms they'll receive from their partner when they defend their life choice.
- In pairs. Make it clear that pairs choose and prepare one life choice between them. As pairs prepare, monitor and help with vocabulary and ideas as necessary.

b) Speaking: practice

- Ask students to make new pairs with a student who has made a different life choice. Use the instructions and the example to make the activity clear. Tell students to put forward the advantages of their new life choices while their partners try to dissuade them.
- With smaller classes, ask pairs to act out their conversations for the class. With larger classes, ask pairs to do this in groups. In the feedback ask the class or groups to identify which students gave the best arguments for or against each new life choice.

Coursebook page 31

4 **The beautiful game**
Grammar: practice

- This exercise revises grammar, structures and vocabulary from Units 1–3: Present Perfect Simple with *for* and *since*; Present Perfect Simple contrasted with the Past Simple; *used to / would*; *much / many*; verb + *-ing*; First Conditional; adjectives / phrases for describing people; Past Continuous; modifying strong and base adjectives; adjectives derived from nouns; *there is / are*; Present Continuous for definite future arrangements; Present Simple contrasted with the Present Continuous.
- Revise or give further input on the structures or vocabulary from Units 1–3 which you consider might cause students problems before they do the activity. Alternatively delay review activities until students have completed the exercise as this will help to identify problem areas.
- Focus on the title of the activity and the photo. Elicit from students the subject of the article. You could point out that the photo shows Newcastle United supporters at St James's Park in the early 1980s.
- Make sure students understand the instructions. Point out the examples in paragraphs 1 and 3.
- Students could do the activity for homework or individually in class. Then check in pairs.
- In the feedback elicit answers from the whole class. Go into more detail with areas which seem to cause a lot of students problems. You could refer individual students to exercises from Units 1–3 which deal with the structures that are still causing difficulty.

> **Key** **1** for **2** took **3** used to **4** much
> **5** going **6** don't **7** we'll leave **8** look
> **9** was wearing **10** absolutely **11** amazing
> **12** crowded **13** atmospheric **14** colourful
> **15** traditional **16** exciting **17** noisy
> **18** dangerous **19** friendly **20** welcoming
> **21** I've been **22** there **23** I'm taking
> **24** think **25** agreed

> Encourage students to learn the new words from Units 1–3 on Coursebook pages 122–124 and do Puzzle 1 on Coursebook page 120 before you give them Progress test Units 1–3 on page T136.

④ *How do you do that?*

Grammar / structures	Verb + -*ing* as a subject, after a preposition and after some verbs; past ability: *could, was able to, managed to, succeeded in*
Topic / vocabulary	Genius and intelligence; talking about skills, abilities and learning; jobs and work; word building; linkers
Wavelength pages	**Writing for work and pleasure 2** *I am writing to apply . . .*: writing a CV; writing a letter of application

Coursebook page 32

Great minds

1 a) Warmer
- With books closed check *genius* and *profession*. Set the scene by asking students to name people they consider to be geniuses and to describe their professions and achievements. Does the whole class agree?
- In groups. Ask students to look at the pictures on page 32 and discuss the questions. Help with *psychoanalyst* if necessary.
- Feedback and elicit as much information as possible about each genius.

> **Key** 1 **Mozart:** composer 2 **Edison:** inventor
> 3 **Freud:** psychoanalyst 4 **Einstein:** scientist
> 5 **Picasso:** artist

> **Optional extras**
> **After 1a) Speaking: practice**
> - In groups. Ask *Who is the most important genius from your country?* In multilingual classes make groups with students of different nationalities and ask the students to explain to each other who they think is the most important genius from their country. In monolingual classes, see if students can agree within their group.
> - Feedback with the class.

b) Reading: preparation
- Remind students not to read the article. Ask individual students in the class for their own ideas about the questions. If you've got a larger class, put students into groups of 4 or 5 and give them a few minutes to discuss their ideas.
- Write students' ideas on the board but don't feedback or you'll pre-empt Exercise 1c).

c) Reading: for detail
- Before students read, emphasise that they should scan the text quickly for information rather than trying to understand all the details or trying to deduce the meaning of unfamiliar words from the context.
- Feedback with the whole class and compare students' ideas on the board with the ideas given in the article.

> **Key** 1 No, geniuses often come from an unhappy background. (lines 4–9) 2 Yes, geniuses are incredibly productive. (lines 14–16)

Coursebook page 33

2 a) Reading: for detail
- Before students read the text again check they understand the phrases *have got in common* and *come to nothing* in the questions.
- Feedback with the class. When eliciting answers, point out that the information presented in the article is not given in an absolute or categorical way. This is done through devices such as the use of questions (lines 1, 10, 12–13, 26) and words like *perhaps* (lines 2, 10).

> **Key** 1 All lost parents before they were 10 years old. (lines 6–7) 2 Perhaps stress makes children escape into their own private worlds – they feel different from other children and so decide to become even more different. Or perhaps they work hard to please parents who aren't there. (lines 10–13) 3 No, Freud had his breakthrough about the importance of dreams after spending years on another project which finally came to nothing. (lines 18–20)
> 4 It seems that geniuses have always worked hard in their chosen areas for at least a decade before they create their first masterpieces. (lines 23–25)

b) Vocabulary: practice

- Ask students to do this activity individually and then compare answers in pairs.
- Feedback with the class. With books closed, elicit suggested answers from the class (the order isn't important) and write them on the board. Then ask other students to give the meaning of the words.

> **Key** 1 background 2 childhood 3 poverty
> 4 abuse 5 failures, fail 6 breakthrough
> 7 masterpieces 8 childlike

After 2b) Vocabulary / Writing: practice

- Write this table on the board or you could use an OHT.

Verb	Noun	Adjective	Person
			producer
	failed		(same as noun)
		connected	–
		creative	
invent		inventive	

- Then ask the students to copy the table into their notebooks.
- Elicit one or two words from the students as examples. Then tell them to fill in the gaps in the table with the correct words from the article. Draw attention to the fact that there isn't a person for the adjective *connected*. Students could use dictionaries to help them if necessary.
- Feedback by eliciting the answers and completing the table. Then ask students to write 5 sentences using words from the table for homework.

> **Key**
>
> | Verb | Noun | Adjective | Person |
> |------|------|-----------|--------|
> | produce (line 16) | productivity (line 16) | productive (line 14) | producer |
> | fail (line 18) | failure (lines 17 and 18) | failed | (same as noun) |
> | connect (line 22) | connection (line 10) | connected | – |
> | create (line 24) | creation (line 22) | creative | creator (line 5) |
> | invent | invention (line 15) | inventive | inventor (line 15) |

c) Reading / Speaking: practice

- In pairs. Students use dictionaries if necessary. Encourage them to explain the meaning rather than interpret the words literally.
- Feedback by asking students to say why they agree or disagree with the quotation. Students could link the quotation to information in the article, e.g. the "ten-year rule".

> **Key** The quotation means that ideas which show genius are mostly the result of hard work rather than creative thinking.

d) Speaking: practice

- In pairs. Encourage students to express themselves. There are no right or wrong answers.
- Feedback with the class.

3 a) 〔oo〕23 (Recording script Coursebook page 150)
Listening: for gist

- Students read the rubric before playing the recording. Set the scene by asking questions and eliciting the answers in brackets, e.g. *What kind of school is it? (It's a school for geniuses.) What is it trying to achieve? (To produce geniuses.) Why do people send their children to schools like this? (They think they're suitable for their children / they'll help their children to do well in life.) Do you know any schools or places like this?* If students answer yes, ask for details.
- Play the recording. Then feedback with the class. Students will have to deduce the answer to question 2 from the sound of Professor Blunt's voice and the way he hesitates rather than from what he actually says.

> **Key** 1 At the beginning of the interview they're concerned about Lucy's progress at the school. They wonder if Lucy really is genius material and don't know whether to take her away from the school. By the end of the interview Professor Blunt has convinced them that they're not wasting their money by sending Lucy to the school so they pay for another year. 2 Not very well. She doesn't sound very intelligent or interested and she's not very good at mathematics. Professor Blunt implies that her writing, reading and drawing aren't very good either and that she hasn't got many friends. Also she's quite angry and physical – Professor Blunt probably means physically destructive!

b) 🔊 23 (Recording script Coursebook page 150)
Gap fill / Listening: to check
- Students could try to fill in the gaps in pairs or groups. Point out that not all the phrases in the Word Box are used in this exercise. Play the recording for students to check. If necessary play the recording again. Feedback.

> **Key** 1 quite good at 2 hopeless at
> 3 extremely good at 4 good at
> 5 not bad at 6 very good at

c) Vocabulary: presentation
- Focus on the form of the verb following the phrases in the Word Box in Exercise 3b): verb + *-ing*.
- Feedback with the class.

> **Key** 1 extremely good at 2 very / really good at 3 good at 4 quite good at 5 not bad at 6 not very good at 7 hopeless / useless at

> **After 3c) Speaking: practice**
> - Write quotations 1–3 on the board or an OHT.
>   1 "Genius and regularity are utter enemies and must be to the end of time." (Thomas Gainsborough, 1772)
>   2 "Genius is only a greater aptitude for patience." (Comte de Buffon, 1803)
>   3 "The true genius is a mind of large general powers, accidentally determined to some particular direction." (Samuel Johnson, 1781)
> - In groups. Ask students to read the quotations and explain their meaning using dictionaries if necessary.
> - Monitor and give help as necessary.
> - Feedback by asking group members to say if they agree with the ideas expressed in the quotations and to give reasons why they agree or disagree with the ideas.

Tell me all about yourself

4 Speaking: practice
- In groups of 4. Ask the students to look at the relevant pages.
- Monitor students as they read and fill in the gaps. Encourage them to tell the truth, think about what they're good at and how / when they learnt things.

- When they've written their own information, they may need help writing a question for each sentence, e.g. *What can you do really well?* from Student C's sentence *I can . . . . . really well.*
- In smaller classes, students go round the class asking for and exchanging information. In larger classes, ask students to make groups of 4.
- In the feedback elicit anything remarkable or unusual students found out.

Coursebook page 34

Nice work if you can get it

5 a) Warmer
- Elicit / teach the meaning of *stand-up comic* and *advertising executive*. Ask students what they know about these jobs before they read the rubric and job descriptions.
- Explain the activity and read through the 2 short job descriptions. In pairs. Students discuss the questions. Ask pairs to write short notes about their discussions. Tell students to focus on any possible similarities. Don't let them dismiss the 2 jobs as having nothing in common and don't let them get distracted by discussing the more obvious dissimilarities.
- Feedback and make a summary of students' ideas on the board.

> **Key Possible answers:** The good and bad sides of Frank's job could be that Frank's job gives him a lot of freedom and he's his own boss but he doesn't have a lot of job security. The good and bad sides of Alan's job could be that Alan's job is well-paid and interesting but it's stressful and he has to work long hours. What the 2 jobs have in common could be that they're both stressful jobs where you have to think quickly.

b) Listening: preparation
- Go through the sentences quickly and elicit / teach the meaning of *stressful, work in a team, criticism, security.*
- In the same pairs. Students try to predict what Frank and Alan say. Point out that both Frank and Alan could both say the same thing about their jobs, so students can tick both boxes.
- Feedback and ask pairs to justify their answers by relating them to the kind of jobs that Frank and Alan do.

c) 🔊24 (Recording script Coursebook page 150)
Listening: to check
- Play the recording twice as it's quite long. Ask students to tick the boxes individually and then compare answers in pairs. Point out to students that they have to listen for the ideas expressed in sentences 1–10, not for the exact words. If students don't agree, play the recording again.
- Elicit answers from the class. Then ask follow-up questions: *How many answers did you predict correctly? Which of the 2 jobs would you prefer?*

> **Key** **1** Frank and Alan. FRANK: . . . I'm quite good at dealing with people. ALAN: You have to get on well with your colleagues. **2** Frank and Alan. FRANK: . . . it's so stressful. ALAN: There's a lot of stress . . . **3** ALAN: You have to work in a team here, too. **4** FRANK: You have to take criticism . . . **5** Frank and Alan. FRANK: . . . you have to think on your feet and quickly say something funny . . . ALAN: . . . you have to . . . make decisions quickly. **6** ALAN: . . . it's very well-paid. **7** Frank and Alan. FRANK: . . . it's a really demanding job . . . on a good night . . . it's fantastic. ALAN: I can work under pressure . . . work hard . . . I really enjoy doing what I do. **8** Neither. FRANK: . . . there's no job security. ALAN: . . . if I lose [my clients] . . . I might lose my job. **9** ALAN: . . . I have to look smart . . . **10** FRANK: . . . I love the freedom. Nobody tells me what to talk about . . . I don't have to get up early – no timetable . . . I can wear what I want . . .

6 a) Vocabulary: practice
- Before students underline words / phrases in Recording script 24 check the pronunciation and meaning of any new words / phrases.
- Write the headings from the table on the board.
- Go through one or two example words / phrases and elicit where they should go in the table. Point out the grammatical restrictions implied in the table, e.g. *It's . . .* must be followed by an adjective, *There is / are . . .* and *You get . . .* must be followed by nouns or noun phrases.
- When students finish, elicit answers and fill in the table on the board.
- Point out that the categories in the table aren't definite as there are variations in people's use of English, e.g. we can say *We **get** a rise every year* (*get = receive*) or *There is an annual rise* which is a more general, less personal statement.

> **Key**
>
> | It's . . . | a demanding job, stressful, well-paid, never boring |
> |---|---|
> | There is / are . . . You get . . . | a lot of pressure, job security, an annual pay rise, a lot of stress, perks, regular bonuses, long holidays |
> | You have to . . . | deal with people, take criticism, think on your feet, look smart, be available, deal with problems, make decisions |
> | You work . . . | for a company / an agency, in the marketing department, under pressure, long hours, in a team |

b) Writing: practice
- Make sure students use the table with the words and phrases from the Word Box in Exercise 6a). Ask them to write just a short paragraph.
- Students could write the paragraph for homework or in class. When they finish, tell them to swap their paragraphs with another student and proofread each other's work.
- Collect the paragraphs. Correct difficult mistakes but underline other errors you think students can correct themselves. Return the work and ask students to write a corrected final version.

Coursebook page 35

Verb + *-ing*
7 Grammar: presentation
- Point out that there are 3 tasks in this exercise: reading the Language Box, finding examples of verb + *-ing* in sentences 1–6 and categorising the uses exemplified in sentences 1–6.
- When students have read the Language Box, check they recognise the 3 uses by giving additional examples at random and asking which use, a), b) or c), the sentence illustrates, e.g. *I don't like living in a city* = use c).
- Students work individually. When they finish, ask them to compare their answers in pairs. Then feedback with the whole class.

> **Key** **1** b leaving **2** c speaking **3** a Working **4** c working **5** a Sitting **6** b meeting

Just the job

8 a) Reading: for detail

- Introduce the topic by explaining that the phrase *just the job* is a British English expression meaning *exactly what is needed or wanted for a particular situation*, e.g. *That laptop you lent me for the weekend was just the job.* Explain also that an employment agency is an agency you pay to help you find a job. It isn't the actual employer. In interviews at the agency applicants have to make themselves look good so that the agency will recommend them to employers for a particular job that's available.
- Students skim the introduction at the beginning of the Dynamic Jobs application form quickly.
- Feedback by asking students to identify how the agency advertises itself. Elicit that it uses questions *Tired of the same old nine to five? Looking for new challenges?* to show it's offering different kinds of job. Also the agency's name *Dynamic Jobs* and the phrases *out of the office and into the circus, from the concrete jungle to the real jungle* and *off the bus and . . . into a hot-air balloon* hint at the unusual nature of the jobs the agency offers.

> **Key** It advertises challenging and unusual jobs.

b) Reading / Writing: practice

- Tell students to be honest as they fill in their forms with their personal details. Then the agency can have a good idea of their skills and abilities and find them the right job.
- Monitor and help with any new vocabulary.

c) Speaking: practice

- This exercise is a light-hearted activity in which students interview each other for dynamic or exotic jobs. In pairs: Pair A and Pair B. Refer pairs to the relevant pages. Make sure pairs don't look at each other's information.
- Check students understand the instructions.
- Pairs then discuss the 3 jobs. When they finish, tell students to make groups of 4 (Pair A and Pair B). Ask the students in Pair A to swap their application forms with the students in Pair B. Go through the examples with the class but encourage students to think of their own questions. Help students to think of appropriate questions for the jobs they've got to offer.

- When students are ready, tell Pair A to interview Pair B. Remind Pair A not to say what the 3 jobs are so that the interviewees don't try to angle their replies towards a particular job. Pair B then interviews Pair A. Remind Pair B not to reveal what the 3 jobs are. Finally pairs decide which job to offer each student interviewed and explain why. As pairs work, monitor the interviews, the decision about which job to give each student and the explanation to the candidate.
- Although working in pairs when preparing and interviewing gives more speaking practice and more opportunity for students to help each other with ideas and language, the preparation can be done individually and the interviews can be done in pairs.
- In the class feedback ask each student *Which job were you given? Are you happy with it? Do you think you'll do it well or badly?*

Coursebook page 36

The sweet smell of success

9 a) Warmer

- Draw attention to the title *The sweet smell of success.* Point out that *success* is an abstract noun and ask students why they think it's described as having a *sweet smell.*
- Whether students consider the characters in the cartoons to be successes or failures will depend to some extent on individual points of view.
- Feedback with the class. Do students all agree which ones are about success and failure? Which cartoons do they think are funny? Can they say what makes them funny?

b) Writing / Speaking: practice

- Keep this activity light-hearted and short. Point out that the aim is for other students to be able to guess which cartoon situation they're continuing when they act out their conversation later for the class.
- If students need help to start them off, choose one of the cartoons and ask *Who do you think speaks next? What does he / she say? How does the other person reply?*
- When the students have got an idea, let them work on their own conversations. Monitor pairs as they work and help with vocabulary and structures as necessary.

c) Speaking: practice
- When pairs are ready ask them to act out their conversations for the class or to large groups in larger classes. Don't let students read their conversations. Make sure they perform live to give their conversation a spontaneous feel. The other students listen and try to guess which cartoon each conversation is based on.
- Ask the class to comment briefly on the strengths of each conversation, e.g. good intonation, amusing dialogue, as well as the weaknesses, e.g. particular language errors.

Past ability and linkers

10 a) Vocabulary: gap fill
- Ask students to skim the story and to say what Laurence Vague's job is. In the feedback on the question ask students to justify their answer, e.g. *He spent all his time as a young boy reading plays and acting them out.*
- Ask the students to fill in the gaps individually. They could use dictionaries if necessary.
- When students finish, ask them to compare and try to agree on their answers in pairs. Don't feedback or you'll pre-empt Exercise 10b).

> **Key** He's an actor.

b) 🔲 25 Listening: to check
- Play the recording for students to check their answers. Then elicit answers from the class.
- Ask students to read the text again. Draw attention to some of the phrases Laurence uses to link together his success story, e.g. *as a baby, by the time, anyway, after a while, finally, it was then that I . . . , after several phone calls, after years of pain and struggling . . .*

> **Key** **2** = e) **3** = d) **4** = b) **5** = a) **6** = h)
> **7** = i) **8** = g) **9** = f) **10** = j) **11** = n)
> **12** = m) **13** = o) **14** = k) **15** = l)

> **Coursebook page 37**

11 Grammar: presentation
- After students have read the Language Box, ask questions to elicit the key differences between these 5 ways of expressing past ability, e.g. *What's the difference between* **could** *and* **was / were able to**?

- Ask students to fill in the gaps.
- Elicit answers from the whole class. The answer to sentence 4 is *was able to* rather than *managed to* as *quickly and easily* makes it clear that success wasn't achieved after difficulty or effort. However you could accept *managed to* if students can justify their answer!
- Refer students to the Grammar reference on page 118 for information on modal verbs (ability).

> **Key** **1** could **2** managed to **3** couldn't
> **4** was able to **5** succeeded in

> **After 11 Photocopiable activities**
> - See 4 The rise and fall of Mimi Mee, page T116.

Rags to riches

12 Writing: practice
- To set the scene begin by eliciting / explaining the meaning of the title *Rags to riches*.
- Focus on linkers students know, e.g. *after that, as soon as . . .* and the linkers in Laurence Vague's success story (see Exercise 10b) teaching notes). Write them on the board.
- Encourage each pair to choose a different title, if possible. Tell students to use the phrases to express past ability in Exercise 11 and the language in Exercise 10a) as well as the other linkers from the board to help them organise their story.
- In pairs. Students prepare their stories. When they're ready, ask them to write their stories in class or for homework.
- Display the stories or ask students to pretend they're giving a speech at an awards ceremony about their (or their pet's!) dizzy rise to world fame and success. Students read their stories out to the class (or to groups in larger classes). Students say which story they like best and why.

> **After 12 Speaking: practice**
> - In new pairs. Students take it in turns to be the interviewer and the successful person and interview each other about their success stories for a TV or radio chat show.
> - If possible photocopy each pair's story so each interviewer can have a copy to use as notes on which to base his / her questions.

Writing for work and pleasure
② I am writing to apply . . .

Topic / vocabulary	CVs; job advertisements and applications
Writing skills	Presenting information in a CV; writing a formal letter of application

Coursebook page 38

Writing a CV

1 a) Warmer
- Explain / elicit that a CV is a document which sets out a person's personal details, academic qualifications, work experience and gives brief details of their other skills and interests. Elicit that *CV* stands for *curriculum vitae*.
- Students discuss the question in pairs.
- Feedback and write suggestions on the board but don't comment on them at this stage.

b) Reading: for detail
- Ask students to skim Ana's CV to find out if their predictions about the qualifications and skills she needs for her job were correct.
- When students finish, elicit their answers and compare them to the predictions on the board.

> **Key Qualifications / skills:** school leaving certificate, qualifications in and knowledge of Portuguese, qualifications in and knowledge of English, computer literate, dealing with bookings and billing, providing tourist information

2 Reading: gap fill
- Check the headings 1–10. Students fill in the gaps.
- Feedback. Then ask other questions about the details in Ana's CV, e.g. *How old is Ana? Why didn't she get a degree?*, etc.

> **Key   a)** = 9   **b)** = 6   **c)** = 4   **d)** = 8   **e)** = 5
> **f)** = 1   **g)** = 7   **h)** = 2   **i)** = 10   **j)** = 3

3 Reading / Speaking: practice
- Elicit / pre-teach *essential, coordinate* and *standardised procedures*.
- Write the headings from the table in the Key on the board. Students copy them into their notebooks. Students then read the 3 job ads to find out what each job involves and the qualifications / skills needed. Students fill in the table.

- Feedback and fill in the table on the board.
- In groups of 4. Students use the information in the table and in Ana's CV to discuss the most suitable job for Ana.
- Feedback and ask groups to justify their choice. Point out that a CV should be relevant to the job you're applying for with a clear layout.

> **Key**
>
> | | The job involves . . . | Qualifications / skills |
> |---|---|---|
> | **Restaurant manager** | making reservations for guests by fax, telephone, e-mail and in person | good standards of English and Portuguese; some knowledge of Japanese an advantage |
> | **Museum assistant** | speaking to visitors in English | interest in history and art; a degree |
> | **Booking manager** | coordinating the work of 3 booking clerks using standardised procedures | computer literate; fluent in Portuguese and English; used to dealing with members of the public |
>
> **Booking manager** is the most suitable job for Ana as she is computer literate, fluent in Portuguese and English, has experience with bookings and billing and is used to dealing with members of the public.

Coursebook page 39

Writing a letter of application

4 Reading: gap fill
- After students read the Writing Box, go through it with the class. Point out that if a name to write to is given in the job ad, we begin the letter *Dear Mr / Mrs / Ms* + surname (NOT *Dear* + first name because a letter of application is formal).
- Students work individually to fill in the gaps and then compare their answers in pairs.
- Feedback and point out that, although the layout of letters can sometimes vary, students will be correct if they follow this layout.

> **Key   b)** = 8   **c)** = 1   **d)** = 7   **e)** = 5   **f)** = 3
> **g)** = 6   **h)** = 9   **i)** = 2

5 a) Reading: matching

- In groups. Give students one minute to brainstorm pairs of formal / informal words, e.g. *man / guy, friend / mate,* etc. Elicit pairs of words, write them on the board and ask the class to say which words are formal and which are informal.
- Elicit that letters of application are formal because you're writing to a stranger / strangers who you want to give you a job.
- Draw attention to the example. Students work in pairs and then compare their answers with another pair.
- Feedback and ask students to identify and note down useful formal phrases in sentences 1–10, e.g. *at your convenience, I would be grateful if you could . . . , I am writing in response to . . . , I look forward to . . . ,* etc.

> **Key** **b)** = 9 **c)** = 1 **d)** = 3 **e)** = 2 **f)** = 6
> **g)** = 10 **h)** = 4 **i)** = 8 **j)** = 7

b) Writing: preparation

- Write these 4 headings on the board: *e) why you're writing, f) information about your suitability for the job and why you want the job, g) additional information, h) closing.*
- Students match sentences 1–10 to the 4 headings.
- Feedback and write the sentences under the correct headings.

> **Key** **2** = e) **3** = f) **4** = h) **5** = e) **6** = h)
> **7** = f) **8** = g) **9** = g) **10** = f)

c) Writing: practice

- Elicit from the students that sentences 2 and 5 will go in section e), the first part of Ana's letter of application for the job of booking manager. Elicit that sentence 5 will come first.
- Students write Ana's letter following the layout of the formal letter of application in Exercise 4. Tell students to address the letter to the Personnel Manager at Nine Star Airlines and to use today's date. Encourage them to link, adapt and add to the sentences as necessary so that the letter sounds natural.
- Monitor students as they write the letter and help and correct as necessary. You could ask students to swap letters as they finish each section. Students then correct the previous section and write the next section. When students finish, feedback on common problems or difficulties.

> **Key   Possible answer:**
>
> > Rua Bartolomeu da Silva, 35 – Lapa
> > 05065 – 110 São Paulo SP
>
> The Personnel Manager
> Nine Star Airlines
> Av. Paulista
> São Paulo
>
> (today's date)
>
> Dear Sir / Madam
>
> I am writing in response to your advertisement for a booking manager in *The State of São Paulo* on 26th July and I would be grateful if you could give me further information concerning the post.
>
> I am currently working as a senior duty receptionist at Hotel Excelsior, São Paulo where I am responsible for a small team of reception staff. Although I enjoy this aspect of my work and I am happy in my current position, I would like a post with more responsibility.
>
> My work involves a variety of duties, including dealing with bookings and billing and providing tourist information. Please find enclosed my curriculum vitae.
>
> Thank you for considering my application. I look forward to hearing from you and I am available for interview at your convenience.
>
> Yours faithfully,
>
> Ana Ortiz

6 Writing: practice

- Before students write in pairs, highlight the tips in the Remember! Box. Remind students that their aim is to impress the employer so that they get the job they're applying for! Check students understand the meaning of the 3 jobs.
- Pairs write the CV and letter of application. Alternatively pairs prepare the information in class and for homework one student writes the CV, the other the letter. Pairs then check each other's work when they bring it to class.
- Collect pairs' work. Concentrate on errors of layout, organisation and formality when you correct. Then ask students to write corrected final versions of their CV and letter for display.

(5) *Culture vultures*

Grammar / structures	Subject and object questions; comparative adjectives; modifying adjectives and nouns; Present Perfect Continuous
Topic / vocabulary	Arts, culture and artists
Pronunciation	Stressing for emphasis
Wavelength pages	**Conversations** *I'm not sure . . .*: language of doubt and hesitation
Take to class	Photos of 2 well-known personalities for Exercise 10a)

Coursebook page 40

Art for art's sake

Optional extras
Before 1a) Warmer
- Draw attention to the title of the unit and elicit / check *vulture = a large bird which eats dead animals*.
- Discuss what kind of person students think a *culture vulture* is. Elicit as many ideas as possible and don't criticise reasonable suggestions which aren't correct. If necessary explain that a *culture vulture* is a person who is very interested in all kinds of arts and probably especially modern and avant-garde art. Point out that the phrase is often a criticism rather than a compliment.
- Ask students what kind of arts (not just the visual arts but theatre, music, literature, etc.) they're interested in and what kind of artistic activities they've taken part in, even if it was just singing a song in a school concert.

1 a) Warmer
- Check meaning / pronunciation. Explain that *programme* refers to a TV programme, *cultural object* refers to an exhibit in a museum and a *gig* is an informal popular music or jazz concert. You could also explain that paintings, sculptures, music, etc. of a very high quality are examples of *fine art*.
- Students discuss the question in groups. You could point out that Tate Modern opened in 2000 and specialises in contemporary art.
- Feedback and check students' pronunciation.

> **Key Possible answers:** painting, photography, film, installation, sculpture, video

b) Vocabulary: matching
- Point out that we usually use *music venue* for the place where you see rock and pop concerts, even though they're concert halls.
- In pairs. Encourage students to use vocabulary based on their own experiences and knowledge as well as the words in the Word Box.
- Feedback. Accept answers students can justify.
- Ask students for examples of the arts they've got or can experience in their homes.

> **Key Possible answers: a)** painting, photography, film, installation, sculpture, video, cultural object **b)** concert, play, dance, ballet **c)** concert, dance, opera, ballet, gig **d)** painting, photography, installation, sculpture, video, cultural object **e)** literature, poetry **f)** all answers are possible

Coursebook page 41

2 a) 📀 26 (Recording script Coursebook page 151)
Listening: matching
- Play the recording. Students compare answers in pairs before the whole class feedback.

> **Key 1** = b) **2** = c) **3** = d) **4** = f) **5** = e) **6** = a)

b) 📀 26 (Recording script Coursebook page 151)
Listening: for detail
- Play the recording again. Students compare answers in pairs before the class feedback.
- Check / elicit meaning and pronunciation. If necessary play the recording again and / or ask students to look at Recording script 26.

> **Key 1** front row, performance **2** stage **3** exhibit **4** presenter, remote **5** back issues **6** artist, sculptor

c) Vocabulary: practice

- Draw attention to the example word map.
- Emphasise that some words can go with more than one word map, e.g. *aisle* can go in a word map for b) theatre and for c) music venue / concert hall / opera house.
- In the class feedback ask individual students to elicit vocabulary from the class and make word maps for each of the 5 places on the board.

> **Key   Possible answers: b) theatre** PLACES / THINGS: aisle, front row, back row, performance, box office, stage, backstage, interval; PEOPLE: actor, playwright, director, author, audience **c) music venue / concert hall / opera house** PLACES / THINGS: aisle, front row, back row, performance, box office, stage, backstage, interval; PEOPLE: composer, audience **d) museum** PLACES / THINGS: exhibit, exhibition; PEOPLE: visitor, attendant, artist, sculptor **e) library** PLACES / THINGS: shelf, reference book, back issues; PEOPLE: playwright, author, librarian **f) home (computer / TV)** PLACES / THINGS: computer, website, remote (control); PEOPLE: actor, director, presenter

3 Speaking: practice

- In groups. Appoint a secretary in each group to write notes on the discussion. If appropriate you could give students additional questions to discuss, e.g. *Which of the places a–e in Exercise 1b) have you never been to? Are there examples of each of the places a–e in the town / city you're in? Do you ever use a computer in connection with the arts?*
- Feedback with the whole class. Compare and contrast the experiences and opinions of the different groups.

Subject and object questions

4 a) 🔊27 (Recording script Coursebook page 151)
Listening: for detail

- Play the recording twice for students to note the answers. Students could compare answers in pairs after the second listening.
- Feedback with the whole class.

> **Key   1** Mario doesn't understand the play. He's a bit lost and is finding it all rather complicated. **2** Sarah is John's wife. Rebecca is John's lover. Terry is John's brother and his killer.

b) 🔊27 (Recording script Coursebook page 151)
Listening: gap fill

- If students ask about the difference between subject and object questions, tell them to wait for an explanation until after the gap fill.
- Play the recording twice if necessary. Students check in pairs. Feedback on the gap fill.
- When students have read the Language Box, write *Rebecca phoned Sarah* on the board. Students identify the subject (*Rebecca*) and object (*Sarah*). Students then fill in the boxes with *S* or *O*. If students are still unsure, go through the Language Box and emphasise that subject questions don't use the auxiliary *do*. Feedback.

> **Key   1** ☐O What **did** she **say**?   **2** ☐S Who **wrote** the letter?   **3** ☐S Who **killed** John?   **4** ☐S What **made** him do that?   **5** ☐O What **did** Terry **find out** that day?   **6** ☐S Who **told** him?

> **After 4b) Listening: for stress**
> - Point out that the main stress in subject and object questions varies because it depends on what information is important to the person asking the question.
> - Write sentences 1–6 on the board or an OHT without the underlining.
>   **1** What did she <u>say</u>? **2** Who wrote the <u>letter</u>? **3** Who killed <u>John</u>? **4** What made him do <u>that</u>? **5** What did <u>Terry</u> find out that day? **6** Who <u>told</u> him?
> - Read the sentences with the main stress on the underlined word / syllable. Students underline the word / syllable with the main stress. Read the sentences again for students to check.
> - Feedback. Then say the sentences again. Students repeat as a class or individually.

Arts and culture

5 a) Speaking: practice

- Keep this light-hearted. Pairs answer as many questions as they can. Don't let students check their answers or they'll pre-empt Exercise 5b).
- Monitor. Check pairs are writing subject questions.

b) Speaking: practice

- In new pairs. Monitor pairs as they work.
- Feedback. Check answers on Coursebook page 133.

Coursebook page 42

Valerie and Mallory
Comparative adjectives

6 **Grammar: revision**

- This activity quickly revises the spelling and form of comparative adjectives. Ask students to work individually or set this as a homework task.
- Feedback. If students have made common errors, briefly revise rules for the formation and spelling of comparative adjectives.

Key		
Adjective + *-er*	*More* + adjective + *than*	Irregular
bigger	more unusual than	better
darker	more boring than	worse
braver	more famous than	further / farther
lazier	more impressive than	
smarter	more creative than	
harder	more insecure than	
livelier	more attractive than	
softer	more useful than	
nicer	more enthusiastic than	
cooler	more colourful than	
brighter	more skilful than	
	more comfortable than	
	more entertaining than	

7 **a)** **Speaking: preparation**

- First elicit that Valerie and Mallory are in an art gallery. Students then speculate about what they're saying, e.g. *I've never seen anything so dramatic as this picture.* Ask students to describe Valerie's and Mallory's personalities, based on the picture. Ask questions to prompt, e.g. *What do you think they're like? serious? intellectual? pretentious? Why?*
- Ask students if they've ever seen or heard snobbish art connoisseurs who consider themselves to be very discriminating about art and fashion in galleries or if they know anyone like this. Be careful not to be too negative!
- Elicit the similarities and differences between the 2 paintings. They're both black and white, but John Frank's painting is a black circle on a white background and Yi Mo's painting is a white circle on a black background.

b) ⊙⊙ 28 (Recording script Coursebook page 151)

Listening: for detail

- Play the recording.
- Elicit answers from the class.

> **Key** Valerie likes the painting of a white circle on a black background by Yi Mo, the Chinese artist. Mallory likes the painting of a black circle on a white background by John Frank.

c) ⊙⊙ 28 (Recording script Coursebook page 151)

Listening: gap fill

- Draw attention to the example sentence to highlight the language area that students are listening for.
- Ask students to read the gapped sentences 1–10 before they listen to the recording. Check / elicit *snob* and *stuff*.
- Play the recording twice. Students fill in the gaps.
- In pairs. Students compare answers before the whole class feedback.
- Go through the key points of the Language Box after students have read it. Ask questions about the information, e.g. *What's the difference in meaning between **so** and **such**?* to elicit that there is no difference in meaning. Both words are used to make the words that follow them stronger. Ask *What's the difference in grammar between **so** and **such**?* to elicit that *so* is followed by an adjective and *such* is followed by *a / an* + noun. Ask *What's the difference between **far** and **a bit**?* to elicit that *far* (and also *much* and *a lot*) are used with comparative adjectives to show big differences in comparisons e.g. *Don is **far** taller than Mick. A bit* (and also *slightly*) are used with comparative adjectives to show small differences in comparisons, e.g. *Mick is **a bit** taller than Sarah.* Point out that *a lot* and *much* are more common in informal conversation than *far*.
- At the end of the discussion on the Language Box, ask *Who do you think is the boss – Mallory or Valerie?* Elicit students' views.

> **Key** 1 such an 2 so 3 a lot 4 much more
> 5 so 6 such a 7 far more 8 far less
> 9 quite as 10 nearly as

Pronunciation: sentence stress

8 [oo] 29 Listening: for stress / to repeat

- Feedback. Then play the recording again. Students listen and repeat as a class and individually.
- After students have read the Language Box, explain that the words are stressed because Valerie and Mallory think that they're giving important information. They're adding to the meaning of the adjectives and comparative adjectives by emphasising them.

> **Key** 1 <u>such</u> 2 <u>so</u> 3 <u>lot</u> 4 <u>much</u> 5 <u>so</u>

Coursebook page 43

9 Speaking: practice

- Students could do the pair work in the characters of Valerie and Mallory to practise stressing for emphasis but don't suggest it if it would embarrass them.
- Tell students they can use adjectives from Exercises 6 and 7 but encourage them to use adjectives of their own as well. Tell them to point to the paintings / chairs or use the number of the photos to make it obvious what they're describing, e.g. *The chair in photo 5 is much harder than the chair in photo 4.*

10 a) Speaking: practice

- Bring in 2 photos of well-known personalities. Use them to illustrate the activity by eliciting comparisons from the class.
- Remind students to use ways of modifying adjectives in their comparisons.
- Monitor pairs as they work.

b) Speaking: practice

- Go through the example with the class to encourage students to reply to the sentences they hear with suitable comparisons or observations of their own.
- Pairs make groups of 4 and discuss and compare the items / people they've chosen. Feedback.

> **After 10b) Writing: practice**
> - In the same pairs. Ask students to write 3 or 4 comparisons about the same items they chose in Exercise 10. Remind them to use ways of modifying adjectives.

The people's art

11 Speaking: preparation / practice

- This activity consolidates practice of arts vocabulary, ways of modifying adjectives and comparative adjectives.
- Students will need support when preparing for this activity but it gives students an opportunity to discuss and give opinions.
- The instructions for the activity specify 4 pairs: Pairs A, B, C and D. However you don't have to use all 4 sets of instructions. You can choose the instructions you want and the activity can be done with different group sizes according to the number of students in your class.
- Read the scenario in the rubric and build up the context and atmosphere of the activity, e.g. by talking about well-known (and controversial if possible) pieces of public art in the place where you're teaching. Ask students if they thought the city planners made a good or bad choice for the piece of art and ask them to give reasons.
- Tell students that they now have a chance to give their opinions about who or what should represent art and culture in their area.
- Make sure students are absolutely clear about what they have to do by asking the whole class to look at Pair A's instructions on page 141. Go through the instructions for both parts of the activity: the preparation and the meeting itself. However, don't elicit ideas for possible people as you'll take away some of the surprise element in the meeting when all 4 pairs present their ideas. If necessary, go through part a), the preparation for the meeting, for Pairs B, C and D as well.
- Pairs then look at their different pages and begin to prepare. It's important that pairs try to anticipate possible objections to their choices so that they can fight for their choice. Monitor pairs and help with ideas for people or works of art and vocabulary.
- In groups of 8, made up of Pairs A, B, C and D. Before pairs present their ideas at the meeting, remind them to fight for their choice. Tell them to compare their choice with the other pairs' ideas, to say why their idea is definitely the best choice and to find reasons to criticise other group members' ideas.
- In the class feedback ask each group to announce their final idea and to give reasons for their choice.

Famous for fifteen minutes

12 a) Reading: for detail

- Focus on the photo. Ask students if they have heard of Andy Warhol and if so, what they know about him, e.g. *What was he famous for?* If students have seen his art, do they like it?
- Students skim the text quickly.
- Feedback with the class.

> **Key** The 1960s

b) Reading: for detail

- Point out to students that they need to read the text carefully to decide which of the jobs 1–13 Andy Warhol did. Students can make logical deductions from the information, e.g. *His paintings and prints are all of well-known people and things* means that Andy Warhol must have been a painter and print maker.
- Feedback. Ask students for evidence from the text.
- After the feedback ask students to explain the title *Famous for fifteen minutes*. Elicit that it's a reference to Andy Warhol's famous quotation *In the future, everyone will be famous for fifteen minutes* and that his MTV programme *Andy Warhol's Fifteen Minutes of Fame* was based on this quotation.

> **Key** **The jobs mentioned:** **2** painter **4** film director **5** record producer **7** publisher **8** philosopher **9** television presenter **11** writer **12** print maker

c) Reading: for detail / Vocabulary: presentation

- Students do this activity individually without using their dictionaries.
- Students compare their answers in pairs and then close their books. Read out the meanings of adjectives 1–8 from Exercise 12c) in random order. Elicit the correct adjectives and spelling and write them on the board. Students then check their answers.

> **Key** **1** well-known **2** everyday **3** hard **4** nervous **5** fashionable **6** avant-garde **7** never-ending **8** unsuccessful

13 a) Speaking: practice

- In groups. Students brainstorm the names of people who are famous for more than one thing. Point out to students that the people can be internationally famous or famous in the place where you teach. Emphasise that the idea is to produce a list of people and the things that they're famous for, not to compare the importance of different famous people.
- Explain to students that they're going to write about the people, what they did and why this person is important, as this might affect students' choice of names.

b) Writing: practice

- Ask students to do this activity for homework. Encourage the students to look at the article on Andy Warhol and to use it for ideas on how to organise their own writing.
- When students have completed and corrected their work, display it in the classroom. Ask students to read the texts and say which they find the most interesting and why.

Is that all?!

14 a) Grammar: presentation

- Elicit the meaning of *portrait* and ask students to look at the picture and read the speech bubbles. Elicit that Duncan isn't impressed because he probably thinks that his friend, Nigel, is rather slow at painting.
- Tell students to answer the questions in pairs using short answers.
- Feedback with the class.

> **Key** **1** Six months. **2** One.

b) Grammar: practice

- Ask students to work individually to write the 2 sentences. Then tell students to check their answers in pairs.
- In the class feedback elicit the answers and write them on the board.

> **Key** **1** Nigel has been painting this series of portraits for six months. **2** Nigel has painted one portrait.

c) Grammar: presentation

- Tell students to read the questions carefully as they work through them in pairs.
- Give students time to read and process the information in the Language Box. In the feedback make sure students have understood that sentences in the Present Perfect Continuous focus on an activity which began in the past and which is still continuing in the present. Although the activity might not be complete and may even hint of a continuation into the future, it shows some kind of present result or effect that you can see, e.g. if someone has been cooking you can see the food they've produced even if they aren't cooking at the moment of talking.
- **Language note:** you could also contrast the meaning of the same verb in the Present Perfect Simple and Present Perfect Continuous, e.g. *I've lived here* compared to *I've been living here*. Tell students that some verbs, e.g. *live,* can be used with either tense without much difference in meaning, although the continuous aspect can give more of a temporary feeling, e.g. *I've been living here for 3 weeks.*
- Refer students to the Grammar reference on pages 112 and 113 for information on the Present Perfect Simple and the Present Perfect Continuous.

> **Key**   **1** = sentence 2   **2** = sentence 1
> **3** = sentence 1   **4** = sentence 2

15 ⊙⊙ 30 (Recording script Coursebook page 151)
Listening: for detail

- Before you play the recording, check students remember that *go* becomes *been* in the Present Perfect Simple when it refers to a place a person has visited and returned from.
- Play the recording twice for students to identify the tenses.
- In the feedback elicit the correct tense. Then ask students to expand the prompts 1–9 to make complete sentences.

> **Key**   **1** C I've been creating art.   **2** C I've been making films.   **3** S I haven't finished a whole film.   **4** C I've been writing a novel.   **5** S How much have you written?   **6** C I've been exploring New York.   **7** S I've been to lots of places.   **8** S Have you been to the Museum of Modern Art?   **9** C I've been working on a series of portraits.

After 15 Grammar: matching

- Write the sentences 1–5 and the sentences a–e on the board or use an OHT.
- Ask the students to match what the different people have been doing (1–5) to what they've actually achieved (a–e).
  1 She's been working here for a month.
  2 She's been training to become an astronaut.
  3 She's been collecting money for charity for the last 3 weeks.
  4 She's been painting her house since Sunday.
  5 She's been researching a book about e-commerce.

  a) She's visited 2 websites.
  b) She's raised £4000.
  c) She's watched *Star Wars* twice.
  d) She's had 3 promotions.
  e) She's finished one door.
- Feedback with the class.

> **Key**   **1** = d)   **2** = c)   **3** = b)   **4** = e)   **5** = a)

16 a) Speaking: preparation

- Check the instructions with the class and illustrate the activity using the example. Go through the list of projects 1–6. Elicit / explain the meaning of the phrases *break into the (music business), a healthier, fitter, more spiritual me* and *perfect partner*. Point out that students will have a chance to swap roles in Exercise 16b).
- In pairs. Students choose a project from the list and prepare to have a conversation about it. Tell them to decide who is like Nigel and who is the impatient friend. Students think of at least 4 rather feeble things the person like Nigel has done in order to achieve his / her goal.
- Students then act out their conversation in pairs.
- Monitor and give help as necessary.

b) Speaking: practice

- Students swap roles and choose a different project. They then prepare their new conversation.
- Feedback with the class.

> ### After 16b) Photocopiable activities
> - See 5 *Right or wrong?*, page T118.

⑤ *Conversations* *I'm not sure . . .*

Grammar/ structures	Language of doubt: *look* + adjective; *look like* + noun (phrase); *look as if* + clause
Functions	Conversation strategies to express doubt and hesitation
Pronunciation	Stress and intonation when expressing doubt
Take to class	2 encyclopedias for Exercise 5

Coursebook page 46

What do you think it is?

1 a) 👀 31 (Recording script Coursebook page 152)
Listening: for gist

- Before students read the instructions, ask them to look at the photos. Ask *What are these objects? Where would you find them?*
- Play the recording. Before students listen a second time, elicit some of the things the 2 friends say about the sculpture, e.g. *it looks warm; that looks like a giant ear* (it doesn't matter if students don't give the exact words).
- Play the recording again and elicit which sculpture the 2 friends are discussing from the class. Ask students to say which clue helped them the most to identify the correct sculpture.

> **Key** They're discussing sculpture 4.

b) 👀 31 (Recording script Coursebook page 152)
Grammar: presentation / Listening: gap fill

- Tell students to try to fill in the gaps before they listen. Some of the gap fills might be quite easy but others, e.g. *looks as if,* may be new to the students.
- Play the recording for students to fill in the gaps. Students check their answers in pairs. Feedback.
- Focus on the Language Box. Double-check the 3 different structures using the word *look.*
- Use the board to highlight the use of short answers when we aren't sure about something:

Wh- questions	Short answers
What do you think it is?	I'm not sure. I don't know. I've got no idea.
Yes / No questions	Short answers
Do you think it's . . . ?	I'm not sure. I don't know. I've got no idea. I suppose so. Maybe.

- Focus on the *Look!* section of the Language Box to show how you can say both *It looks as if he's getting angry* (which focuses on the fact of getting angry) or *He looks as if he's getting angry* (which focuses more on the person who is getting angry). Point out that the verb after *looks as if* can be in any tense relevant to the context.
- **Language note:** draw attention to the fact that *sort of* in inexact description is used in speech more than in writing.

> **Key** 1 looks 2 no idea 3 suppose, sort of
> 4 look like 5 think 6 looks as if 7 looks like
> 8 Maybe 9 might be

Coursebook page 47

Pronunciation: stress and intonation

2 a) Pronunciation: preparation

- When pairs finish underlining the stressed words / syllables, ask them to circle the words / syllables they think are stressed more in each sentence. Don't feedback or you'll pre-empt Exercise 2b) but ask them to think about which words carry the most important information.

b) 👀 32 **Listening: to check and repeat**

- Play the recording, pausing if necessary.
- Feedback by playing the recording again and eliciting the answers from the class.
- Highlight the tentative intonation, e.g. *I'm not really sure*; the stressing of *think* to show uncertainty; the lengthening of the second syllable in *suppose*.
- Elicit from students the typical gestures and facial expressions that accompany the language of doubt. Tell them to use these when they practise.
- Play the recording. Students repeat the exchanges.

> **Key** (underlining = stress, bold = main stress)
> **1** A: <u>What</u> do you think it **is**? B: I've got **no** <u>idea</u>.
> **2** A: Do you <u>know</u> what it **is**? B: I'm <u>not</u> really **sure**
> . . . but I <u>think</u> it's some sort of **dog**. It <u>looks</u> as if
> it's **mov**ing. **3** A: Do you <u>think</u> it's a**live**?
> B: I sup**pose** so. It **might** be.

c) Pronunciation: practice
- Students practise the exchanges in pairs. Encourage them to exaggerate the stress and intonation and to use typical gestures and facial expressions for the language of doubt.

3 Speaking: practice
- Ask students to pretend they're in a gallery.
- Tell the students to use as many of the different phrases as possible from the Language Box in Exercise 1b) and to include the stress and intonation practised in Exercise 2.
- Practise a conversation with one or two students to illustrate the activity before the students work in groups.

What's the answer?

4 a) Speaking: practice
- Use examples of some well-known local quiz shows together with the picture and the instructions to create the atmosphere for this activity. Check *contestant* and *general knowledge quiz*.
- Students discuss the questions in pairs. Then feedback. Focus on students who have won a prize in a general knowledge quiz or who think they're good at quizzes. Ask for details.

b) ⟦oo⟧33 (Recording script Coursebook page 152)
Listening: for detail
- Play the recording. Students note down the answers to questions 1–4. Monitor to see if they need to hear the recording more than once. Then ask students to compare their answers in pairs before the feedback.
- Ask additional questions to elicit the answers in brackets, e.g. *What does Geoff keep doing as the time to answer the question passes?* (*He asks for more time and tells the quizmaster to be quiet.*) *How does the quizmaster's attitude change?* (*He's very friendly at first but by the end he's very angry.*) *What happens to the contestant in the end?* (*He's taken away by security.*)

> **Key**   **1** £10,000 (ten thousand pounds).   **2** What is the capital of Iceland?   **3** 10 seconds.   **4** No.

c) Speaking: practice
- Elicit the correct answer. Students then check it.

> **Key**   Reykjavík is the capital of Iceland.

d) ⟦oo⟧33 (Recording script Coursebook page 152)
Listening: gap fill
- In monolingual classes ask which fillers students use in their own language.
- Ask students to try to fill in as many gaps as they can before the listening. Don't worry if they can't fill in all the gaps and don't feedback yet.
- Students listen to the recording and fill in all the gaps. Students compare their answers in pairs. Play the recording again for students to check.
- **Language note:** highlight that it's not a good idea to leave long silences in conversations in English. Focus on the meaning and use of the hesitation phrases in the Language Box and phrases 1–6 in Exercise 4d). They're useful for recognition purposes even if students don't use them in their own conversations.
- Point out that we use the filler *Don't tell me!* when we're trying to think of an answer to a question and don't want to be told the answer.
- Demonstrate the stress and intonation in the hesitation phrases and ask the students to repeat them.

> **Key**   **1** think   **2** tell   **3** tip, tongue   **4** Wait   **5** see   **6** Just

Your time's up!

5 Speaking: practice
- Divide the class into 2 teams. Give each team an encyclopedia. Ask the teams to read their instructions on writing questions and then tell both teams to read the rules for the quiz on page 138.
- Monitor the teams as they read questions 1–4 and then write their own 4 questions. Their questions can be about vocabulary covered in previous units of the course but the quiz will work better if they're general knowledge questions about famous people or places, recent history, popular culture, etc.
- The questions must have answers that can be checked. Emphasise that teams must know the answer to every question they ask.
- When the questions are ready, the teams play according to the rules. Emphasise that you want the proceedings to be entirely in English, then let the teams get on with the competition with as little intervention from you as possible.
- Feedback with the whole class.

⑥ Skin deep

Grammar / structures	Revision of superlative adjectives; Second Conditional with *would, could, might*; *wish* + Past Simple / *could* / *would*; infinitive of purpose and *by* + verb + *-ing* for methods
Topic / vocabulary	Fashion and beauty
Wavelength **pages**	**Day to day English** *If I were you . . .*: suggestions and advice
	Reading for pleasure 2: *"Oh, really!"*
	Do you remember? Units 4–6

Coursebook page 48

The way we were

> **Optional extras**
> **Before 1a) Warmer**
> - In groups of 4: Pair A and Pair B. Pairs look at each other for 30 seconds. Pair Bs then go out of the classroom. Each pair writes down exactly what both students in the other pair are wearing.
> - Pair Bs return to their group and students discuss their descriptions.

1 a) Warmer
- Before students open their books, describe one or two students' clothes. Ask the class to guess who you're describing.
- Teach / check *decade*. Then ask students to look at photos 1–6. In pairs. Students discuss which decade they think each photo is from.
- Feedback and ask students to justify their answers. Help with vocabulary as necessary.

> **Key** **1** = 1970s **2** = 1940s **3** = 1980s
> **4** = 1950s **5** = 1990s **6** = 1960s

b) Speaking: practice
- In groups. Monitor the conversations and encourage students to give details.
- Feedback with the class. Ask students to justify their likes and opinions.

> **After 1b) Speaking: practice**
> - Write on the board: *Which other fashions do you connect with the decades in the photos? Can you describe current popular fashion in your country? What do you think of it? Which current fashions do you think are cool? ridiculous?* Students discuss the questions in pairs.
> - Feedback with the class.

2 a) Vocabulary: presentation
- Before students match the Word Boxes to the photos, write words from the Word Boxes on the board. Then ask students to come to the board and draw the item of clothing. Remind students that they can use the *Longman WordWise Dictionary* to help them if necessary.
- In the feedback deal with pronunciation and stress. Use the photos to consolidate meaning.
- Then ask students to describe the clothes that you're wearing.

> **Key** **a)** = 3 **b)** = 4 **c)** = 1
> **d)** = 5 **e)** = 6 **f)** = 2

b) Speaking: practice
- Tell students they can use their dictionaries if necessary.
- Feedback with the whole class on the first part of the exercise. Check that students have found items 1–6 by asking them to point out each item in the photos.
- Check that students understand the second part of the exercise. Draw attention to the example and elicit more clothes that can have sleeves, e.g. *jumper, top, T-shirt, dress, blouse*, etc.
- Feedback with the whole class by listing on the board or on an OHT students' suggestions for clothes that can have items 1–6. You could also teach / elicit other items which aren't shown in the photos, e.g. *hood, zip*, etc.

> **Key** **1** collar (photos 1, 2, 3, 4): shirt, jacket, blouse, top, etc. **2** button (photos 1, 2, 4): jacket, shirt, trousers, jeans, etc. **3** pocket (photos 1, 2, 3, 4, 5): jacket, trousers, shirt, suit, etc. **4** buckle (photos 1, 3): belt, jacket, skirt, shoes, etc. **5** laces (photo 5): trainers, boots, shoes, etc. **6** shoulder pad (photo 3): jacket, dress, etc.

Fads and fashions

3 a) Superlative adjectives: gap fill

- Revise the form (including spelling changes) and use of superlative adjectives with the whole class.
- Monitor students as they fill in the gaps. Check vocabulary as necessary.
- Students compare answers in pairs before the class feedback.

> **Key** 2 the most expensive   3 the newest
> 4 the best   5 the worst   6 the strangest,
> the stupidest / the most stupid, the wildest
> 7 the coolest, the most stylish   8 the most
> unattractive

b) 🔊 34 (Recording script Coursebook page 152)
Listening: for gist

- Before students listen, remind them that they don't have to understand every word.
- Feedback with the class.

> **Key** Amy is answering question 6.
> Tim is answering question 4.

c) 🔊 34 (Recording script Coursebook page 152)
Listening: for detail

- Emphasise that the sentences express what Amy and Tim said. The sentences don't give their exact words. If students find this difficult, play the recording twice. If students still have difficulty, play the recording again and pause as necessary.

> **Key** 1 = T 2 = A 3 = T   4 = T
> 5 = T   6 = A 7 = T   8 = A

d) Speaking: practice

- If necessary, students could work in groups.
- Feedback with the whole class. Elicit any unusual or interesting answers.

> **After 3d) Writing / Speaking: practice**
> - In groups. Students write 4 questions for a questionnaire using superlative adjectives. Groups then swap questionnaires, ask and answer the questions and feedback to the whole class.

Rich and famous

4 a) Speaking: practice

- Ask the students what they understand by *style icons*. Elicit that style icons are famous people who represent a type and often an era and that style icons fascinate and influence the general public's clothes, attitudes and general lifestyles.
- In pairs. Give students time to try and identify the style icons. You could list the names from the Key on the board in random order if necessary.
- Feedback on the identity of the style icons. Students then discuss if they think the style icons in the photos are / were influential.
- Feedback and then ask students to list other people, past or present, who they consider to be style icons.
- Feedback with the whole class by listing students' suggestions for style icons past and present on the board and discuss why they chose them. Ask students if they think that style icons influence styles and fashions or if they think that they copy them. Do any of the style icons influence the students themselves?

> **Key** **top left:** Mick Jagger   **top right:** Madonna
> as Marilyn Monroe   **centre left:** David Beckham
> and Victoria Beckham (Posh Spice)   **centre**
> **right:** Frank Sinatra   **bottom:** Audrey Hepburn

b) Speaking: practice

- Check the meaning and pronunciation of the words in the Word Box as necessary.
- Ask students to give examples of rich and famous people during their discussion.
- Ask students to think of possible advantages and disadvantages connected with each of the ideas in the Word Box, e.g. *an advantage of therapy: you can afford the best therapists to help you with any problems; a disadvantage of therapy: you probably need it because of all the stress.*
- Monitor and help pairs as necessary but don't worry about students' grammar in the discussion. If they use Second Conditionals, that's fine. However as they're talking about real examples of rich and famous people, there's no need for the Second Conditional at this stage.

Second Conditional

5 a) 🔵 35 (Recording script Coursebook page 152)
Listening: for gist

- Play the recording and feedback on the answer to question 1.
- Then play the recording again. Feedback with the class on question 2 and elicit from students the ideas that Tina and Ryan mention.

> **Key** **1** Tina sees the advantages. **2** Tina mentions: plastic surgery; clothes; lifestyle. Ryan mentions: therapy; marriage; privacy; the press; the public.

b) 🔵 35 (Recording script Coursebook page 152)
Matching / Listening: to check

- Students match individually, then compare their answers in pairs.
- Students then listen and check. Feedback with the whole class.

> **Key** **2** = d) **3** = c) **4** = a) **5** = e)

c) Grammar: presentation

- Students answer the questions.
- Feedback and then ask students to read the Language Box on page 51.
- Remind students of the form and use of the Second Conditional. Highlight the unreal / very unlikely nature of the Second Conditional (it's the opposite of the real situation) and the time (although the verb is in the Past Simple, the time is the present or the future).
- **Language note:** you could point out that we usually use the Past Simple in the *if* part of the sentence in the Second Conditional, but that we can also use the Past Continuous. You could also highlight the fact that with the verb *be* we usually use *were / weren't* with all subjects, but we do sometimes use *was / wasn't* with *he / she / it* in conversation.
- Refer students to the Grammar reference on page 116 for information on the Second Conditional.

> **Key** **1 No**, they're not rich and famous.
> **2** They're talking about **unreal** situations.
> **3** The sentences refer to **the present / future**.
> **4** The **Past Simple** tense is used in the *if* part of each sentence.

Coursebook page 51

6 **Writing: practice**

- Focus students' attention on the 2 examples. Go through them with the class and highlight the difference between the real situation and the imagined, unreal situation.
- Ask students to work individually. Then tell them to compare their answers in pairs.
- Feedback with the class.

> **Key** **1** If she were taller / tall enough, she could get modelling jobs. **2** If they weren't too / so busy, they could / would spend more time together. **3** I could afford a car if I earned more / enough money. **4** If my wife weren't so famous, the press wouldn't bother me all the time. **5** If Joe could sing, he would be a singer in a rock band.

After 6 Listening: for stress

- Write the 2 example sentences from Exercise 6 on the board or on an OHT.
- Read each sentence aloud twice. Individual students come to the board and underline the stressed words / syllables and circle the main stress. Several students may need to do this before you elicit the correct answers.
- Elicit from the class that the most important information is in the part of the sentence that doesn't begin with *if*, i.e. the result clause, not the condition.
- Model the sentences again for the class and then individual students to repeat.

> **Key** **(underlining = stress, bold = main stress)**
> **1** I'd <u>live</u> on a <u>tropical</u> **is**land if I were <u>rich</u>.
> **2** If he <u>didn't</u> need the <u>money</u>, he'd <u>leave</u> his **job**.

After 6 Reading / Writing: practice

- Students write 4 short real or imagined problems. In pairs. Students swap problems and take it in turns to make suggestions / give advice and encouragement using Second Conditionals.
- Monitor pairs as they work and give help with vocabulary as necessary.
- Feedback with the class.

My fantastic life

7 a) Speaking / Writing: practice

- Before pairs write, brainstorm some questions with the class. Elicit different types of Second Conditional questions, e.g. questions using *could* and negative questions. Elicit questions that deal with both the positive and negative aspects of the lives of the rich and famous, e.g.:

 1 Home: *Where would you live? What would your home / homes be like? What wouldn't it / they be like? How would you decorate it / them? What extras would you install? Would you install fences and security systems? Would you buy homes for other members of your family? for your friends?*

 2 Appearance: *Where would you buy your clothes? your shoes? your jewellery? other fashion accessories? Would you have any designers working for you? Would you become bored with fashion? Would you employ a personal dresser? hairstylist? beautician?*

 3 Leisure: *What would you do for fun? Where would you go in the evenings? on holiday? Where wouldn't you go? Would you buy a yacht? a private plane? a helicopter? a glider? Who would your friends be? Who wouldn't your friends be?* Encourage students to give some names if they can.

 4 Lifestyle: *What would you do every day? What would you never do again? What food would you eat? What would you drink? What problems would you have that you haven't got now? What problems wouldn't you have that you've got now?*

- Monitor students as they write their questions and remind them not to answer them! Give help as necessary and encourage them to identify and correct their own mistakes.

b) Speaking / Writing: practice

- Make sure students work in new pairs.
- You could ask students to take short notes about their partner's answers. Monitor students as they interview each other.
- Tell students to write their paragraph about their partner in class or for homework.
- Students could also write about *My fantastic life* for homework, describing what their life would be like and how it would be different if they were rich and famous.

After 7b) Writing / Reading: practice

- Write these 2 questions on the board or on an OHT:

 1 Would he / she be happier, not as happy, or exactly the same if he / she were rich and famous?

 2 What are the most interesting or the most surprising things he / she said about his / her new life as a rich and famous person?

- Students write answers to the 2 questions about the partner they interviewed and wrote about in Exercise 7b) on a separate piece of paper. Tell students not to include their partner's name in their answers.
- Collect all the papers. Read answers from different papers to the class, or ask students to come up to the front and read them, or use an OHT. The rest of the class then guesses who the answers are about.
- Alternatively you could display the papers round the classroom and ask students to write the name of the person they think it's about on each paper.

Wish + Past Simple

8 a) 🔲36 Listening: gap fill

- Play the recording and ask students to fill in the gaps individually.
- Feedback with the class.

> **Key** I **wish** I **could** live on an island like that.

b) Presentation

- Feedback on questions 1 and 2 before students read the Language Box. Draw attention to the fact that both *wish* + Past Simple and the Second Conditional deal with unreal situations.
- Students read the Language Box. Check the form and use of *wish* + Past Simple. Point out that *wish* can also be followed by *could* and *would*.
- Refer students to the Grammar reference on page 116 for information on *wish* + Past Simple.

> **Key** 1 Ryan can't live on an island. Presumably because he hasn't got enough money. 2 Yes, he would like his situation to be different.

c) Writing: practice

• The aim of the activity is for students to demonstrate that they understand the concept and can manipulate the form by expressing the wishes of these people.

• Make sure students understand that there is more than one possible wish for each sentence.

• Feedback and accept all plausible answers.

> **Key** **Possible answers:** **1** She wishes she were taller / tall enough. She wishes she could get modelling jobs. **2** They wish they weren't too / so busy. They wish they could spend more time together. **3** He / She wishes he / she could afford a car. He / she wishes he / she earned more / enough money (to buy a car). **4** He wishes his wife weren't famous. He wishes the press wouldn't bother him all the time. **5** He wishes he could sing. He wishes he could be a singer in a rock band.

I wish . . . I wish . . .

9 **a)** Speaking: preparation

• Check *genie* by drawing attention to the picture. Set the scene for the exercise.

• Give students time to think about their 3 wishes. Emphasise that students should talk about their present lives and wishes for the present, not about regrets from the past.

b) Speaking: practice

• Students go round the class and talk to each other about their wishes. Monitor students to make sure that they only talk about their present lives and wishes for the present.

• Feedback with the whole class and ask the students if anyone said anything that surprised or impressed them.

> **Coursebook page 52**

> **Before 10 Warmer**
> • Have a class discussion about the meaning of the saying *Beauty is only skin deep.* Encourage the students to think of and express in English examples of popular sayings about beauty from their own cultures. Ask them to explain what the sayings mean.

10 Warmer

• Divide students into groups. Give students one minute to brainstorm as many words as they can think of associated with beauty, e.g. words connected with make-up, hairstyles, facial appearance, beauty techniques, clothes and fashion accessories. At the end of one minute collect the lists from the groups.

• Feedback and ask students to suggest headings / categories for the words they listed.

• Ask students questions about their own beauty treatments, e.g. to all students: *What is the last beauty product you bought?* to male students: *Do you shave every day?*

• In groups, ask students to think of more questions associated with beauty now and in the past, e.g. *Do you go to a gym? How much is it for reasons of appearance rather than fitness? Have you ever dyed your hair? What features do you think make a man handsome? a woman beautiful? What features do you think made a man handsome / a woman beautiful in other decades?*

• Monitor and make sure that the questions aren't about personal areas students wouldn't wish to talk about. Then tell the students to take it in turns to ask and answer questions in pairs.

• In groups. Students discuss what different things people do / have done to their body to improve / change their appearance. Groups then feedback.

11 **a)** Reading: for gist

• With books closed, explain to the students that they're going to read an article called "The History of Beauty". Write the title on the board. In small groups, ask students to predict in general terms the contents of 5 paragraphs they would expect to find in an article with this title. When they finish, write their suggestions on the board.

• With books open, check that students understand sentences 1–5. Elicit from the students a theme word for each sentence: *1 = baths; 2 = underwear; 3 = teeth; 4 = suntans; 5 = hairstyles.* Ask students to read the article quickly and match the sentences to the appropriate paragraphs. Emphasise that students shouldn't focus too much on unknown words at this point.

• After the feedback with the class compare students' suggestions on the board with the contents of the article.

> **Key** **1** = d) **2** = e) **3** = b) **4** = a) **5** = c)

b) Reading: for detail

- Pre-teach as necessary vocabulary which doesn't pre-empt the reading task, e.g. *ingredient, protective, pumice stone*.
- Discourage the use of dictionaries. Remind students to read the first sentence of paragraphs a–e from Exercise 11a) as they read the whole article. In pairs. Students note down the answers as they read. Monitor and give help as necessary. Ask students questions to encourage them to deduce the meaning of unfamiliar words.
- In different pairs. Students compare answers before the whole class feedback.

> **Key 1** Paragraph a): twentieth century, sixteenth century, 1533–1603, eighteenth-century Italy   Paragraph b): Tudor days, seventeenth century   Paragraph c): 1770s   Paragraph d): the beginning of the last millennium, the sixteenth century, 1633–1703   Paragraph e): Georgians (= the people who lived in the Georgian period 1714–1830), medieval Britain, modern **2** Lead and arsenic. **3** (Tooth) enamel. It eventually removed the enamel completely. **4** decay **5** The pig fat in the wigs attracted the mice. Their skins were used for false eyebrows. **6** Wine, milk and puppy's urine. **7** ignoring, damage **8** It was very difficult to stand or walk in platform shoes and wearers often twisted their ankles. It was very difficult to breathe in corsets and wearers often fainted.

After 11b) Vocabulary: practice

- In groups of 3. Ask students to choose a word from the article. Tell them to write 3 definitions for the word: one true definition and 2 false ones which aren't definitions of any other words in the article. Monitor and give help as necessary.
- Groups take it in turns to read out their 3 definitions. The rest of the class says which definition is true and identifies the word from the article.

12 Speaking: practice

- During the discussion make a note of errors of pronunciation or use for the feedback.
- Elicit a selection of answers to the questions in the feedback. Encourage students to give reasons for their opinions. Feedback on errors.

Coursebook page 53

Verb forms for *Why?* and *How?*

13 a) Presentation

- Elicit answers to questions 1 and 2 from the class. Students then read the Language Box.
- **Language note:** emphasise that a sentence containing an infinitive of purpose (*to* + infinitive) expresses a purpose or a reason and is often used to answer a question beginning *Why*. A sentence containing *by* + verb + *-ing* gives information about a method used to do something and is often used to follow a question beginning *How* meaning *by what method*.

> **Key 1** To make them look very pale – almost white. **2** By wearing platform shoes.

b) Gap fill

- Ask students to fill in the gaps individually.
- Feedback with the class.

> **Key 1** by washing **2** to make **3** by not eating **4** by developing **5** to get off

After 13b) Writing: practice

- Read out or write these questions on the board / an OHT: *Why do people wear make-up? How can you get rich? Why do people dye their hair? Why do people read? How can you get fit? How can you learn good English?*
- Elicit as many answers for each question as possible using *to* + infinitive or *by* + verb + *-ing*.
- In pairs. Students think of 2 similar questions, one beginning *Why* to elicit a purpose or reason and the other beginning *How* to elicit a method. Pairs write each question at the top of a separate piece of paper.
- Monitor and give help as necessary.
- Put the pieces of paper round the room. Ask students to go round and write an answer for each question on each piece of paper.
- In the class feedback comment on the accuracy of the students' language and the appropriateness of the ideas.

After 13b) Photocopiable activities

- See 6 *Leave it with us!*, page T120.

⑥ Day to day English *If I were you . . .*

Grammar / structures	Suggestions: *You could . . . , Why don't you . . . ?, Try / How about . . . + - ing?*; advice: *You should / ought to . . . , If I were you . . . , You'd better . . .* ; orders: *You must / have to . . .*
Topic / vocabulary	Phrases for minor illnesses / injuries, treatments

Coursebook page 54

Suggestions and advice

1 **oo** 37 (Recording script Coursebook page 153)
Listening: for detail
- Pre-teach *audition*. Help with other vocabulary as necessary but let students deduce *skinny* and *fainted* from the context of the listening.
- Before playing the recording elicit suggestions or pieces of advice students could give Tony but don't insist on accurate form at this point.
- Feedback with the whole class.

> **Key** **1** For people to appear in a TV commercial.
> **2** He thought he was too thin for the job. **3** To try to look bigger and stronger by wearing lots of jumpers. **4** He got overheated and fainted.

2 a) Matching
- Explain that each picture shows a suggestion or piece of advice for dealing with a particular problem. In pairs. Ask the students to read the 12 different suggestions / pieces of advice and to choose the 6 suggestions / pieces of advice that match the 6 pictures. Focus on the example.
- Feedback but don't identify the problems illustrated in the pictures or you'll pre-empt Exercise 2b).

> **Key** **B** = 5b) **C** = 1a) **D** = 6b) **E** = 3a) **F** = 2b)

b) Matching
- Students read the problems. Before students do the matching, ask them to match the problems to the pictures A–F in Exercise 2a). Then go through the example with the class.
- In pairs. Students match the problems to the suggestions / advice 1–6 and compare answers with another pair before the whole class feedback.

> **Key** **b)** = 1a) and b) **c)** = 3a) and b) **d)** = 2a) and b) **e)** = 4a) and b) **f)** = 5a) and b)

3 Speaking: practice
- In groups. Students discuss the ideas in Exercise 2a) and make other suggestions.
- Feedback with the class. Elicit any strange or wonderful cures or remedies for the problems.

4 a) oo 38 **Listening: for detail**
- Students read the suggestions / pieces of advice and predict the order. Then play the recording for students to check their predictions.
- Play the recording again. Use it as a drill to focus on the changes in intonation and stress as suggestions / pieces of advice get stronger.

> **Key** **a)** = 4 **b)** = 2 **c)** = 1 **d)** = 5 **e)** = 3

b) Gap fill
- Students fill in the gaps.
  Feedback and go through the Language Box.
- **Language note:** point out how we stress the verbs *must* and *have to* for emphasis but if we want to make *should / ought to* stronger we usually stress modifying words like *really*.

> **Key** Why **don't you** drink some hot lemon juice?
> **Try** drinking some hot lemon juice. How **about** drinking some hot lemon juice? If **I were you**, I'd see a doctor.

5 a) Speaking / Writing: practice
- Check vocabulary before students prepare their suggestions and advice for each problem.
- In pairs. Students discuss and then write their suggestions / pieces of advice.
- Encourage novel remedies for each problem 1–6.

b) Speaking: practice
- In groups. Students read out their suggestions or advice without saying which problem they're for. The other students guess the problem.
- Monitor and note down errors for feedback at the end of the activity.

Wavelength page

Reading for pleasure
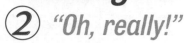
② "Oh, really!"

Vocabulary *baguette, besides, bitter, blast* (n), *by the way, camembert, cashier, caviar, checkout, chilli, collapse, crab, crocus, daylight robbery, delight* (n), *disbelief, display* (n), *either, figure, frivolous, frozen, give in to something, glue, goat, herb, hesitantly, ingredient, magnificent, oregano, oven, Parma ham, passion, penny, perfume, pity* (n), *produce* (n), *profit* (n), *quality, respectable, risk* (n), *row* (n), *saffron, salami, scales* (n pl), *seal up, section, seed, select, silk, slim* (adj), *slip something into something, solidarity, speciality, spice, sticker, superior, temple, temptation, thrill* (n), *tricks of the trade, tuna, yawn* (n)

> **Coursebook page 55**

Before reading

1 Presentation
- In pairs or groups. Students discuss what kinds of people shop outside normal opening times.
- Feedback and elicit any interesting ideas.

2 ◉◉ 39 (Recording script Coursebook page 55)
Reading and listening: for detail
- Pre-teach vocabulary. Students read and listen.
- They could work in pairs. Feedback.

> **Key** **1** Probably because he wants to park his car in a safe and convenient place. **2** Its name was lit up in coloured neon lights and it was the only place open in the neighbourhood. **3** He loved the displays of food and he was fascinated by the people who chose to shop late at night.

3 Reading: for gist and detail
- Pre-teach vocabulary. Check *Robin Hood*.
- Students read the story and answer the questions.

> **Key** **1** He put them on the scales and pressed the symbol for potatoes. **2** 2 baguettes.
> **3** To the cheese section. **4** A young woman with an almost empty trolley. **5** He put the goat's cheese into one of the baguette bags, the Parma ham into the other baguette bag and the jar of caviar into his pocket. **6** Because there was a special offer of 2 tins of tuna fish for the price of one. **7** Because she hadn't noticed the mountain of tins of tuna fish. **8** Because she had moved into a new flat that day and before then she had always lived with her parents.
> **9** To help her buy the basic things she needed.
> **10** Because she hadn't got that much money.

> **11** A tiny packet of saffron. **12** He opened up a box of cheap soap and one of expensive soap, exchanged the contents and sealed up the boxes with glue. **13** He was wearing a silk suit.
> **14** He said that he enjoyed it, it gave him a sense of power and it was an art. **15** His wallet and car keys had gone from his pocket.

After reading

4 Speaking: discussion
- Feedback on the answers to Exercise 3. You could ask more questions. Students justify their answers.
  1 Do you feel sorry for Ambrose at the end?
  2 What do you think Ambrose did next?

5 Vocabulary: practice
- Students list the items that Ambrose:
  1 was prepared to pay for: *herbs, bag of oranges, 3 grapefruit, 2 baguettes, camembert, salami, bird seed, 6 tins of tuna fish.*
  2 didn't pay full price for / stole: *4 mangoes, a goat's cheese, a packet of Parma ham, a jar of caviar.*
  3 chose for Julia: *2 packets of spaghetti, a packet of rice, 2 tins of tomatoes, pepper, dried chillies, oregano, breakfast cereal.*
  4 didn't pay full price for / stole for Julia: *a packet of saffron, a box of expensive soap.*

6 Personalisation
- Discuss these questions with the class.
  1 Ambrose says he is robbing the rich to give to the poor. Do you think wealth should be more equally distributed?
  2 What would you do if you saw a shoplifter?
  3 What measures do shops take to try and prevent shoplifters?

⑥ *Do you remember?* Units 4–6

Grammar / structures / vocabulary
1 Second Conditional
2 Arts and culture vocabulary
3 Grammar / structures / vocabulary from Units 4–6

Coursebook page 56

1 Difficult choices

a) 🔊 40 (Recording script Coursebook page 153)
Listening: gap fill

- In pairs. Before students listen, ask them to think of 10 things people do nowadays to try to make themselves more attractive.
- Students listen to the recording. Point out that the question the 2 people are answering isn't in the recording. Students have to try to work out what the question was.
- Students may have problems giving the exact words of the question if they don't know the word *tattoo* or if they're confused by the construction *had to have* because of the repetition of the 2 meanings of *have*. If students can't supply the missing words of the question you could prompt them by writing 3 possible questions on the board and asking them to choose the correct one.

> **Key**   If you had to **have** a **tattoo**, what **would you have** and where?

b) 🔊 40 (Recording script Coursebook page 153)
Listening: for detail

- Play the recording again for students to answer the question.
- Feedback with the whole class.

> **Key**   **1** He would have his surname, Wong, in Chinese on the top of his right arm.   **2** She would have a small, delicate, green and red flower on her ankle.

c) Speaking: practice

- Don't be afraid to give students sufficient time to think about their ideas and opinions and to work out how to express their answers in English.
- As students work, monitor and support, supplying any necessary vocabulary and noting errors.

d) Writing: practice

- Monitor as each pair writes an additional question.
- Feedback. Write the new questions on the board.

e) Speaking: practice

- In groups. Students discuss the questions. You could ask one student in each group to take notes for the class feedback.
- Feedback with the whole class and elicit any unusual or interesting ideas.

> **Optional extras**
> **After 1e) Speaking: practice**
> - Play *Who's going to jump out of the balloon?* and elicit the names of 6 historical heroes or villains from the class. List them on the board.
> - Explain that the 6 people are in a hot-air balloon. The balloon is going down quickly and 2 people must jump out.
> - Students discuss who they want to stay in the balloon and who they want to jump out. Encourage students to use the Second Conditional, e.g. *If I had to choose a person to jump out I would choose X because . . .*

2 The Arts Café

a) 🔊 41 (Recording script Coursebook page 153)
Listening: for detail

- Focus on the picture. Remind students of Valerie and Mallory from Unit 5 Exercise 7a). Elicit what they're like, i.e. very pretentious and excitable, very serious about art, etc. Ask students what they think the journalist is like, to elicit that he doesn't look as if he gets very excited by anything.
- Establish the context of the discussion. Then play the recording for students to listen and tick the kinds of artists and performers Valerie and Mallory are looking for.
- In the class feedback elicit that Valerie and Mallory are quite ambitious and perhaps impractical in their plans for their arts café as they're looking for all the artists / performers listed in the Word Box apart from *actor* and *singer*.

> **Key**   actor ✗   musician ✓   photographer ✓
> painter ✓   dancer ✓   video artist ✓
> sculptor ✓   writer ✓   singer ✗   poet ✓

b) 🔘🔘 41 (Recording script Coursebook page 153)
Listening: for detail

- Students write the kinds of art and entertainment 1–6 from Exercise 2b) in their notebooks before they listen and discuss possible answers.
- Students listen to the recording and make notes. Play the recording again if necessary.
- Feedback with the whole class. Elicit that Valerie and Mallory don't want singers and don't want the customers to dance because they think that both are too downmarket.
- You could play the recording again for students to list some words / phrases which show that Valerie and Mallory want to establish a high quality arts café, e.g. *a showcase for hot young talent, the best of modern dance,* etc.

> **Key** **two kinds of live music:** jazz, classical
> **one kind of dance:** modern dance **four kinds of visual art:** painting, sculpture, video installations, photography **one thing connected with literature:** poetry evenings **one kind of performer they definitely don't want:** They don't want singers. **one thing they don't want their customers to do:** They don't want them to dance.

c) Speaking: preparation

- Establish the context. In pairs: Pair A are Valerie and Mallory; Pair B are artists / performers.
- Pair As read their instructions and prepare their questions. Monitor and help as necessary.
- Pair Bs read through their instructions and each student chooses a different artist / performer. Emphasise that the artists' past experiences aren't very impressive. Encourage students to help each other to exaggerate their past experience so that they have a chance of getting the job. Monitor and help with ideas and names.

d) Speaking: practice

- In groups of 4. Make sure Valerie and Mallory interview 2 different artists from 2 different pairs. Encourage the 2 artists to compete for the job. Make notes for the class feedback.

e) Speaking: practice

- Groups of 4 make pairs. Artists point out the difference between their real and imagined experience to each other while Valerie and Mallory discuss the artists and choose one for their arts café.

- In the same groups of 4. Valerie and Mallory tell the artists which one they chose and why.
- In the feedback ask Pair As to report to the class on who they chose and why. Elicit any particularly amusing made-up past histories from Pair Bs. Feedback with the class on language points that you noted during the role-play.

> **Coursebook page 57**

3 *You don't need to lose weight!*
Grammar: practice

- This exercise revises grammar, structures and vocabulary from Units 4–6: First / Second Conditional; modifying adjectives and nouns; Present Perfect Simple / Present Perfect Continuous; skills and ability; subject questions; *wish* + Past Simple; infinitive of purpose and *by* + verb + *-ing*; verb + *-ing*; past ability.
- Revise the structures or vocabulary from Units 4–6 which you consider might cause students problems before they do the activity. Alternatively delay review activities on the structures until students have completed the exercise.
- Draw attention to the title of the activity and the photo. Elicit from students the subject of the conversation. Students could do the activity for homework or individually in class before checking their answers in pairs.
- Feedback with the class. Go into more detail with areas which seem to cause problems to a lot of students. You could refer individual students to exercises from Units 4–6 which deal with the structures that are still causing problems.

> **Key** **1** I'll lose **2** so **3** I've been following **4** lost **5** much **6** can't **7** have to **8** hearing **9** Who says **10** having **11** that were **12** You're being **13** don't think **14** to lose **15** to lose **16** were **17** would **18** eating **19** doing **20** jogging **21** at **22** in losing **23** so **24** Going **25** could

> Encourage students to learn the new words from Units 4–6 on Coursebook pages 124–126 and do Puzzle 2 on Coursebook page 120 before you give them Progress test Units 4–6 on page T139.

(7) *Can we talk?*

Grammar / structures	Past Perfect Simple and Past Simple in narratives; reported speech: *say, tell, ask*; *because* and *so*
Topic / vocabulary	Means of communication; phrasal verbs and expressions for telephoning
Pronunciation	Sentence stress
Wavelength pages	**Writing for work and pleasure 3** *Guess what!*: telling a story

Coursebook page 58

Communication

> **Optional extras**
> **Before 1 Warmer**
> - In 4 groups. Give students one minute to list as many means of communication as they can.
> - Elicit the words / phrases. Write them on the board. The group with the most wins.

1 Speaking: practice
- Before students look at the questions elicit brief descriptions of the different frames of the cartoon and help with vocabulary as necessary.
- Read through the questions with the class. Students then discuss the questions in pairs.
- In the feedback, ask students to justify their opinions. Discuss the cartoon's message that there is less, not more, communication because of mobile phones.

2 a) Vocabulary: gap fill
- In pairs. Students read the comments that people have made about different means of communication and fill in the gaps.
- Feedback and then highlight / elicit the typical verbs used with each kind of communication:
  1 use, go off, turn off; 2 watch, turn down, be on; 3 read, say, write; 4 be on (something), crash; 5 reply, delete, attach.
- Elicit other words which are associated with the different means of communication, e.g. notes: *get, leave*; computers: *turn on / off, shut down, file, screen, desk top*; e-mails: *send, get, draft*; mobile phones: *ring, turn on, recharge, text message, text* (v); television: *turn on / off / up / over*, etc.

> **Key** **1** mobile phones **2** television **3** notes **4** computers **5** e-mails

b) Vocabulary / Speaking: practice
- Students could work individually and then discuss their ideas with the whole class.

> **Key** **Possible answers:** **1** I use it all the time: computers, e-mails **2** Could you turn it down, please?: computers, mobile phones; It's always on in the background: computers **3** It said, "Meet at cinema – at 7 p.m.": e-mails, mobile phones **4** I'm on it for hours: mobile phones **5** I'm not going to reply to it: notes, mobile phones; I deleted it by accident: computers

c) Vocabulary / Writing: practice
- Students brainstorm means of communication in pairs if you didn't do the Before 1 Warmer. Elicit and write the words / phrases on the board.
- Pairs then write the sentences from Exercise 2a) which can be about the means of communication they chose, e.g. the Internet, radio, phone calls, letters, etc. If several pairs chose the same one you could suggest an alternative.
- Encourage students to use their own ideas to write 3 more sentences. Monitor and help as necessary, e.g. the Internet: *get on-line, surf, chat, type in*; the radio: *listen to, turn it up / down / on / off, get good reception*; phone calls: *make, take, get cut off, phone-in, bad line*; letters: *send, receive, tear up, fold, enclose, post*.
- Make sure each student has a copy of the 3 sentences he / she has written in pairs.

d) Speaking: practice
- In groups made up of students from different pairs. Students take it in turns to read their sentences without saying the name of the means of communication. The other students listen until the speakers finish (even if they can guess after one sentence) and guess which means of communication the speakers are describing.
- Feedback. Write useful words, phrases and collocations on the board next to the appropriate means of communication.

Coursebook page 59

Telling stories

3 a) Reading: preparation

- Check students understand that Felix is a terrible storyteller and the main events of the story.

b) 👀 42 (Recording script Coursebook page 153)
Listening: for detail

- Play the recording. Ask students to confer in pairs. Play the recording again. Pairs confer a second time before the whole class feedback.

> **Key**   Event 1 and event 4.

c) 👀 42 (Recording script Coursebook page 153)
Listening: for detail / Grammar: presentation

- Play the recording. Students underline the correct tense and decide which event happened first.
- Feedback with the whole class.
- Go through the Language Box with the class.
- Refer students to the Grammar reference on page 113 for information on the Past Perfect Simple.

> **Key**   **1a)** took   **1b)** had forgotten   **2a)** started
> **2b)** had given   Event b) (both pairs)

4 a) Speaking / Writing: practice

- Check students understand the situations. Go through the examples.
- In pairs. Students identify which 2 sentences in each story need the Past Perfect Simple. Elicit the sentences with the correct verbs. Ask why they need the Past Perfect Simple to elicit that they show that something happened before another event in the past.
- Students practise telling each other the stories in their pairs. Student A tells story A and Student B tells story B. Then ask them to close their books and tell each other the stories again, swapping the stories they tell so that Student A tells story B and Student B tells story A.
- Students write both stories in their notebooks without referring to their books if possible.
- Monitor students both as they speak and write.

> **Key**   **Story A:** sentences 2 and 4   **Story B:**
> sentences 1 and 4   **Story A:** **3** decided   **4** had
> taken   **5** went   **Story B:** **1** had missed   **2** ran
> **3** saw   **4** hadn't told   **5** was

b) Grammar: presentation / Speaking: practice

- Highlight how *so* and *because* are used to connect cause and result by writing on the board: *The weather was hot* (cause) *so I opened the window* (result). *I opened the window* (result) *because the weather was hot* (cause).
- Focus on the examples. Explain that when the sentence is in the past, the clause after *because* often sounds better in the Past Perfect Simple as it's the (previous) cause of the result, e.g. *He saw that the room was empty* (result) *because someone **had stolen** everything* (cause).
- **Language note:** if the events are in the order they happened, the Past Perfect Simple isn't always necessary, e.g. *She arrived late* (cause) *so she ran upstairs to the meeting* (result) compared to *She arrived late because she had missed her train.*
- In pairs. Students could do this either as a speaking or writing activity or both. Feedback.

> **Key   Possible answers:**   **A** He saw that the room was empty **so** he decided to phone the police.   He decided to phone the police **because** he saw that the room was empty.   Someone had stolen everything **so** he decided to phone the police.   He decided to phone the police **because** someone had stolen everything.   The thief had taken the telephone **so** he couldn't phone the police.   He couldn't phone the police **because** the thief had taken the telephone.   The thief had taken the telephone **so** he went to the next-door flat.   He went to the next-door flat **because** the thief had taken the telephone.   He decided to phone the police **so** he went to the next-door flat.   He went to the next-door flat **because** he (had) decided to phone the police.   Someone had stolen everything **so** he went to the next-door flat.   He went to the next-door flat **because** someone had stolen everything.
> **B** Jilly missed her train **so** she arrived at the office late.   Jilly arrived at the office late **because** she had missed her train.   Jilly had missed her train **so** she ran upstairs to the meeting.   Jilly ran upstairs to the meeting **because** she had missed her train.   Her secretary hadn't told her **so** Jilly was furious.   Jilly was furious **because** her secretary hadn't told her.   She saw a notice on the door: "Today's meeting cancelled" **so** she was furious.   She was furious **because** she saw a notice on the door: "Today's meeting cancelled".

The funniest thing happened . . .

5 Speaking: practice

- Explain that each pair is going to read a different true story. Then when each student in the pair has remembered all the important details, he / she is going to re-tell the story, not read it, to a student from another pair.
- In groups of 4: Pair A and Pair B. Refer pairs to the relevant pages and ask them to read their instructions and story.
- Pairs then answer the comprehension questions (1–8). The questions focus students on the main details and elicit the use of the Past Simple and the Past Perfect Simple. As pairs read the stories and answer the questions, monitor and give help as necessary.
- When pairs have answered the questions, give them a time limit to practise telling their stories to each other. Remind them to include all the important details of the story so that a listener will be able to answer the comprehension questions (1–8).
- In new pairs with one Pair A student and one Pair B student. Students take it in turns to tell and listen to each other's stories and check each other's understanding by asking and answering the comprehension questions.
- Feedback with the whole class.

> **Key**   **Pair A: 1** letter, note   **2** A Member of Parliament in England.   **3** At a party to meet some of his voters.   **4** A very unattractive woman had followed him everywhere and had asked him stupid questions.   **5** Because he thought she had written "Horseface" at the end of her letter after her name.   **6** "To Horseface, with best wishes, Geoffrey Dickens."   **7** Because the woman hadn't written "Horseface" after her name, his secretary had written it.   **8** Awful and very embarrassed.   **Pair B: 1** e-mail   **2** In Bermuda.   **3** He was on a short business trip.
> **4** Because the flight was / had been terrible.
> **5** To his wife because she was going to join him the following day.   **6** To Mrs Joy Elkson. He had made a mistake with his wife's e-mail address because she had recently changed it.
> **7** Because her husband, Henry, had died a few months before.   **8** She fainted because she thought her dead husband had sent her an e-mail from hell.

Coursebook page 60

What did they say?

6 a) Warmer

- To set the scene, elicit where Mandy and Sam are now and where they were 10 days ago.
- Pre-teach / elicit *jury* and *innocent*. Students then discuss the 2 questions in pairs.
- Feedback with the whole class.

> **Key**   Mandy is speaking to the mechanic. She's angry because she's got a bill for £900 and the mechanic said it wouldn't cost more than £150.   Sam is writing to the lawyer.   He's angry because he's in prison and the lawyer told him he didn't have to worry about anything.

b) Grammar: presentation

- In pairs. Students compare the sentences and thoughts and discuss what happens to the verb when a sentence is reported.
- Write sentences a) and b) and 1 and 2, and then f) and g) and 6 and 7 on the board. Underline the main verbs in each sentence. Elicit that we usually move the main verb back one tense when we report information.
- Point out that Sam is reporting the information in f) and g), so *I / me* refers to Sam and *you* refers to the lawyer.
- Ask students to read the Language Box.
- **Language note:** point out that we don't have to move the main verb back one tense if the reporting verb is in the present and the information is still true, e.g. *He told me **she's still living** in Warsaw.*

c) ◉◉ 43 Grammar: practice / Listening: to check

- Students work individually and then check their answers in pairs. Elicit answers from the class and write them on the board but don't feedback or you'll pre-empt the listening.
- Play the recording. Students listen and check.
- Feedback and compare answers with the answers written on the board.

> **Key**   **c)** You told me I hadn't done any serious damage.   **d)** You said it only needed one or two new parts.   **e)** You told me you could fix it in a day.   **h)** You told me the other side didn't have a case.
> **i)** And you said the jury would find me innocent.
> **j)** Then you told me you'd fixed everything.

After 6c) Grammar: practice

- Write sentences 1–5 on the board. In pairs. Students report the sentences beginning *She said . . .* You could give students support by underlining the words they need to change.
  1 <u>I</u> arrived <u>yesterday</u>.
  2 <u>My</u> boyfriend phoned <u>me</u> three days <u>ago</u>.
  3 <u>I</u> don't think <u>this</u> is <u>mine</u>.
  4 <u>We</u> will win <u>today</u>.
  5 <u>I</u> speak better English than <u>you</u> <u>now</u>.
- Feedback with the class.

> **Key**   1 She said <u>she</u> had arrived <u>the day before</u>.   2 She said <u>her</u> boyfriend had phoned <u>her</u> three days <u>before</u>.   3 She said she didn't think <u>that</u> was <u>hers</u>.   4 She said <u>they'd</u> win <u>that</u> day.   5 She said <u>she</u> spoke better English than <u>you</u> / <u>me</u> / <u>him</u> / <u>her</u> <u>then</u> / <u>at that time</u>.

Coursebook page 61

7 a) Grammar: presentation

- Students work individually and check their answers in pairs. Feedback with the class.

> **Key**   3 = S   4 = M   5 = M   6 = S   7 = M   8 = S

b) Grammar: presentation

- Students work in pairs and then read the Language Box. Feedback. Focus on the examples and information in the Language Box.
- Highlight that if the reported question is in the past then we usually move the tense back, even if the direct question is about the present, e.g. *He asked me what my name was* NOT *He asked me what my name* ~~is~~
- **Language note:** point out that we don't have to move the main verb back one tense if the reporting verb is in the present and the information is still true, e.g. *They're asking everybody who they're going to vote for.*
- Refer students to the Grammar reference page 115 for information on reported speech.

c) Grammar: practice

- This activity can be done in class or for homework. Point out that *jury* is a singular collective noun.
- In the feedback relate the answers to the information in the Language Box.

> **Key**   3 Sam asked (the lawyer) if they would win.   4 Mandy asked (the mechanic) what was the problem with it.   5 Mandy asked (the mechanic) if / whether he was going to look at the brakes.   6 Sam asked (the lawyer) if she'd spoken to the newspapers.   7 Mandy asked (the mechanic) if / whether he could check the tyres.   8 Sam asked (the lawyer) why the jury was looking at him like that.

He lied to me!

8 a) Reading: for detail

- Ask students to read the article about Dickie Garret quickly. Don't let them use dictionaries.
- Feedback and check *con-artist* and *con* (v). Make sure students understand that Dickie Garret isn't a thief. He gets money by gaining people's trust so they give the money willingly.

> **Key**   He's a con-artist.   He has conned innocent victims out of thousands of pounds throughout the British Isles.

b) Speaking: preparation

- If your students need support, write *Names* on the board. Elicit and write under the heading the names Dickie Garret was known as which are mentioned in the article. Then write *Stories* on the board. Ask the students how they think Dickie got money from his victims as each of the different characters. Elicit ideas and write them under the heading. You could elicit other ideas for names and stories and write them on the board.
- Check that students understand the prompts. In pairs, students prepare their stories.

c) Speaking: practice

- Focus on the examples. Point out that contrastive stress is used when the speaker emphasises a new subject or new information to make it stand out from a previous subject or information.
- In groups: 2 sets of pairs with different stories about Dickie Garret. Students swap stories about how Dickie Garret tricked them.
- If your class is strong enough, you could split the pairs up. Ask one student from 2 different pairs to work in a pair and to exchange stories. The original pair of students then get back together and tell each other the stories they've heard.
- Monitor the groups / pairs. Feedback.

9 Writing: practice

- Set up the situation in class whether students do the writing for homework or in class. Make sure students understand that the letter is informal. Elicit some ideas for scenarios.
- In pairs. Students decide on their situations. Monitor and help with ideas and language.
- Students write their letters individually. When they finish, students make groups. Each group chooses a letter to read to the rest of the class.

After 9 Photocopiable activities
- See 7 *How did you get into this mess?!*, page T122.

Coursebook pages 62 and 63

I'm on the phone!

10 a) Speaking: preparation

- Before students read the phone conversation taking 4 different routes, make sure they understand that the conversation ends with *Success! Connection!* or *Failure! No connection!* each time. If necessary, read the conversation with a student taking one of the routes.
- Monitor pairs as they read. Encourage students to use lots of expression.

b) Vocabulary: matching

- To set the scene for the activity elicit brief examples of formal and informal expressions and the difference in context when such expressions would be appropriate and inappropriate.
- In pairs. Students do the matching.
- In new pairs. Students check their answers.
- Feedback with the class.
- **Language note:** point out that *all right* can be a more formal alternative to *OK,* that *cheers* is a very informal way of saying *thank you* in British English and that *thanks* is an informal alternative to *thank you* used in both American and British English.

> **Key** **1** I'm afraid Mr Rocco is out at the moment. **2** Could I ask who's calling, please? **3** Certainly. This is Trevor Trink. **4** Could you tell him that Trevor Trink called? **5** I'm afraid I can't say, sir. **6** Can I take a message? **7** Could I have your phone number, please? **8** Could you hold a moment, Mr Trink? **9** Certainly. **10** All right. Thank you very much.

c) Vocabulary: practice

- In pairs. Students find out or guess the meanings of the phrasal verbs and put the 3 sentences in each group in a logical order.
- Students close their books. Feedback by asking an individual student to tell you each phrasal verb and another student to explain its meaning.
- Students open their books. Elicit the sentences in each group in their correct logical order.

> **Key** **A a) look up** = find **b) hang up** = finish a phone conversation by putting the phone down **c) ring up** = phone **B a) put through** = connect someone to someone else on the phone **b) take down** = write down **c) call back** = phone again **C a) get back** = try to phone someone again later **b) cut off** = suddenly not be able to hear someone that you were speaking to on the phone **c) get through** = succeed in reaching someone by phone
> **A** = a), c), b) **B** = b), a), c) **C** = c), b), a)

After 10c) Speaking: practice

- In pairs. Students make up a short story about a good or bad experience they had on the phone using at least 6 of the phrasal verbs from Exercise 10c). Tell them both to make notes as they prepare their story.
- Ask pairs to think about the first line of their story. Give an example if necessary, e.g. *I rang up an ex-boyfriend last night.*
- Monitor as students make up their story.
- In new pairs. Students take it in turns to tell each other their stories and to react, e.g. *Oh, really? Did he? You're joking!* Feedback.

11 a) 🔊 44 (Recording script Coursebook page 153)
Listening: for gist

- Explain that the aim of this activity is to help students identify formal and informal phone calls. Elicit some of the expressions students might expect in formal / informal phone calls.
- Play the recording. Students fill in the boxes and confer in pairs. Then play the recording again.
- Feedback. Students may have difficulty with message 3. Elicit that although it's a message left at a company, the message itself is informal.

> **Key** **2** = I **3** = I **4** = I **5** = F

b) 📼 44 (Recording script Coursebook page 153)

Listening: for detail

• Play conversation 1 twice if necessary.

• Feedback with the class.

> **Key** She included necessary information that helps Mr Gibson to know what to do or what's happening, i.e. names, times, dates, numbers, places, etc.   She ignored any information extra to the basic message.

c) 📼 44 (Recording script Coursebook page 153)

Listening: for detail

• Draw the table in the Key on the board with only the headings *Who called? To speak to . . . ?, The message, Phone number* and the numbers 2–5 filled in. Then ask students to copy it into their notebooks. Point out that there won't be entries under each heading.

• Play conversations 2–5. Students fill in the table. Students check in pairs. Play them again.

• Feedback by eliciting answers and filling in the table on the board. Highlight the difference between taking notes from a recorded message you can play again and from a live speaker when you can ask questions. Elicit questions you could ask, e.g. *Could you repeat that? Could you speak more slowly, please? How do you spell that?*

Key Who called?	To speak to . . . ?	The message	Phone number
2 Jason	Sally	Take his book *Intellectual Capital* to his flat this evening. Ring if you can't.	987253
3 Mr Jones	Mrs Jones	He rang. Might ring back later this afternoon or will see you at home. Nothing important.	–
4 Jill	Jane	Are you going to the cinema tonight? Ring her.	–
5 Stan Baker, Coffer Enterprises	Martin Sands (Sales)	Ring him before 10 a.m. Thursday about order 614ZX. Important.	08706 21730 Extension 9

Pronunciation: sentence stress

12 a) 📼 45 **Listening: for stress**

• Play the recording for students to underline the stressed words / syllables.

• Feedback by writing the sentence on the board and eliciting the stressed words / syllables. Focus on how the secretary stresses the same information in her speech that she writes down in her message.

• In pairs. Students repeat the sentence to each other. Go round the class and monitor students' stress and intonation, making sure they copy the rise before each comma and the fall at the end of the sentence.

> **Key**   So that's Mr <u>Pear</u>son, on <u>Fri</u>day, at e<u>le</u>ven <u>thir</u>ty, room <u>seven</u> <u>oh</u> <u>six</u>.

b) Pronunciation: practice

• Monitor pairs to make sure they stress the important information. Encourage them to exaggerate the rise before each comma and the fall at the end of the sentence.

13 Speaking: practice

• Divide the class into 2 groups: Student As and Student Bs. Students read their instructions and the information about their 2 phone calls (one formal and one informal). Ask students in each group to discuss the messages and exchange ideas. Go round and help as necessary.

• When they finish, ask students to make AB pairs.

• Students sit back to back to make their phone calls or use phone lines if you've got them. Remind them to use formal or informal language as appropriate. Make sure students swap roles after Student A has left his / her 2 messages.

• An alternative is to ask the students to record their messages onto a cassette, as if they were speaking to an answering machine. The other student in the pair can then listen to the cassette and make notes but he / she won't be able to ask for spelling or repetition.

• As you monitor, check students' pronunciation of the alphabet during the spelling of names. It may need some quick revision.

• Feedback with the class.

Writing for work and pleasure

③ Guess what!

Topic / vocabulary	A story about a robbery
Writing skills	The use of linkers and different past tenses to show the order of events in a story; expressions to make a story flow smoothly

Coursebook page 64

Telling a story

1 a) Reading: gap fill
- Before students open their Coursebooks, remind them of linkers, e.g. *and, so, but*. In pairs. Give students one minute to brainstorm as many linkers as they can. Feedback with the class and write the linkers on the board.
- Focus students on the instructions and the linkers. Compare the linkers (a–n) with the list of linkers on the board.
- Ask students to read the letter quickly without filling in the gaps to get an idea of what the letter is about.
- Check students' general comprehension by asking questions about Heather's letter to Andy, e.g. *Who came to the town? What happened in Bill Mortimer's shop?*
- In pairs. Ask students to fill in the gaps.
- Make sure students understand that linkers a–g are for gaps 1–7 and linkers h–n are for gaps 8–14. When students finish, ask them to compare their answers with another pair.
- Feedback with the class.

> **Key** **2** = g) **3** = c) **4** = a) **5** = f) **6** = b)
> **7** = d) **8** = l) **9** = m) **10** = h) **11** = j)
> **12** = n) **13** = i) **14** = k)

b) Reading: for detail
- Ask students to read the instructions and sentences. Check / elicit vocabulary as necessary or ask students to use their dictionaries.
- In pairs. Ask students to put the events in the story in the order in which they happened. Tell pairs to compare their answers in groups of 4 and to discuss any differences.
- When students have agreed on their answers, feedback with the class. Ask students to justify their answers by referring to the letter.

> **Key** **1** = e) The town found out that the film crew were coming. **2** = b) People painted their houses. **3** = i) The film crew arrived. **4** = d) Tom and Jo walked round town wearing their trendiest clothes. **5** = j) The young man asked to film a robbery in the shop. **6** = g) The young man started to film. **7** = f) Three masked men put jewellery into bags. **8** = a) The men drove off in a car. **9** = h) Bill realised that the men were robbers. **10** = c) Bill phoned the police.

Coursebook page 65

c) Reading: for detail
- Students read the questions 1–6.
- Ask the students to write the answers to the questions individually. Tell them to write the answers using whole sentences.
- When students finish, ask them to compare their answers in pairs.
- Feedback with the class.
- Then ask students to read the Writing Box. Go through the information on writing or telling stories. Draw students' attention to the use of linkers, other expressions and different tenses to show the order of events in a story. Give or elicit from the students further examples if necessary.

> **Key** **1** Lots of people had painted their houses and tidied their gardens before the film crew arrived. **2** The film crew had been in town for a couple of days when the young man visited Bill Mortimer. **3** Three of the men were wearing masks when they robbed the shop. **4** One of the masked men was carrying a gun. **5** The young man was filming with a video camera while the men were stealing from the shop. **6** Bill called the police when he realised that the men weren't actors.

d) Grammar: analysis
- Ask students to re-read the section of the Writing Box about the use of different tenses to show the order of events.
- Feedback with the whole class. Elicit from students that we use the Past Simple to talk about single finished events, we use the Past Continuous to describe activity which was already in progress when the other event happened and we use the Past Perfect Simple to show that something happened before another event in the story and to give background information.

> **Key** 1 Past Perfect Simple   2 Past Perfect Simple   3 Past Continuous   4 Past Continuous   5 Past Continuous   6 Past Simple

2 Writing: practice
- In pairs. Students develop a story from one of the basic plots.
- Give students a word limit of 120–180 words. Remind them to use different past tenses to show the order of events and to use at least 6 linkers from Exercise 1a).
- Go round the class and monitor students as they work. Help with ideas, language and story-telling techniques as necessary.

Making a story more interesting

3 a) Vocabulary: practice
- Go through the example with the whole class. Elicit other adverbs and adjectives which could be used in place of those used in the example. Highlight the strong adjective *tiny* and elicit the base adjective *small*. Ask students for other examples of base and strong adjectives, e.g. *funny* and *hilarious, cold* and *freezing, tired* and *exhausted, bad* and *awful / terrible, angry* and *furious, hungry* and *starving, hot* and *boiling*.
- In pairs. Students add adverbs, adjectives and strong adjectives to sentences 1 and 2 to make the stories more interesting and dramatic. Ask each student to write down his / her own copy of the story.
- Monitor pairs as they work and give help with ideas and vocabulary as necessary.
- Feedback with the whole class. Elicit students' sentences and only give the suggested answers from the Key if you feel they would be helpful.

> **Key   Possible answers: 1** Tim woke up **suddenly** one **still, quiet** night, heard a **loud, crashing** noise downstairs, **quickly** picked up a **large, heavy** object and walked **silently** down the stairs.   **2** A **smart, handsome** man drove into a **sleepy, country** town, parked his **sports** car outside a **small, quiet** pub, went **quickly** inside, sat down **immediately** at a table and started talking to a **nervous young** woman.

b) Reading: practice
- When students have finished adding adverbs, adjectives and strong adjectives to sentences 1 and 2, organise the class into groups of 4. Make sure that students from each pair from Exercise 3a) are in different groups. Tell students to take it in turns to read their stories. Students compare stories and decide which is the most interesting or dramatic.
- Feedback with the class and ask students to vote for the most interesting or dramatic story.

4 Vocabulary: practice
- In the same pairs as in Exercise 2. Pairs swap stories with another pair and add the adjectives and adverbs.
- Each pair then gives the story with the adjectives and adverbs added back to the pair that originally wrote the story.
- Pairs compare their original stories from Exercise 2 with the new, more interesting stories and say whether they approve of the changes.
- Feedback with the class.

5 Writing: practice
- Go through the instructions and read through the first and last lines of the story with the class. Check *incredible, decade* and *trip of a lifetime*.
- Before students begin, draw their attention to the Remember! Box. Then ask them to prepare a plan for their letter to a friend telling him / her a story.
- When students finish their individual plans ask them to take it in turns to go through the plan in pairs. Tell students to make suggestions for ideas and improvements. Monitor the discussions and help as necessary.
- Students could write their letter for homework. Display the finished letters for the class to read.

⑧ Life, death and the universe

Grammar / structures	*Will* + infinitive for prediction; *going to* + infinitive for prediction based on present evidence; Third Conditional for regret, relief and blame
Topic / vocabulary	Speculating and making predictions about the future; expressing regrets and relief about the past; *otherwise, in case*
Pronunciation	Weak forms and linking in Third Conditional sentences
Wavelength pages	**Conversations** Points of view: persuading, refusing persuasion, giving opinions, agreeing / disagreeing, interrupting

Coursebook page 66

Visions of the future

Optional extras
Before 1a) Warmer
- Encourage students to make short-term predictions about themselves by writing questions on the board, e.g. *What time will you get home today? Which clothes do you think you'll wear on Tuesday? Where do you think you'll be in one year's time?* Students write their answers on pieces of paper.
- Collect the papers and read out some answers. Students guess who wrote each prediction and justify their guess.
- Ask students which was the most difficult question to answer and why. (It was probably the one furthest in the future as it's the most difficult to predict.)

1 a) Reading: for gist
- In groups of 4. Tell students not to use a dictionary but to focus on overall meaning.
- Monitor groups as they read and discuss.
- Feedback with the whole class.

> **Key** They're all about predicting the future.

b) Reading: for detail
- Students read the quotations again.
- Feedback with the class. Students identify which phrases in the quotations enabled them to answer the questions.

> **Key** Quotation 4 focuses on what makes a machine work. Quotation 2 is about planes. Quotation 1 is about phones.

c) Reading: for detail
- Ask students when the first moon landing took place. Then tell them to calculate how many years passed between the prediction and man first walking on the moon. Elicit suggested answers before students check on Coursebook page 141.

> **Key** 12 years. Man first walked on the moon in 1969.

d) Speaking: practice
- Elicit / check *futurology, undoubtedly* and *futurologist*. Ask students to give reasons why they agree or disagree with Steven Pinker's comment, e.g. *You can see from some of the predictions made in the other quotations that predictions about the future can sound very silly when the future arrives.*

2 Reading: for gist
- Elicit / check the meaning of *summarise*. Before students read, elicit that a word or phrase which is relevant to the text and gives a good idea of its overall content, not just a small part of it, is a good title for a text. Remind students to read the text quickly and not to use a dictionary. Tell them to focus on the overall meaning of the text, not the meaning of individual words.
- Give students 2 minutes to read the text. When the time is up, ask students to check their answer in pairs.
- Feedback and elicit the answer from the class. Ask students to give reasons why they didn't choose titles 1 and 3. Elicit that the title *Transport in the twenty-first century* only refers to the first paragraph and that the title *The future looks bright!* is too general and doesn't reflect the content of the extract.

> **Key** 2 We're no good at predicting the future.

Coursebook page 67

3 a) Reading: for detail

- Check students understand the reasons (a–f). Students then read the text again and answer the questions individually in their notebooks. Monitor students' work. Students then confer in pairs before the feedback.
- Elicit answers from the class. Ask students to justify their answers by referring to the text.
- Ask questions to focus on the meaning of words in the text, e.g. *Which word in the text means (a period of a thousand years)?* and about details, e.g. *Why does the writer say "But forget fly-driving for a cup of coffee in a sky café"?*

> **Key**   1 disappointed   2 a), f)

b) Speaking: practice

- Encourage as much debate as possible and ask students to justify their views.

4 a) Grammar: presentation

- Ask students to read the Language Box.
- **Language note:** you could point out that native speakers also say *He's going to have a heart attack before he's forty.* Explain that there's sometimes no clear distinction between *will* and *going to* except in the way that a speaker perceives the event. If a speaker is thinking in general terms, reflecting his / her knowledge and experience of the world, he / she may say *The doctor will probably give her an injection.* On the other hand, if a speaker thinks there are clear grounds for predicting a particular action in a specific situation then he / she may use *The doctor's going to give her an injection.*
- The problem for students is that they don't always have the knowledge to know when *going to* or *will* may not be appropriate. So what is needed is a safe framework within which to operate. Students need to learn the cases when the alternative (*will* or *going to*) sounds wrong. Students will never be wrong if they use *will* (with different modifiers) for predictions based on general knowledge about a situation / person.
- Refer students to the Grammar reference on page 114 for information on the Future.

> **Key**   probably

b) Grammar: presentation

- Focus on the fact that it's impossible to be absolutely certain about some aspects of the future. We therefore often use words like *probably* with *will* or modal verbs like *may / might* to show different degrees of certainty.
- Go through the example and point out that some of the sentences have the same degree of certainty / uncertainty.
- Feedback with the class.

> **Key**   2 = c) and h)   3 = a)   4 = g)
> 5 = f) and j)   6 = d) and i)

c) Grammar: presentation

- Feedback with the whole class.

> **Key**   Word order in positive sentences: *will + probably / definitely +* infinitive   Word order in negative sentences: *probably / definitely + will not / won't +* infinitive

Coursebook page 68

The shape of things to come

5 a) Reading: practice

- Make sure students understand the sentences and the context.
- In pairs. Students read the sentences and give their opinions. They then tick the predictions which have already come true or are happening now.
- Feedback with the class. Do students agree?

> **Key**   2 and 10.

b) Speaking: practice

- Monitor as students discuss.
- Feedback and elicit students' views.

c) Grammar: presentation / Gap fill

- Feedback with the class.
- **Language note:** point out that we use a comma before *otherwise.*
- Highlight the difference between *in case* and *in case of +* noun. We usually use *in case of +* noun = *if there is (this situation)* in formal notices, e.g. *In case of fire, use emergency exits.*

> **Key**   1 otherwise   2 in case
> 3 in case   4 otherwise

Coursebook page 69

6 a) 🎧46 (Recording script Coursebook page 154)
Listening: for detail

- Remind students of the context. It's New Year's Eve, 1799 and Professor Karl and Max are discussing predictions about the future.
- Ask students to speculate about the answers. Write suggestions on the board.
- Play the recording for students to answer the questions. Play it again if necessary. Elicit answers and compare them to the suggestions.

> **Key** They're discussing prediction 3: we will find a cure for all diseases. Max is working on a very strong medicine. The mixture explodes.

b) 🎧46 (Recording script Coursebook page 154)
Listening: gap fill

- Students try to fill in the gaps before they listen. Remind students to note down the evidence that the professor has to support his predictions. Then play the recording. Ask students to check their answers in pairs. Play the recording again if necessary.
- In the feedback link the form of the 2 predictions (*going to* + infinitive) to the evidence in front of the professor (clouds for prediction 1 and smoke for prediction 2).
- Ask other questions about the recording to elicit the answers in brackets, e.g *What are the different attitudes of the 2 speakers? (Max is young and enthusiastic and interested in the future. The professor is sceptical and interested in the present.) What has improved enormously recently? (The microscope.) Why does the professor call Max a fool? (Because Max thinks the professor means his discovery will lead to an explosion of scientific knowledge but the professor means the chemical mixture is going to explode.) Why does Max say "Professor" 3 times? (Because he can't see the professor after the explosion and he's starting to get worried.)*
- After students have read the Language Box, emphasise the link between the present evidence and information in the example situation (*The brakes aren't working! We've lost control of the car!*) and the prediction (*We're going to crash*). Elicit other contexts where clear and immediate evidence can be used to make specific predictions using *going to* + infinitive.

- Focus students' attention on the *Look!* section of the Language Box. Use the examples to compare the more general nature of predictions using *will* + infinitive as opposed to the more specific, more immediate nature of predictions using *going to* + infinitive.
- **Language note:** many students feel frustrated that there's no clear difference to learn between *will* and *going to*. Very often we can use either form in a prediction as all predictions are based on some kind of knowledge / belief / evidence. It's often impossible to say that one piece of evidence is only general while another is only present / immediate / specific. Encourage students to remember the circumstances where one or other structure is wrong, e.g. it would be wrong for Professor Karl to say *I mean it ̶w̶i̶l̶l̶ explode! Look at it!* because the prediction is clearly based on present evidence, directly in front of him.
- Refer students to the Grammar reference on page 114 for information on the Future (*going to* + infinitive and *will* + infinitive) and to Unit 3 page 25 for the other main use of *going to* + infinitive: future plans and intentions.

> **Key** 1 There**'s going to** be a terrible storm tonight! 2 That**'s going to** explode! Evidence for prediction 1: clouds. Evidence for prediction 2: smoke.

7 Grammar: matching

- The aim of this activity is to sensitise students to contexts which highlight when to use *going to* + infinitive and when to use *will* + infinitive.
- Ask students to check their answers in groups before the whole class feedback.

> **Key** 1 = d) 2 = a) 3 = c)
> 4 = f) 5 = b) 6 = e)

After 7 Writing: practice

- Ask students to produce their own versions of Exercise 7 for homework. Students think of 3 contexts which require *going to* + infinitive (with 3 example sentences) and 3 contexts which require *will* + infinitive (with example sentences).
- Collect and check their work. Students swap exercises and do each other's activity.

8 a) Writing: practice

- In pairs. Students write predictions based on the evidence of what's happening at present. Encourage students to write as many predictions as they can for each picture.
- Monitor and help as necessary. Make sure the predictions arise naturally out of the contexts shown and that students use *going to* + infinitive.

b) Speaking: practice

- Make groups of 4 from 2 sets of pairs. Ask the students to take it in turns to read out their predictions. Tell them only to read out sentences which don't repeat previous predictions. When both pairs have finished, ask them to discuss the evidence on which they made their predictions.
- Feedback and elicit predictions and evidence.

> **Key Possible answers: 1** She's going to leave him. She's going to take off her ring. He's going to be alone. They're going to get a divorce. They're going to separate. **2** The piano is going to hit him. The piano is going to drop / fall on him. He's going to die. He's going to get hurt / injured. There's going to be an accident.
> **3** She's going to get a ticket. They're going to take her car away. They're going to clamp / wheel-clamp her car. She's going to have to take a taxi.

After 8b) Speaking: practice

- Each student writes 3 predictions about the future of the world. Collect the predictions.
- Divide the class into 3 teams: A, B and C.
- Read out the predictions at random. Teams make alternate pessimistic and optimistic comments about them within a 30-second time limit, e.g. Prediction 1 *Human beings will probably live in space colonies in the next 100 years.* Team A's pessimistic comment: *That's a bad thing because it will cause pollution in space.* Team B's optimistic comment: *That's a good thing because the Earth will be less crowded.* Each team then makes optimistic or pessimistic comments in turn, i.e. prediction 2 will be followed by Team C's pessimistic comment and Team A's optimistic comment.
- Give one point for each appropriate comment, correct in form and made within the time limit. The team with the most points wins.

Coursebook page 70

Looking back

9 a) 🔊47 (Recording script Coursebook page 154)
Listening: for gist

- Students listen to the recording and fill in the boxes. Point out that only 3 of the 4 people are speaking in the recording.
- Feedback with the whole class and ask students if their predictions in Exercise 8 were correct. Revise reported speech by eliciting sentences from individual students in which they compare one of their predictions with what actually happened, e.g. *I said (the piano) was going to (hit the man). In fact, (the piano missed him because he stopped to read the poster).*

> **Key a)** isn't one of the speakers
> **b)** = 1 **c)** = 2 **d)** = 3

b) 🔊47 (Recording script Coursebook page 154)
Listening: for detail

- Ask students to try to fill in some or all of the gaps before they listen to the recording if they think they know the answers. Don't feedback or you'll pre-empt the listening.
- Play the recording. Ask students to check their answers in pairs after they've listened. If their answers aren't complete or they can't agree, play the recording again.
- Feedback with the whole class. Elicit and highlight the form of the verbs in both clauses of each of the sentences 1–3.
- You could focus on some of the vocabulary and expressions used in the recording. Play the recording again or refer students to Recording script 47. Ask students to explain the meaning of these remarks:

MAN 1: It makes me feel sick to think about it!
MAN 2: Ten years of marriage down the drain.
WOMAN 2: These people are so pathetic. Why aren't they out catching the real criminals?

> **Key 1** If I hadn't **stopped** to read this poster, it **would have** hit me! **2** If I'd **bought** her some flowers or something, she **might not have** done this. **3** If I hadn't **stopped** to buy her a present, this **wouldn't have** happened!

10 a) Grammar: presentation

- The questions in Exercise 10a) help to focus on how we can contrast what really happened with different imagined possible past situations using the Third Conditional.

- Ask students to read the questions individually. Then tell the students to ask and answer the questions in pairs. After students have answered the questions, feedback with the whole class to check that students have clearly grasped the facts in each situation.

- Go through the Language Box with the class. Refer back to the feelings of the 3 people to illustrate how Third Conditional sentences are often used to express relief, regret and blame.

- The form and use of Third Conditional sentences is complex. Reassure students and tell them they'll need time to become proficient and confident at forming Third Conditional sentences.

- Make sure students are aware of the forms of verbs in the 2 clauses of Third Conditional sentences. Point out they can substitute *could / couldn't* for *would / wouldn't* or *might / might not* + *have* + past participle.

- Draw students' attention to the fact that clauses in Third Conditional sentences can be reversed without a change in meaning, e.g. *He would have hit me if I hadn't run away* and *If I hadn't run away, he would have hit me*. Point out the use of the comma at the end of the first clause when that clause begins with *if*.

- Give a few simple situations, e.g. *I was late for work yesterday because I missed the bus* and elicit sentences in the Third Conditional: *If you hadn't missed the bus, you wouldn't have been late for work yesterday*.

- Refer students to the Grammar reference on page 116 for information on the Third Conditional.

> **Key   Possible answers: 1a)** No, it didn't. Because he stopped to read a poster on the wall. **1b)** He feels a huge sense of relief, sick, very shaky and nervous but extremely happy to be alive.   **2a)** Yes, she did. Because he forgot / didn't remember their anniversary after everything that had happened.   **2b)** He feels sad, stupid, regretful and that it's all his fault.   **3a)** Yes, she did. Because she parked in a "No parking" zone. **3b)** She blames Alice, feels angry, thinks it's unfair and not her fault (even though it is).

b) Writing: practice

- Go through the examples and situations 1–5 to check that students understand the activity.

- Students could write the sentences in class or for homework.

> **Key   1** He wouldn't have stopped to look at the poster if it hadn't had a really interesting design on it.   **2** If the rope hadn't broken, the piano wouldn't have fallen to the ground.   **3** If he hadn't been so stressed, he would have remembered their anniversary.   **4** He wouldn't have been so tired if he hadn't worked all weekend on a report.
> **5** She wouldn't have parked in a "No parking" zone if she hadn't been in a hurry.

Pronunciation: weak forms and linking

11 a) ⊙⊙ 48 Listening: to check

- When students have underlined the stressed words / syllables in the Third Conditional example sentences in Exercise 10b), ask them to compare their answers in pairs.

- Play the recording for students to listen and check their answers.

- Feedback with the whole class. Write the example sentences on the board or use an OHT. Ask individual students to come to the board and underline the stressed words / syllables.

- Elicit also that the auxiliary *have* is weakened and the *h* sound is dropped. If students can't tell you this in the feedback, refer them to the Language Box and go through the information and the example sentences with the class.

- In Unit 2 students looked at the pronunciation of *have* as an auxiliary in questions and statements. *Have* can very often be a contraction (*they've, she's*, etc.) so it's obviously weakened. Draw students' attention to the fact that in Third Conditional sentences and after a subject which ends in a consonant sound, *have* doesn't become /v/ as in *they've* /ðeɪv/ but becomes /əv/, e.g. *The men have* /ˈmenəv/ *gone but the women have* /ˈwɪmɪnəv/ *stayed*.

> **Key   (underlining = stress)**
> The pi<u>a</u>no would have <u>hit</u> him if he hadn't <u>stopped</u> to look at the <u>poster</u>.   If he hadn't for<u>got</u>ten their ann<u>iv</u>ersary, she might not have <u>left</u> him.

b) Speaking: practice

- In pairs. Ask students to underline the stressed words / syllables in the Third Conditional sentences they wrote in Exercise 10b).
- Feedback with the class. Write the sentences on the board or use an OHT. Ask individual students to come to the board and underline the stressed words / syllables.
- Ask students to practise saying the sentences they wrote in their pairs. Monitor and encourage them to exaggerate the contrast between weak and stressed syllables and to use the correct pronunciation of *have* /əv/.

> **Key** 1 He wouldn't have <u>stopped</u> to look at the <u>poster</u> if it hadn't had a really interesting de<u>sign</u> on it.   2 If the <u>rope</u> hadn't <u>broken</u>, the pi<u>ano</u> wouldn't have <u>fallen</u> to the <u>ground</u>.   3 If he hadn't been so <u>stressed</u>, he would have re<u>mem</u>bered their anni<u>ver</u>sary.   4 He wouldn't have been so <u>tired</u> if he hadn't <u>worked</u> all week<u>end</u> on a re<u>port</u>. 5 She wouldn't have <u>parked</u> in a "No <u>park</u>ing" zone if she hadn't been in a <u>hurry</u>.

Coursebook page 71

12 a) Reading / Writing: practice

- Give students a set time to read the messages on the website. Ask students to close their books when the time is up.
- In small groups. Students discuss what they can remember about each message. If necessary, write prompt questions on the board, e.g. *Who sent the messages? How old are they? What other details can you remember about the people? What does each person regret?*
- Focus on some of the words and phrases in the messages, e.g. *according to, get involved in, invest, instinct, technical support, sales associate, get off with.* Tell them to discuss the meanings in pairs and to use dictionaries if necessary.
- In pairs. Ask students to identify the mistake or bad decision each person made and the result that it had. Elicit answers from the class.
- Ask students to work individually and write a sentence in the Third Conditional to express the regret / regrets of each person who wrote to Barry Cadish's website.
- Monitor students and point out but don't correct any mistakes in grammar.

b) Reading: practice

- In larger classes students correct their sentences in pairs. In smaller classes, students write their sentences on an OHT. Then go through them with the class. This will result in less discussion but it will produce more exact practice of the Third Conditional form.

> **Key   Possible answers: 1** If he / she hadn't thought that the uses for computers would be very limited, he / she would have learnt about them in the 1970s. If he / she had realised how important computers were, he / she would have invested in them. If he / she had listened to his / her sister, he / she would have become rich (like her).   **2** If he / she hadn't been so unkind, her / his friend wouldn't have stopped talking to her / him.   **3** If Stephanie hadn't got off with her boyfriend's brother, she wouldn't have lost her boyfriend / her boyfriend wouldn't have left her / she and her boyfriend wouldn't have split up. **4** If Isobel's father hadn't got a new job, they wouldn't / might not have had to move (to that stupid place).   **5** If Mark hadn't got angry with his little brother and hit him, his mum wouldn't have sent him to his room and he would have been able to watch TV.

13 a) Writing: practice

- Check students understand they have to describe a mistake or bad decision they made in the past and the result that it had. Remind students to end the story with a Third Conditional sentence which summarises their regret. Encourage students to refer to true regrets about their own lives but they can imagine regrets if that is what they would prefer to do.
- Monitor students and help with ideas, vocabulary and grammar.

b) Speaking: practice

- In groups. Students take it in turns to read their final Third Conditional sentence only. Tell the other students to ask questions and find out the story behind the regret.
- Be sensitive about students' regrets in your feedback with the whole class.

> **After 13b) Photocopiable activities**
> - See 8 The Terry Stinger Show, page T124.

⑧ Conversations Points of view

Grammar/ structures	Language of persuasion and expressing opinion: *go on, come on, no way*; language to accept, reject or concede to opinions: *but what about . . . ?, absolutely, as far as I'm concerned, I suppose so*
Functions	Persuading, refusing persuasion, giving opinions, agreeing, disagreeing, interrupting to make a point
Pronunciation	Stress and intonation for emphasis, particularly when persuading: *oh, p–l–e–a–s–e*

Coursebook page 72

That's easy for you to say!

1 Speaking: practice
- Check *persuade*. Then give examples of your own.
- Monitor. Groups then feedback to the class. Ask students to give reasons for the persuasion, e.g. *My friend persuaded me to go to the party so he could have a lift home.*

2 a) 🔊49 (Recording script Coursebook page 154)
Listening: for detail
- Play the recording. Students compare answers in pairs. Play the recording again. Students check.
- Feedback. Elicit / teach *karaoke* (the activity of singing to recorded music for entertainment).

> **Key** They're in a pub (which has got karaoke). Kath wants Alan to sing. No, but he agrees to do it in the end.

b) Matching
- Ask students to read the sentences 1–7. Check *wimp* (someone with a weak character who's afraid to do something difficult or unpleasant).
- **Language note:** point out that *What have you got to lose?* is most common in this form but can change in person and tense, e.g. *What did they have to lose?* and that *No way!* as a refusal is now common in both American and British English.
- Don't feedback or you'll pre-empt the listening.

c) 🔊49 (Recording script Coursebook page 154)
Listening: to check
- Students listen to the recording again and check their answers to Exercise 2b). Feedback.
- Students fill in the gaps in the Language Box. Feedback with the class. Point out that the set phrase *You only live once* can't usually be changed, e.g you can't say *He only lives once*. You could also draw attention to the fact that *kidding* can replace *joking*.

> **Key** 2 = A 3 = A 4 = A 5 = K 6 = K 7 = K
> **Imperatives / set phrases:** Be a sport. Don't be such a wimp. What have you got to lose? Just have a go. **Set phrases:** You can't be serious! No way! **Stressing that it's you, not the other person, who has to do it:** That's easy for you to say!

Pronunciation: stress and intonation

3 a) Pronunciation: preparation
- Focus on the Language Box and read the example.
- Students underline the "stretched" words individually and then check answers in pairs.
- Don't feedback or you'll pre-empt Exercise 3b).

b) 🔊50 Listening: to check
- Play the recording. Students check. Focus on the intonation as well as the stress. Point out and demonstrate the importance of facial expression and gesture when you're persuading.
- Students practise saying the sentences to each other. Encourage them to overact!

> **Key** 1 Oh go <u>on</u>. Just once. 2 I <u>really</u> want you to do it. 3 It'll be a <u>laugh</u>. 4 Just have a <u>go</u>. 5 What have you got to <u>lose</u>?

Oh, come on!

4 Speaking: practice
- Check *second-hand* and *fancies*. In pairs. Students choose 2 of the situations and take it in turns to be a persuader and someone who doesn't want to be persuaded.
- Briefly focus on the language in Exercise 2c). Tell students to use as many of the persuading and refusing expressions as possible. Encourage them to try to persuade each other eventually! Monitor pairs and encourage appropriate facial expression, gesture and intonation.

Wavelength page

I disagree!

5 a) 🔘 51 (Recording script Coursebook page 154)
Listening: for gist

- Play the recording and elicit the subject of the argument. Teach *nepotism* and ask students to discuss nepotism in groups.
- Feedback. Elicit from students the language they used to give their opinions, interrupt, agree, disagree and write it on the board, however basic, e.g. *No, Yes, I agree, I think, That's right, But,* etc.

> **Key** They're arguing about nepotism, the practice of giving the best jobs to members of your family, regardless of qualifications, when you're in a position of power.

b) 🔘 51 (Recording script Coursebook page 154)
Listening: for detail

- Check the words / phrases in the Word Box.
- Play the recording for students to tick the words / phrases. Play it again if necessary.
- Ask students to compare answers in pairs before the whole class feedback.

> **Key** You can't seriously believe . . . Hold on. I think . . . Yes, but what about . . .? If you ask me, . . . I see what you mean. As far as I'm concerned, . . . Come on. The thing is, . . . But really, . . . As I said, . . . I disagree.

c) Vocabulary: practice

- Monitor students and give help as necessary.
- Feedback with the class.
- **Language note:** give students as much of the following additional information as you feel they can cope with (bold = main stress).
  Giving an opinion: the most common way to give an opinion in English is to say *I think . . .* Teach also *In **my** opinion* and *To **me**, . . .,* e.g. *To **me**, it's wrong to give jobs to your family just because they're your family. To **me** can also finish short sentences, e.g. It seems like a good idea to **me**.*
  Interrupting (to make a point): the main aim is to get into the conversation quickly and effectively without being rude. Overuse of *But . . .* to interrupt can be rude whereas *If I could **just** say . . . , **Yes**, but . . . , **Yes**, and . . .* are effective and acceptable.

Accepting an argument: *I see what you **mean**, I sup**pose** so* can also be used to agree or disagree. Agreeing: we use *You're **quite** / **so** right* and *I can't argue with **that*** to express strong agreement with an argument.
Disagreeing: *You must be **jok**ing / You can't be **se**rious* also show disagreement. *That's **rub**bish* is an informal expression which we use to show strong disagreement.
You could also elicit / teach words and phrases used when we aren't sure, e.g. *You **could** be right, **may**be, per**haps**.*

- Check the stress and intonation of all the words / phrases. Point out that the main stress is on the first person in opinion phrases, e.g. *As far as **I'm** concerned, I think . . .* Contrast this with the stress on *think* when expressing doubt, e.g. *Is Jane coming? I **think** so. Where's Sam? Well, I **think** he's . . .*

> **Key Possible answers (bold = stress):**
> **1** I think . . . If you ask **me** . . . As far as **I'm** concerned . . . The thing **is** . . . **2** Hold on. Yes, but what about . . . ? But **real**ly, . . . **3** As I **said**, . . .
> **4** That's **true**. Absolutely! I a**gree**. **5** I see your **point**. I see what you **mean**. I sup**pose** so.
> **6** You can't **se**riously believe . . . I don't think so. Come **on**. You're **jok**ing! I disa**gree**.

6 Speaking: practice

- Before the discussions make it clear that the aim of the activity is to practise the language of agreement and disagreement. Explain that students will take turns to agree and disagree whether they agree or disagree with the situation in reality. Encourage them to get into the mindset of the discussion and perhaps even exaggerate their opinions.
- Students read situations 1–6. Check meaning as necessary, e.g. *gamble, cheat, tax form, campaign, affair, be fired, wipe (a computer file).*
- Remind students to use phrases from pages 72 and 73. If necessary, illustrate the activity for the class by having a brief discussion with a student.
- Pairs discuss the 6 situations and take it in turns to agree and disagree.
- Monitor students' discussions and make notes on their use of language.
- Feedback with the class.

⑨ It's a family affair

Grammar / structures	*Should / shouldn't have done; wish / if only* + Past Perfect Simple; Present Continuous + *always* to express criticism / irritation
Topic / vocabulary	Family celebrations; giving reasons, contrasting and criticising
Wavelength pages	**Day to day English** *Isn't it?*: question tags to check and confirm information
	Reading for pleasure 3: *Dear Sue*
	Do you remember? Units 7–9
Take to class	Photos for Exercise 1

Coursebook page 74

Say "cheese"!

1 Warmer
- To set the scene bring to class personal / family photos. Students comment and ask questions.
- Focus on photos A–E to present the topic of family celebrations. Check the expression *say "cheese"* which is used to get people to smile when they're having their photo taken.
- Students discuss the questions in pairs and show each other any photos they've got. Feedback.

2 a) Vocabulary: matching
- Check the pronunciation and stress of the words in the Word Box. Ask students to look up any words they don't understand in their dictionaries.
- Elicit the family occasions. Students then match the words in the Word Box to the photos.
- In the feedback, point out that the couple in picture E are celebrating their golden wedding (50th wedding anniversary).

> **Key** **A** guest, host, relative / relation, celebration, turkey **B** ceremony, relative / relation
> **C** newborn baby, couple **D** gift / present, cake, guest, birthday, balloon, celebration, candle, party, decorations **E** anniversary, decorations, couple
> **Words not in the photos:** wedding, bride, champagne, bridegroom

b) Writing: practice
- Students work individually or in pairs and choose one of the photos A–E.
- Focus on the instructions, example and the deliberate mistake. Encourage students to be as subtle as possible with their mistakes.
- Ask students to write a description of at least 5 sentences. Remind them to use the vocabulary from the Word Box in Exercise 2a).

c) Speaking: practice
- In groups. Students read out their descriptions and identify the mistakes. If a group can't identify the mistake ask the student to read out the description to the whole class. Feedback.

3 Speaking: practice
- Start off the discussion with your own anecdote.
- Feedback after the group discussions.

Coursebook page 75

You shouldn't have done that!

> ### Optional extras
> **Before 4a) Speaking: practice**
> - Students bring in photos of family occasions. Put the photos up round the room. Students identify the occasions and match the correct student to each photo.

4 a) ⊙⊙ 52 (Recording script Coursebook page 154)
Listening: matching
- Go through the instructions with the class.
- Then play the recording. Students compare answers in pairs. Play the recording again.
- Feedback with the whole class.

> **Key** **1** = children's party **2** = birth of a baby
> **3** = 25th wedding anniversary **4** = wedding
> Problem in 1: Timmy, a little boy, is feeling sick. According to his mother it's because he ate too much cake. Problem in 2: the wife is upset because her husband missed the birth of their child. Problem in 3: the husband doesn't like the music. Problem in 4: the idea of a circus wedding has gone wrong. The house is on fire, there are elephants in the garden and the bride's mother has been attacked by a monkey.

b) 🔊52 (Recording script Coursebook page 154)
Listening: for detail

- In pairs. Students fill in as many of the boxes and gaps as they can. Students may point out that a bride can also be a wife and a wife can also be a mother. Tell students that the woman on her wedding day is a bride, the other women talking to their husbands are wives and the woman talking to / about her son is a mother.
- Play the recording. Students fill in the boxes and gaps. Play it again if necessary. Feedback.

> **Key** **a)** = 3 wife **b)** = 1 mother
> **c)** = 4 bridegroom **d)** = 4 bride
> **e)** = 2 wife **f)** = 3 husband

5 Grammar: presentation

- Elicit answers before students read the Language Box and fill in the gaps. Go through the Language Box. Give / elicit additional examples if necessary.
- **Pronunciation note:** point out to students that they shouldn't expect to hear the word *have* clearly in these sentences. Highlight that *should* isn't a long sound. It's pronounced /ʃəd/ or /ʃʊd/ and the *l* is silent.
- Refer students to the Grammar reference on pages 117 and 119 for information on *wish / if only* + Past Perfect Simple and *should / shouldn't have done.*

> **Key** A mistake in the past. Criticism, regret and blame. **Language Box:** We can express **criticism**, **regret** and **blame** about events in the past in different ways.

6 Grammar: practice

- Students could do this for homework or in class.
- Feedback with the class. Elicit the answers and write them on the board. Discuss any errors.
- Students close their books. Read the answers on the board and the beginning of sentences 1–5 in Exercise 6. Elicit the complete original sentences in brackets, e.g. *1 I shouldn't have drunk so much. It was wrong of me. (It was wrong of me to drink so much.)*

> **Key** 1 I shouldn't **have drunk so much.**
> 2 She wishes **she hadn't come to the party.**
> 3 I should **have bought him a present.**
> 4 If only we **hadn't invited Gary.** 5 I wish **we'd hired a DJ (so the music was better).**

7 Speaking / Writing: practice

- Organise students into A, B, C and D pairs.
- Pairs read their instructions and examples and look at their pictures. Check students understand.
- Pairs write 3 sentences for the man and 3 sentences for the woman. Give help and monitor. Make sure students aren't criticising the present situation, e.g. *I wish I weren't here* but are expressing blame or regret about the past. Remind them to give just enough information in each sentence so that the other students will be able to guess a bit more about the situation with each sentence. Explain that the activity is similar to 20 questions but uses sentences instead of words.
- In groups of 8, each containing Pair A, B, C and D. Pairs take it in turns to read the sentences for the man and the woman. The groups try to guess the situations. Students ask *Yes / No* questions if they can't guess the situation after all the sentences have been read. Use only 2 pictures for smaller classes. Pairs then make groups of 4 or read their sentences to the class.

> **Key** Possible answers: **Pair A:** MAN: I should have looked at the map. I should never have listened to her. I should have asked the way. WOMAN: If only I'd brought a coat / an umbrella. I wish we'd set off earlier. He should have checked the water. **Pair B:** MAN: I wish we'd taken the cable car. I shouldn't have brought her. She should have worn something more suitable. WOMAN: If only I hadn't worn these shoes. I wish I hadn't said I loved hiking. He should have told me it was difficult. **Pair C:** MAN: I should have looked at / read the instructions. I wish I hadn't taken it apart. I wish I'd phoned an engineer. WOMAN: He should have asked an expert to look at / repair it. I should have done it myself. If only he'd listened to me. **Pair D:** MAN: If only I'd worn a hat. I wish I'd brought some suntan lotion. I should have checked the plane before we took off. WOMAN: I should have brought a map. I should have brought more water. I should have worn something more suitable.

After 7 Photocopiable activities

- See the song, 13 *It should have been me,* page T134.

Coursebook page 76

Let's get married

8 Vocabulary: presentation / Speaking: practice
- Check *wedding reception*. Explain that there's food and people make speeches at a traditional reception. Some receptions also have music and dancing.
- Students could use dictionaries if necessary.
- Feedback on the people (a–e) in the picture.
- In groups. Students then discuss the questions. In multilingual classes ask students to compare different ceremonies and customs. To encourage discussion you could ask *Where do the couple get married in traditional weddings in your country? How long does the wedding ceremony usually last? What happens? Is there a party afterwards?*
- Feedback with the class.

> **Key   a)** bridesmaids   **b)** bride's father
> **c)** best man   **d)** bride   **e)** bridegroom

9 a) ⊙⊙ 53 (Recording script Coursebook page 155)
Listening: for gist
- Check *cultural difference*. Play the recording.
- Students check their answers in pairs before the whole class feedback.

> **Key   1** Martin's from England. His wife's from
> Spain.   **2** Wedding presents.

b) ⊙⊙ 53 (Recording script Coursebook page 155)
Listening: for detail
- Play the recording. Students write the answers. Play the recording again if necessary.
- Students check in small groups. Feedback.

> **Key   1** Ana's aunts gave them £1200 and her
> cousin gave them £200.   **2** A toaster.   **3** No. It's
> perfectly normal as a wedding present in England
> but Martin was embarrassed because a toaster
> from his closest family seemed so small compared
> with all the money from Ana's aunts and cousin.

c) Vocabulary: practice
- Students could work in pairs and use dictionaries to check the various meanings of *get*.
- Feedback with the class.

> **Key   1** arrive   **2** obtain   **3** receive   **4** become

10 Grammar: presentation / practice
- Students read the Language Box. When they finish, use the example sentences to make sure students are aware of the different structures which follow the different connectors to give reasons and make contrasts.
- **Language note:** explain that *so* is less formal than *so that* and can be used to express reasons / intentions and also for consequences. *So that* can only be used for intentions and reasons, e.g. *They saved money **so that / so** they could get married* (intention / reason). Compare *They were in love **so** they got married* (consequence) where *so that* isn't possible. Point out that we can say *He married her to / in order to be rich*. We can't say *He married her for to be rich*.
- Students fill in the gaps with connectors from the Language Box. If students need extra help, write 3 options (a–c) for sentences 1–6 on the board or on an OHT.

1 a) because	b) because of	c) why
2 a) although	b) however	c) in spite of
3 a) although	b) even though	c) despite
4 a) for	b) to	c) so that
5 a) in spite of	b) because of	c) because
6 a) for	b) to	c) in order to

- Feedback with the whole class.

> **Key   1** because   **2** although / even though / in
> spite of the fact that / despite the fact that
> **3** despite / in spite of   **4** to / in order to
> **5** because of   **6** for / because of

> **After 10** Writing / Speaking: practice
> - Students complete each sentence so that it's true for them, using one of the possibilities in brackets. Students then discuss the sentences and situations in pairs.
>   1 I think marriage is a good / bad thing . . . (in spite of / because of)
>   2 I'm studying English at the moment . . . (because / although / so that)
>   3 I eat / drink (a type of food or drink) . . . (even though / to)
>   4 I was / wasn't a hard worker at school . . . (because / even though)
>   5 I can't stand / really like (a person) . . . (despite the fact that / because of)
> - Feedback with the class.

Coursebook page 77

11 a) Reading: for detail

- Give students a strict time limit to make sure they skim the texts and don't read intensively. Elicit the answers immediately the time is up.

> **Key** In the USA (ads a) and c) in Las Vegas and ad b) in New York).

b) Reading: for detail

- Make sure students understand the questions. In pairs. Students read the ads and answer the questions. Encourage students to focus on the activity rather than the vocabulary in the text.
- Feedback with the class and elicit the answers. Ask students to justify their answers.

> **Key** **1** = b) one of the most spectacular views on Earth; c) the view when you skydive is also spectacular **2** = a) your choice of a Super Stretch Limo or Pink Cadillac; c) private use of a passenger jet liner **3** = a) Elvis himself will . . . sing his most memorable tunes **4** = c) a beautiful spring bouquet **5** = a) "The King" . . . will be your guide for one hour **6** = b) free admission . . . on their anniversary **7** = a) Elvis (an actor impersonates the famous singer) **8** = c) skydiving

c) Speaking: practice

- Tell students they can change any of the details, e.g. they could change the famous person from Elvis to their favourite film star and then get married in their favourite film star's home or they could change the Empire State Building to the Parthenon, etc.
- Feedback and elicit a selection of preferences and ideas. Discuss any interesting suggestions.

d) Speaking: preparation

- Check *Titanic, haunted house, Hawaiian paradise* and *Wild West* with the students.
- Discuss another theme wedding, e.g. a Chicago gangster wedding, as an example with the class to give students some ideas if necessary. Elicit ideas for the settings, clothes, the ceremony, the events, etc.
- In pairs. Ask students to discuss the theme weddings. Monitor and help as necessary.
- Feedback with the class and elicit suggestions / ideas about the different weddings.

12 Speaking: practice

- In Pair As (couples) and Pair Bs (interviewers). Explain the activity. Give some examples as you go through the preparation questions. If students come up with their own idea for a theme wedding all the better!
- If there are too many men / women in your class to make couples you could make pairs of husbands / wives whose partners have left them because of their disastrous wedding. Tell them that they both had the same wedding on the same day and that the same thing went wrong. Their partner left because he / she didn't even want a wedding like that!
- Pairs prepare their stories or questions. Monitor and help with ideas. If interviewers finish their preparation first, encourage them to think of expressions to use with their guests, e.g. *Good evening; Welcome to the show; Please sit down; Well that sounds great; Thank you for coming on the programme; Good luck!*
- Pairs make groups of 4 for the chat show interviews. Groups act out their interviews for the class or in large groups if you have a larger class.
- In the class feedback elicit which wedding sounded the most interesting, romantic, awful, dangerous, exotic, etc.

> **After 12 Speaking / Writing: practice**
> - In groups, ask students to design their own website ad for a theme wedding. Tell them to follow the instructions in Unit 3 Exercises 12a) and 12b) where students designed a theme restaurant website ad.

Coursebook page 78

Parents and kids

13 a) Reading: for detail

- Point out that extract A is a film script. Make sure students read the extracts quickly. The aim is to practise reading for specific detail, leaving aside unfamiliar vocabulary.
- In the feedback, elicit the answers from the class. Ask students to indicate the sections in the extracts where they found the answers.

> **Key** In extract A the people are at home, probably in the dining room. In extract B the people are in the daughter's flat.

b) Reading: for detail

- Read through the instructions and questions and check that students understand. Point out that answers to the question *How do the different characters feel?* are debatable and that students should use examples from the extracts to justify their answers.
- In pairs. Students read the extracts again and answer the questions.
- Feedback and elicit suggested answers from the whole class. Ask other students if they agree / disagree with the answers and to give reasons for their opinions.
- **Language note:** point out *elevator* in extract A and elicit from the class the British English equivalent, *lift*. In extract B draw students' attention to *Alsatian* (a large breed of dog also called a German Shepherd) and to *ruby wedding* (a wedding anniversary celebrating 40 years of marriage).

> **Key** **1** Extract A: father, mother, husband, wife, parents, daughter   Extract B: mother, daughter
> **2** The family issues illustrated are:
> b) communication (extracts A and B)
> c) boyfriends / girlfriends (extract B)
> d) sharing jobs round the house (extract A)
> e) respect / politeness / manners (extracts A and B)
> g) freedom / independence (extract B)
> h) parental control (extracts A and B)
> **Possible answers** to *How do the different characters feel?*   Extract A: The daughter, Jane, feels put upon because she wants to be more independent. (*Do we always have to listen to this elevator music?*)   The mother, Carolyn, feels put upon because she wants more help round the house. (*As soon as you've prepared a nutritious yet savoury meal that I'm about to eat, you can listen to whatever you like.*)   The father, Lester, feels put upon because no-one's interested in him. (*Well, you want to know how things went at my job today?*)   Extract B: The daughter, Bridget, is cross and frustrated because her mother tries to interfere in her life. (*Why oh why did I give my mother a key to my flat? . . . I said through clenched teeth . . . she said, as if I were thirteen.*)   Bridget's mother probably feels frustrated because Bridget won't accept her help and advice. (*What on earth are you doing, silly? Now, come along, darling, let's not start . . .*)

Coursebook page 79

14 Reading: for detail
- Make sure students understand the definitions / phrases 1–5. Don't let students use dictionaries.
- Feedback with the class.

> **Key** **1** nutritious yet savoury   **2** You couldn't possibly care less, could you?   **3** taken aback   **4** burst in   **5** keep someone company

15 a) 〔OO〕54 (Recording script Coursebook page 155)
Listening: for gist
- Check students understand the instructions and the questionnaire.
- Play the recording for students to identify which question each person is answering and the opinion of each speaker.
- Feedback and elicit from the students the vocabulary / phrases they heard which helped them to identify the question, e.g. 1 *I'm one of three* = b), 2 *I left home . . .* = d), 3 *I think children – teenagers – should rebel . . .* = c).
- Play the recording again while students read the recording script on page 155. Answer any queries about vocabulary.

> **Key** **1** = b)   **2** = d)   **3** = c)   Speaker 1 thinks 2 (or 4 if you've got a lot of money) is the perfect number of children to have.   Speaker 2 thinks children should leave home after 17 years old.   Speaker 3 thinks teenagers should rebel against their parents in a positive way.

Before 15b) Writing: practice
- In pairs. Students write one more question for the questionnaire related to the theme of parents and kids. Use these questions as well as questions a–f from Exercise 15a) in Exercise 15b).

b) Speaking: practice
- In groups. Ask one student in each group to record the main points of the discussion for the feedback. Some groups will be more interested in the topic than others. End the discussion when most groups seem to have finished.
- Feedback with the whole class by reading out the questions students discussed and by listening to a selection of the views expressed.

I'm fed up with him!

16 a) 👓 55 (Recording script Coursebook page 155)
Listening: for gist
- Play the recording once only for this activity. Ask students to confer in pairs before eliciting answers from the whole class.

> **Key** The people are a daughter, a mother and a son. The problem is that the daughter and son are arguing because the son never gives the daughter her phone messages. The mother is trying to keep the peace.

b) 👓 55 (Recording script Coursebook page 155)
Listening: gap fill
- Ask students to read the sentences and try to fill in the gaps. Don't feedback and don't worry if they haven't filled in all the gaps.
- Play the recording for students to fill in the gaps. Then play the recording again. Feedback.
- Ask students to read the Language Box. When they have finished, elicit additional examples of the use of the Present Continuous and *always* to express criticism of a habit which happens a lot and is irritating. Also point out the different structures which can follow *tired of, sick of* and *fed up with*.
- **Language note:** highlight the use of the Present Continuous and *always* in contrast to the use of the Present Simple and *never* to express criticism and irritation.
- Refer students to the Grammar reference on page 110 for information on the use of the Present Continuous with *always*.

> **Key** **1** You're **always taking** his side. **2** You're **always protecting** him. **3** I'm so tired **of** this argument. **4** I'm sick **of** answering the phone for you. **5** She's **always trying** to cause trouble. **6** I'm fed up **with** it.

17 a) Speaking: preparation
- Set the scene with the statement *Living with people is difficult.* Elicit some of the things that have really irritated your students about friends, family, flatmates, etc. they've lived with. You could give examples of your own.
- Explain the activity. Tell students to refer back to the extracts for ideas of how others can be irritating. Remind them to use the language from Exercise 16b).

- In pairs. Students prepare their arguments. Tell them to list 2 things each person does that are irritating. They then work these irritating habits into an argument where they complain to each other. Help them to start off their argument. Tell students that the argument probably starts off in a friendly way but then it becomes more heated as they both come out with their different complaints. You could give an example:
(*Student A is sitting on the sofa when Student B comes in.*)
STUDENT A: Um . . . there's something I'd like to talk to you about . . .
STUDENT B: Sure. Go ahead.
STUDENT A: Well, you know you're always . . .

b) Speaking: practice
- Students act out their conversations for the class or for large groups. At the end of each argument ask the class / group to say who they are and what they're arguing about.
- Feedback with the class.

18 Writing: practice
- Elicit all the possible characters from the extracts. Extract A: the father, the daughter, the mother. Extract B: Bridget Jones, her mother.
- If students choose Bridget Jones tell them not to write simply a new version of the diary extract on page 78!
- This activity makes use of all the language in the unit so remind students of what they've covered: how to criticise, blame, express regret and irritation, give reasons, make contrasts, talk about marriage, etc. Build up the activity with the class and encourage students to pour their hearts out in their diaries.
- Give students some guidance. They could start with one incident from that day, e.g. *I came home from work* . . . and then use that to broaden out into their major moans about their family. You could elicit a few example sentences to start students off.
- When students have written their diary extracts, ask them to swap with a partner and proofread each other's work before giving it in.

> **After 18 Photocopiable activities**
> - See 9 *What's the missing word?*, page T126.

⑨ *Day to day English* *Isn't it?*

Grammar / structures	Question tags; use of *actually*
Functions	Checking information and asking for agreement
Pronunciation	Intonation in question tags

Coursebook page 80

A family reunion

1 a) Matching
- Check *reunion* and explain that the people at the reunion will have to do a lot of checking of information because they don't know each other that well.
- Don't feedback or you'll pre-empt Exercise 1b).

b) 🔘🔘56 Listening: to check / Presentation
- Play the recording for students to check their answers. Feedback with the whole class.
- Students read the Language Box. How question tags are used to confirm or check information will be covered in more detail in the intonation work which follows. Emphasise at this point how common question tags are in spoken English.
- Go through the Language Box with the class. Then focus on the different forms of short answers we can use with question tags. Explain that we reply with the same short answers that we'd use for an ordinary question, e.g. *Yes, that's right. No. I don't. Yes, she has.*
- Remind students that speakers who use questions with negative question tags expect listeners will probably agree with or confirm the question whereas speakers who use questions with positive question tags are checking information they aren't sure about.
- **Language note:** focus on the use of *actually* when correcting and explain that its use makes you sound polite, instead of possibly abrupt. Explain that *actually* means something like *This is the reality* or *This is the fact* and can be replaced by *in fact. In fact* gives slightly more emphasis and is usually used at the beginning of the sentence, e.g. *He's your sister's boyfriend, isn't he? No, he's my husband, actually. In fact, we've been married for 10 years.*

> **Key**   **2** = D   **3** = C   **4** = B   **5** = E
> **a)** = 5   **b)** = 4   **d)** = 2   **e)** = 3

Pronunciation: intonation in question tags

2 🔘🔘57 Presentation
- Play each recorded sentence a few times. Students say which of the questions has got rising intonation and which has got falling intonation. Students then repeat the sentences.
- Feedback on who is expecting agreement and who is checking information.
- Focus students' attention on the Language Box. Highlight the attitude of the speakers and remind students that we can use falling question tags for making conversation, for involving the other person, for asking for agreement, as well as for confirming information.

> **Key**   The question tag in question 1 rises at the end.   The question tag in question 2 falls at the end.   The person asking question 1 is checking information he isn't sure about.   The person asking question 2 is asking for agreement.

3 a) Speaking: preparation
- Begin by saying a few sentences with question tags about students. Make sure students recognise when you're really unsure and checking information and when you're confirming. e.g. *Marco, you play the guitar, don't you?* (falling intonation, confirming) *Josefina, your mother's a doctor, isn't she?* (rising intonation, checking). Ask students to write 3 sentences that check or confirm information they aren't sure about and 3 to ask for agreement with information they think is true.

b) Speaking: practice
- Review examples of short answers to question tags and the use of *actually* for politeness before students go round the class.
- Monitor students' answers. Check they sound polite and that they're using the correct rising / falling intonation.
- Feedback with the class.

Wavelength page

Reading for pleasure
③ Dear Sue

Vocabulary *amazement, annoyed, apparently, blush (v), broadcasting, bump into, bunch, cappuccino, certainly, cheer someone up, daffodil, daisy, deep, desktop, disaster, doormat, efficiently, fellow, free server, giggle, hoot (v), instead, joy, kick off, leap, lower (v), make someone go weak at the knees, mountain bike, pearl, personal column, print something out, put together, raindrop, rip (v), rose, scroll down, secret admirer, sentimental, shoot (a film / programme), skim, skip (v = miss), stare, tease (v), tendency, text message, violet, voicemail, weep, windscreen, Yellow Pages*

Coursebook page 81

Before reading

1 Presentation
- Check *untraceable* and *a free server*.
- In groups. Encourage students to be inventive.
- Feedback and note down students' suggestions.

2 [oo] 58 (Recording script Coursebook page 81)
Reading and listening: for detail
- Students read and listen to the recording. They could work in pairs before you feedback.
- Elicit the usual meaning of *AD (Anno Domini)*, used to show that a date is a particular number of years after the birth of Christ. Check *blue = sad*.

> **Key** **1** She was in her car in a traffic jam.
> **2** It was raining. **3** Because her ex-boyfriend, Dave, told her that their relationship was over 2 weeks ago. **4** A mysterious Mr Sunshine.

3 Reading: for gist and detail
- Pre-teach vocabulary as necessary.
- Students could read the whole story and answer the questions for homework.

> **Key** **1** To celebrate the special award that the news programme Sue worked on had won.
> **2** She'd been too miserable to go. **3** She thinks her friend, Fran, had gossiped and told the whole of News Spot. **4** Mr Sunshine. **5** Roy. **6** Roy was an old friend and had been like a brother to Sue for years. **7** The phone on Sue's desk began to ring. **8** Roses are red, violets are blue, sugar is sweet, and so are you . . . Sue. **9** Fran.
> **10** That Roy had got a girlfriend called Esmeralda and had found true love at last. **11** She thought Dave was the most likely person.

> **12** On Tuesday evening she had dinner with Stephen. On Wednesday evening she had a drink with Chris. **13** Her ex-boyfriend, Dave. **14** Mr Sunshine / Roy.

After reading

4 Speaking: discussion
- Feedback on the answers to Exercise 3. You could ask more questions.
  1 What are the different ways Roy sent messages to Sue? Students compare their list with the list of suggestions they made in Exercise 1.
  2 Sue thought that Roy was *married to his profession*. Do you think it's possible to be totally committed to your profession as well as have a successful marriage / relationship?

5 Vocabulary: practice
- Students list the words in the story associated with office equipment: *print out, desk, turn on, computer, e-mail, scroll down, open (the message / a file), free server, close down, print off, file, phone, ring, pick up, put down, voicemail, flash, press (the LISTEN button), dial, desktop, save.*

6 Writing and speaking: practice
- In pairs. Students write the conversation between Dave and Sue when Dave said: *I really like being with you, Sue. But I don't feel ready for a serious relationship.* Students act out their conversations.

7 Personalisation
- Ask students if they have any experience or knowledge of unusual or interesting ways couples have courted each other.
- Students write their own Mr Sunshine poems.

Grammar / structures / vocabulary | 1 Means of communication and reported speech
2 Third Conditional
3 *Should / shouldn't have done, wish / if only* + Past Perfect Simple; language of anger and irritation
4 Grammar / structures / vocabulary from Units 7–9

Coursebook page 82

1 *Tell me more*

a) ⊙⊙ 59 (Recording script Coursebook page 155)
Listening: matching
- Play the recording once only. Students match.
- Feedback with the class.

> **Key** **1** = c) **2** = a) **3** = b) **4** = d)

b) ⊙⊙ 59 (Recording script Coursebook page 155)
Listening: for gist
- In pairs. Play the recording twice. Then ask students to discuss the questions.
- Feedback and elicit suggestions. Ask students to justify their ideas. Note them on the board.

c) Speaking: preparation
- In groups of 4: Student A, Student B, Student C and Student D. Students then work individually.
- Encourage students to prepare, practise and rehearse phrases, information and sentences.

d) Speaking / Writing: practice
- Remind students to tell the person speaking to stop, slow down or repeat what they're saying if they don't understand.
- In their original groups of 4. Give a time limit for each student to report his / her information and remind the students listening to take notes.
- Monitor groups and check that students' notes are full enough.

e) Reading: practice
- All 4 members of the group look at the same original text in turn until they've checked all 4 texts. The 3 note-takers point out to the original teller what he / she forgot or got wrong, according to their notes. Encourage the 3 note-takers to use *say* and *tell* when discussing the differences between their notes and the original, e.g. *You didn't say that . . . Yes, he did but he didn't tell us that she had . . .*

2 A sorry tale

a) Reading: preparation
- In groups of 4: Student A, Student B, Student C and Student D. Students could take notes.
- Monitor students and help with any difficulties.

b) Speaking: practice
- In the same groups. Students take it in turns to tell each other their paragraphs and the group establishes the correct order of the paragraphs.

c) Speaking: practice
- If necessary, briefly revise the form and meaning of the Third Conditional before students discuss.
- Feedback. Elicit who students think was the most / least responsible.

> **Key** Jed and Jemima were under arrest.
> **Possible answers:** If Jemima hadn't talked to her friends, she wouldn't have been late. If Jemima hadn't driven so fast, she wouldn't have crashed the truck. If Jed had fixed the brakes, Jemima wouldn't have had the accident. If Old Pa Welbeck had let Jed and Jemima pay less, a little money every week or accepted chickens or corn, they could have bought his truck. If Jed and Jemima had stopped drinking beer and smoking, they could have saved more and bought Old Pa Welbeck's truck. If Jemima hadn't heard the ad, they wouldn't have gone to "Big Daddy's Truck Bargains". If Jemima had written down the address, Jed wouldn't have had to ask a passerby for directions. If Jed hadn't told the stranger about their money, the stranger wouldn't have robbed them. If they hadn't trusted the stranger and gone with him, he wouldn't have robbed them. If Jed had fought the stranger, they might have got their money back. If one of them had chased the thief, they might have caught him. If the policeman had believed them, they might have caught the thief. If they hadn't asked the policeman for help, they wouldn't have been arrested.

Wavelength page

3 *It's all your fault!*

a) Writing: preparation

- Check *soap opera*. Elicit the over-the-top nature of this kind of programme and emphasise that anything is possible in terms of plot. You could teach *cliffhanger* and elicit examples.
- Go through the instructions. Check / teach *scriptwriter, dysfunctional, dramatic, disastrous*.
- In groups. Students answer the questions and plan their scene. Make sure students don't feel overwhelmed by the activity. Point out that these are short scenes, a maximum of 5 minutes long. Students are just writing a dialogue where several characters have an argument and the scene can be about big issues or lots of little ones. Students shouldn't feel under pressure to make it real drama.
- Students will need to establish where the characters are in one or two lines at the beginning so that they can move on to the drama. You could give an example:

(Bridegroom, Peter, and bride, Sylvia, standing in front of the priest.)

PRIEST: *(to bride)* Do you take Peter to be your husband?

BRIDE: I . . .

MAN: *(bursts in shouting)* No! Stop! It should have been me! Sylvia, you can't marry him!

This results in a terrible row, where even more terrible secrets come out (elicit students' ideas) and everyone blames everyone else.

b) Speaking / Writing: practice

- Allow enough time (15–20 minutes) for students to discuss their ideas and write their scripts.
- Write on the board: *1 Set the scene, 2 Main action, 3 Conclusion.* Explain that parts 1 and 3 should take a maximum of one minute and the main action a maximum of 3 minutes.
- Monitor carefully, helping with ideas, vocabulary and language content. Don't let students try to make the situation too complicated and don't let the scene drag on too long.
- Tell students to decide on the dialogue for their scene together. Remind each student to write a copy of the whole script for himself / herself. You could appoint a group secretary with neat writing and a good language level to write the script but you will then need to produce copies for each student before the groups act out their scenes.

c) Speaking: practice

- Students decide on which parts they will play and practise their scenes.
- Groups then read or act out their scenes.
- At the end of each group performance ask the rest of the class where the characters in the script are, who they are and what happened.
- Ask the class to vote for the best / saddest / funniest or the most dramatic scene.

Coursebook page 83

4 Max's diary

Grammar: practice

- This exercise revises grammar, structures and vocabulary from Units 7–9: Past Perfect Simple; giving reasons and contrasting; Third Conditional, *should / shouldn't have done*; reported speech; *wish / if only* + Past Perfect Simple; criticising; *otherwise* and *in case*.
- Revise the structures or vocabulary from Units 7–9 which you consider might cause students problems before they do the activity. Alternatively delay review activities on the structures until students have completed the exercise.
- Remind students of Max Ranting from Unit 8, Exercise 5a). Students do the activity for homework or individually in class, then check in pairs.
- Feedback with the class. Go into more detail with areas which seem to cause problems to a lot of students. You could refer individual students to exercises from Units 7–9 which deal with the structures that are still causing difficulty.

> **Key** **1** took **2** to **3** order **4** had gone
> **5** even though **6** hadn't / had not been
> **7** would've / have died **8** 've / have put
> **9** 've / have used **10** because of **11** despite
> **12** was doing **13** told **14** had **15** probably
> **16** had come **17** to **18** 've / have listened
> **19** hadn't / had not thought **20** so that
> **21** always **22** why **23** otherwise **24** for
> **25** In spite

> Encourage students to learn the new words from Units 7–9 on Coursebook pages 126–128 and do Puzzle 3 on Coursebook page 121 before you give them Progress test Units 7–9 on page T142.

⑩ *What's going on?*

Grammar / structures	The Passive; the Passive with *get* and with indirect objects; negative questions; modal verbs for laws, rules and social behaviour; verb + *-ing* and verb + infinitive
Topic / vocabulary	News stories and crime; legal language; describing behaviour; word building
***Wavelength* pages**	**Writing for work and pleasure 4** *On the other hand . . .*: writing a report
Take to class	Tabloid and broadsheet newspapers for Exercise 7a)

Coursebook page 84

Have you heard the news?

1 Speaking: practice
- Before the discussion in pairs check general newspaper vocabulary, e.g. *headline, article, sports section, feature, editorial.*
- Tell one student to ask the questions, the other to answer and then swap roles. Alternatively, after answering a question, tell students to ask *How about you?*
- Monitor and encourage students to chat.
- Feedback with the whole class.

2 a) Reading: for gist
- Elicit examples of international, national and human interest news stories to check that students understand the concepts.
- Set a time limit. Remind students to read quickly.
- Feedback with the class.

> **Key**   1 = national   2 = human interest
> 3 = international

b) Reading: for detail
- Check *riot, hamster, (computer) virus* and *bonus.* Students skim for details to answer specific questions without trying to understand everything.
- Students check answers in pairs. Feedback.
- **Language note:** contrast the words *riot, protest* and *demonstration.* Explain that *riot* is used when violence is involved. A peaceful protest or demonstration can become a riot if it gets out of control and becomes violent.
- Elicit the noun, person and verb connected with the words *riot, protest* and *demonstration: riot* (n), *rioter* (person), *riot* (v); *protest* (n), *protester* (person), *protest (against something)* (v); *demonstration* (n), *demonstrator* (person), *demonstrate (against something)* (v).

> **Key**   1 Demonstrators against capitalism and the police.   2 Because he was buried but managed an incredible escape, like the world-famous American escapologist, Harry Houdini.
> 3 As soon as the e-mail was opened, personal computers received over a thousand more messages, causing the systems to crash. People opened it because it was called "Annual Bonus". They thought they were going to get some money.

c) Vocabulary: presentation
- Students could work in pairs using a dictionary.
- Pairs check answers with another pair. Feedback.

> **Key**   **1a)** looted   **1b)** hurled   **1c)** broken into
> **1d)** wrecked   **2a)** coffin   **2b)** hibernating
> **2c)** chewed   **3** virus, sent, e-mail, opened, personal, messages, systems, crash, bug, hit, contacted

Optional extras
After 2c) Speaking: practice
- Give prompt questions to encourage students to share opinions related to the articles in a group discussion, e.g. *Do you agree with the movement against capitalism? Do newspapers in your country have many stories about animals? Have you ever been affected by a computer virus?*
- Feedback with the whole class.

The Passive

3 a) Grammar: preparation
- Feedback. Don't go into the differences in form or you'll pre-empt Exercise 3b).

> **Key**   **a)** = 2   **b)** = 3   **c)** = 1

Coursebook page 85

b) Grammar: presentation

- Feedback with the class when students have answered the 2 questions. It isn't a problem at this point if students don't use the terms *active* or *passive* although they're useful and students should learn them eventually. Encourage students to comment on the differences in the form of the verbs in the sentences, to say that the word order is different and that some words are missing in the sentences in the article. Question 2 ensures that students notice that the person who did the actions, the agent, is missing from the passive sentences.
- Students then read the Language Box. Go through the example sentences and use them to highlight the form and use of the Passive. Use the term *passive* and check students understand *the person who did the action*. Point out that it's a short way of saying *the person who did / does / has done / will do,* etc. *the action*.
- Refer students to the Grammar reference on page 117 for information on the Passive.

> **Key** 1 In Exercise 3a) the sentences are active. In the articles they're passive. 2 The subject or who did the action is missing.

4 a) Grammar: practice

- This activity reminds students that, when they need a Passive form, it's just a question of identifying the tense and then using that tense of the verb *be* together with the past participle of the main verb.
- Elicit the different forms of the tenses of the verb *be* and write them on the board. Students then write the sentences individually.
- Students compare their answers in pairs. Then elicit the answers from the class and write them on the board.

> **Key** 1 Present Continuous: The suspects **are being** interviewed. 2 Past Simple: The money **was** found. 3 Present Perfect Simple: A lot of people **have been** arrested. 4 The Future with *will*: He'**ll / will be** killed if he goes there! 5 Infinitive with *to*: Supplies need **to be sent** to the area. 6 Gerund: I like **being** interviewed.

b) Grammar: practice

- Feedback with the class and elicit the Passive sentences and their tenses or verb forms.

> **Key** 1 Past Simple: . . . shops **were looted** and bricks and bottles **were hurled** . . . Past Simple: Hundreds of police . . . **were brought in** to break up . . . Past Simple: . . . a McDonald's restaurant and a bureau de change . . . **were broken into** and **wrecked** . . . 2 Past Simple: Prayers **were said** . . . and . . . the animal **was buried** . . . The Future with *will*: . . . he'll be called Houdini. 3 Past Simple: The virus **was sent** . . . Past Simple: As soon as this e-mail **was opened** . . . Past Simple: . . . thirty million European workers **were affected**. Present Perfect Simple: We'**ve been hit** . . . Present Simple: Normal business **is made** impossible . . . Infinitive without *to*: . . . customers can't **be contacted** . . .

5 a) 🔁60 (Recording script Coursebook page 155)
Listening: for detail

- Play the recording twice. Ask students to write down their answers.
- Students compare their answers in pairs. Then play the recording again for students to correct.
- Feedback with the class.

> **Key** 1 It's similar to article 1. 2a) 2000 = the police estimate of how many people were on the march 2b) 10 or 11,000 = Planet of Love's estimate of how many people were on the march 2c) 12 = the time the march started 2d) 20 = the number of people who started throwing things 2e) hundreds = the number of police on horseback 2f) 30 = the number of seconds it took for the march to change from a peaceful march to a complete riot 2g) 4:30 = the time of the news broadcast

b) 🔁60 (Recording script Coursebook page 155)
Listening: gap fill

- Play the recording twice. Feedback with the class. Students then read the Language Box. Highlight that *get* with the Passive is used in informal spoken and written English.

> **Key** 1 got 2 got 3 are getting 4 are getting 5 didn't get

Broadcast news

6 Speaking: practice

- This activity can be done in any combination of students or with any group size. However if students prepare their stories in pairs or groups they can help each other with ideas and language.
- Organise students into equal numbers of A, B, C and D students or A, B, C and D pairs. You don't have to use all 4 scenarios, although students probably need at least 3 stories to argue about.
- You could create a pair of editors if you need one extra pair. While the other students are working on their stories the editors can discuss the kind of story they want / don't want, questions they can ask the journalists. Editors then chair the meeting and make the final decision about which story goes first.
- Explain that the programme is on air in 30 minutes. The technicians will need 10 minutes to find the material the journalists need, so students have got 20 minutes to decide on the order of the programme.
- When the groups are ready, bring them together to start their discussions. Warn the students when they've got 5 minutes left and stop the activity after 20 minutes.
- If you've got access to video cameras or tape recorders, record the activity as TV or radio news. Each student / pair presents their story. With pairs, one student is the newsreader, the other a correspondent, or someone being interviewed. Give students 10–15 minutes to prepare.

> **Coursebook page 86**

Scandal

7 a) Reading: for gist

- Bring a selection of newspapers to illustrate the concept of *tabloid* and *broadsheet* newspapers. These could be in the students' first language or you could use British newspapers.
- Ask students to glance at the title and writing style of the article on page 86. Elicit that it's a tabloid newspaper.
- Ask students to read the article quickly and decide if it's for or against Andrew Chalmers.
- Feedback. Ask students to justify their answer.

> **Key** Against.

b) Reading: for gist / Speaking: practice

- Students read the article again and concentrate on Andrew Chalmers' crimes / offences.
- Elicit Chalmers' crimes / offences and write them on the board. In pairs. Students close their books and then explain the meaning of each crime / offence in their own words.
- If your students need more support, write the crimes / offences on the board or on an OHT in one column. In another column, write the definitions from the Key in a different order. Students then read the article and match the crimes / offences to the definitions.
- Feedback with the class.
- **Language note:** point out the difference between *rob, steal* and *mug. Rob* + person or place, e.g. *That man robbed **me** then robbed **the shop**. Steal* (or *take* sometimes in conversation) + items or money, e.g. *He stole (took) **my credit card** and stole £500. Mug* is when someone attacks you or uses violence in a public place, but usually with few witnesses and steals your money or belongings, e.g. *I was mugged outside my hotel and they took my passport.* You could also explain that we usually use the verb *steal* rather than *shoplift*, e.g. *A shoplifter was arrested for stealing* and that in conversation we usually use the phrasal verb *break into* rather than *burgle*, e.g. *Our flat was broken into.*

> **Key Possible answers: 1** drink-driving = driving a vehicle when you've drunk more than the legal limit of alcohol **2** fiddling expenses = giving false information to your employer in order to get money **3** shoplifting = taking things from shops without paying for them **4** burglary = breaking into a building to steal things **5** forgery = illegally copying something to make people think it's real **6** fraud = deceiving people / organisations, usually to get money from them

c) Vocabulary: practice

- Students work individually. Then ask them to check answers in a dictionary in pairs.
- Feedback by writing the answers on the board in random order. Elicit the definitions.

> **Key 1** speeding **2** released **3** the scene of the crime **4** trial **5** jury **6** sentenced

After 7c) Vocabulary: practice

- In groups. Write on the board *1 shoplifter, 2 car thief, 3 murderer, 4 mugger, 5 bank robber, 6 pickpocket, 7 kidnapper, 8 vandal, 9 terrorist.* Ask *What do these criminals do? What are the crimes called? What are the verbs?* Elicit and write on the board *1 a shoplifter steals from shops, shoplifting* (n), *shoplift or steal* (v).
- Students could use the *Longman WordWise Dictionary* to help them. Feedback.

> **Key** **2 a car thief** steals cars, **car theft** (n), **steal** (v) **3 a murderer** kills people, **murder** (n), **murder** (v) **4 a mugger** robs people in the street, **mugging** (n), **mug** (v) **5 a bank robber** takes money from banks, **bank robbery** (n), **rob** (v) **6 a pickpocket** steals from people's pockets and bags in crowds, **pickpocketing** (n), **pick (someone's) pocket** (v) **7 a kidnapper** takes people and holds them in return for money, **kidnapping** (n), **kidnap** (v) **8 a vandal** smashes things in public places, **vandalism** (n), **vandalise** (v) **9 a terrorist** uses violent actions against the public for political aims, **terrorism** (n), verb depends on what a terrorist does, e.g. **bomb**, **shoot**, etc.

d) Speaking: practice

- In groups of 4. Encourage students to justify their opinions based on the information in the article.
- Feedback with the class.

Coursebook page 87

8 a) 〔oo〕 61 (Recording script Coursebook page 156)
Listening: for detail

- Ask students what they think Chalmers' attitude will be when he's interviewed.
- Go through the instructions and the questions. Play the recording. Students confer in pairs, then listen to the recording again to check.
- After the class feedback, ask students if they were surprised by Chalmers' attitude or if it was what they expected.

> **Key** **1** No. **2** Yes. **3** Because he was never informed about how the money was spent by the business director.

b) 〔oo〕 61 (Recording script Coursebook page 156)
Listening: gap fill

- Students listen to the recording again and fill in the gaps.
- Elicit the answers from the class. Then ask students to read the Language Box. Check students understand *indirect object, receiver of the thing, information, gift.*

> **Key** **1** The jury **was given** false information. **2** They **weren't told** the whole story. **3** I **was** never **informed** about how the money was spent.

c) Grammar: practice

- Students can rewrite the sentences in the Passive for homework or in class. Before they do the activity, remind them to write the passive sentence in the same tense as the equivalent active sentence.
- Ask students to correct each other's work in groups. Monitor the corrections to make sure they're accurate and then feedback.

> **Key** **1** I was told to come here. **2** I wasn't given any choice. **3** The Prime Minister will be informed. **4** Jane was told to wait in reception. **5** I was asked a couple of questions.

9 a) 〔oo〕 62 (Recording script Coursebook page 156)
Listening: for detail

- Go through the instructions and the questions with the class. Check *bad excuse, cut off* and *business connection.*
- Play the recording for students to write their answers. Monitor students as they write. Then play the recording again for students to confirm their answers.
- Ask students to swap answers in pairs and agree on their final answers before you feedback with the whole class.

> **Key** **1** Seymour Cripes-Tottingly. It's a bad excuse because Cripes-Tottingly was arrested for fraud when he was 36. Fraud is a serious crime and 36 isn't young. This excuse usually refers to minor silly things we do or mistakes we make when we're at school, college or university. **2** Because "he did those terrible things" and was "Clever, but criminal". He put the money into foreign bank accounts and lied to people who trusted them.

b) 🔊62 (Recording script Coursebook page 156)
Listening: gap fill

- Write the question *Were you the financial director?* on the board. Tell students to listen and notice how the interviewer's question differs from the question on the board. Play the beginning of the recording again for students to hear that the verb is negative.
- Ask students to try to fill in the gaps in sentences 2–4. Then play the whole of the recording so that they can confirm their predictions.
- **Language note:** focus on the attitude of the interviewer to highlight the meaning and use of negative questions, i.e. the interviewer doesn't believe him and she's surprised. Point out that negative questions are used a lot in conversation. Highlight the stress, intonation and facial expression which accompany negative questions.
- Students read the Language Box. Go through the examples and point out that the word order is the same as in ordinary questions but we use a negative question verb (auxiliary or modal). Explain that *Didn't you know?* means *I find it hard to believe / I'm really surprised you didn't know!* and *Isn't that John's car?* means *It looks like John's car. I think it is John's car.*
- **Pronunciation note:** explain that in questions with *be*, we stress the negative verb *be* and the information words (adjective, place, etc.), e.g. **Wasn't** she **scared? Aren't** you from Paki**stan?** With other verbs, we stress the negative auxiliary / modal, the main verb and the information words, e.g. **Did**n't you **real**ise it was **him? Can't** you under**stand** what he **wants?**

> **Key** 1 Weren't 2 Didn't 3 Couldn't 4 Haven't

But haven't you ever . . . ?!

10 **Speaking: practice**

- In groups of 4: Student A, Student B, Student C and Student D. Check students understand the instructions and scenarios.
- Tell students to ask as many negative questions as they can to try to catch the others out, disprove them or just to see if they're really as honest, etc. as they say they are. Point out how often this kind of thing happens in everyday conversations and social situations with friends.
- Monitor and note down common errors.
- Feedback with the class.

It shouldn't be allowed!

11 a) **Vocabulary / Speaking: practice**

- Students read the adjectives. Check for meaning, pronunciation and stress before students discuss the answers in pairs.
- Feedback with the class.

> **Key** 1 The people are in a traffic jam. One driver is sounding his horn. 2 The people are in a cinema. 2 men are talking. 3 The people are in a library. 2 women are talking. Students' use of the adjectives to talk about each picture will vary.

b) 🔊63 (Recording script Coursebook page 156)
Listening: for detail

- Play the recording.
- Students compare answers in pairs. If students don't agree, play the recording again. Feedback.

> **Key** 1 illegal, selfish, stupid 2 illegal, rude, annoying, selfish 3 irritating, polite, anti-social

c) 🔊63 (Recording script Coursebook page 156)
Listening: for detail

- Play the recording twice. Then feedback.

> **Key** b) = 2 c) = 3 d) = 1, 2 e) = 2 f) = 1 g) = 2, 3 h) = 1, 2, 3 i) = 3 j) = 2

d) **Vocabulary: presentation**

- Students cover the Language Box, read expressions a–j in Exercise 11c) and write *L* beside expressions about laws, *R* beside expressions about rules and *B* beside expressions about behaviour.
- Students then read the Language Box and check their answers. Feedback with the class.
- Focus on which verb form is used with each expression and point out that *It's not . . .* and *You're not . . .* are the usual negative forms for these expressions. However the more common negative forms *isn't* and *aren't* can also be used.
- Remind students that we usually use *must* and *mustn't* for direct orders from the speaker to the listener rather than for laws and rules, e.g. *You must stop working so hard.*
- Refer students to the Grammar reference on page 118 for information on modal verbs.

Verb + *-ing* and verb + infinitive

12 a) Grammar: preparation
- Feedback with the whole class.

> **Key** 1 The verb *drive* changes to verb + *-ing* (a gerund) and the word order changes because *driving* is the subject. 2 There's no real difference in meaning.

b) Grammar: practice
- Use the example to illustrate the activity.
- Students work individually, then check their answers in pairs before the whole class feedback.

> **Key** 1 It's illegal to carry a gun. 2 Smoking's not / Smoking isn't against the rules in here. 3 It's not / It isn't against the law to criticise the government. 4 Using a mobile phone in the cinema is anti-social. 5 It's selfish to park on the pavement.

Coursebook page 89

Who do they think they are?

13 a) Vocabulary: matching
- Check the pronunciation / stress of the items in the Word Box. In groups. Ask students to use their dictionaries if necessary.
- Feedback with the whole class.

> **Key** a) = breaking the speed limit / speeding b) = sexism c) = cheating d) = dropping litter e) = jaywalking f) = fiddling taxes g) = fare-dodging h) = queue-jumping i) = stealing from work j) = hitting / smacking

b) 🎧 64 (Recording script Coursebook page 156)
Listening: for gist
- Encourage global understanding by telling students not to focus on the meaning of individual words.
- Play the recording. Ask students to make notes. Play the recording again if necessary.
- Students check their answers in pairs. Feedback.

> **Key** 1 Listening 1 is about jaywalking (picture e). Listening 2 is about fare-dodging (picture g). 2 Listening 1 compares California in America / the USA to "here", i.e. Britain. Listening 2 talks about Italy. 3 See Recording 64.

c) Speaking: practice
- If students are interested in the issues raised, don't be afraid to devote a reasonable length of time to the discussion. Refer students back to Andrew Chalmers' story on pages 86 and 87 to set the scene and warm the students to the theme. Ask *What is your opinion about the "mistakes" Chalmers made? Are they against the law? Do you think they're important?*
- In groups. Check students understand the instructions and questions.
- Monitor the discussions and note down errors.
- Feedback and listen to a selection of answers, opinions and personal experiences before dealing with any language points.

> **Key** 1 In Britain: a) breaking the speed limit is illegal. b) sexism or racism is illegal in a job advertisement. It breaks laws of discrimination / equal opportunities. c) cheating is against the rules. d) dropping litter is illegal. e) jaywalking is against the rules. f) fiddling taxes is illegal. g) fare-dodging is illegal. h) queue-jumping is anti-social and bad manners. i) stealing from work is illegal. j) hitting / smacking is sometimes illegal.

After 13c) Photocopiable activities
- See 10 *Who can go free?*, page T128.

14 Writing: practice
- This writing task can be done now or you could wait until after students have done Writing for work and pleasure 4. Students will then be able to use the language and ideas for organising their writing from pages 90 and 91.
- Check students understand the saying *Rules are made to be broken*. We usually say it when we feel we have to go against accepted ways of behaving / rules. It means sometimes you have to do something illegal and it can refer to minor rules or major laws but it's light-hearted, not a political conviction.
- When students have finished writing about one of the questions, ask them to swap their work with another student and help each other with correction, ideas and comments. Students then write a second draft which you can display in the classroom for students to read.

Writing for work and pleasure

 On the other hand . . .

Topic / vocabulary	How family size affects children
Writing skills	Reports and how they're laid out; organisation of ideas into paragraphs with subheadings or clearly defined gaps; use of linkers; use of formal language

Coursebook page 90

Writing a report

1 a) Speaking / Writing: practice

- To set the scene for the activity, you could elicit from the class what students think is the perfect number of children to have.
- Focus students on the instructions and the word map. Check students understand *conduct a survey*. Ask them to think about the advantages and disadvantages of being an only child compared to the advantages and disadvantages of being a child in a large family.
- In pairs. Students discuss the topic and add their own ideas to the word map.
- Go round the class. Monitor and give help with ideas and language as necessary.
- Copy the word map onto the board.
- Feedback with the whole class. Elicit students' ideas and write them in the appropriate place on the word map.

b) Reading: for gist

- Check students understand the instructions. Then ask them to read the report "How does family size affect children?".
- In pairs. Students compare the ideas they added to the word map in Exercise 1a) with the ideas in the report.
- Feedback with the whole class and ask students to comment on the similarities and differences between their ideas and the ideas mentioned in the report.
- Highlight some of the words and phrases used in the report and elicit / check their meaning, e.g. *gather, burden, isolated, sibling, social skill, tolerance, co-operation, household, sole, unfavourably, tend to, downside, spoilt, adequately, adulthood, viewpoint.* You could ask students to use their dictionaries if necessary.

c) Reading: gap fill

- Draw students' attention to the gaps 1–4 in the report. Ask them to look at the word map in Exercise 1a) and fill in the gaps with the correct heading for each paragraph. Ask students to work individually.
- Feedback with the class.

> **Key** **Paragraph 1** The advantages of being a child in a large family **Paragraph 2** The disadvantages of being a child in a large family **Paragraph 3** The advantages of being an only child **Paragraph 4** The disadvantages of being an only child

Coursebook page 91

d) Reading: analysis

- Before students read the Writing Box, ask them to discuss the question in pairs. Tell them to decide what information the first and last paragraphs of the report contain. When they finish, tell them to compare answers with another pair.
- Feedback with the class.
- Focus students on the Writing Box and go through the information with the class. Highlight the function of the introductory and final paragraphs, the organisation of the report into sections, the use of paragraph headings and the use of clear and impersonal language. Illustrate the features of report writing given in the Writing Box with additional examples from the report or from other sources.

> **Key** The first introductory paragraph says what the report is about and how the information was gathered. The last paragraph summarises the information, gives an opinion and makes a recommendation.

2 a) Vocabulary: practice
- Ask students to copy the table into their notebooks. Go through the headings 1–5 and the examples with the class. Check that students understand what they have to do.
- In pairs. Ask students to fill in the table with the linkers and phrases in green from the report. Then tell them to swap partners and to compare their answers.
- Feedback with the class.

> **Key   2** in addition, Moreover, also, As well as this   **3** despite, on the other hand, In contrast, although   **4** On the whole, In conclusion   **5** I recommend that

b) Vocabulary: practice
- Ask students to use dictionaries to check the meaning of any linkers and phrases in the Word Box that they don't understand. Then tell students to write them in the correct place in the table.
- Feedback with the whole class and then ask students if they can add any linkers / phrases of their own to the table. Elicit suggestions and write them on the board.

> **Key   1** thirdly   **2** furthermore   **3** however   **4** to summarise   **5** I propose that

3 a) Speaking: practice / Writing: preparation
- Read through the 5 topics. Explain any words, phrases or concepts that students don't understand, e.g. *self-employed, gap year*. Point out that an increasing number of students in Britain have a gap year between leaving school and going to university or college. The gap year is often spent travelling, doing voluntary work abroad or earning money to finance travels and further studies.
- In pairs. Students choose and then discuss their chosen topic. Monitor and give help as necessary.
- Feedback with the whole class and elicit a brief selection of students' ideas about each of the different topics.

b) Writing: preparation
- In the same pairs, ask students to make a detailed word map for their topic.

- Tell them to write the topic they've chosen in the middle of the word map. Then ask students to fill in the word map with their main ideas, supporting ideas and examples.
- Monitor pairs and give help as necessary. If students need support with advantages and disadvantages for their chosen topic you could give them some of the following ideas.
  1 If you're self-employed, you can make your own decisions and work when you want to but you don't get the benefits of company pension schemes, health care, etc.
  2 If you have children when you're young, you've got more energy to enjoy them but you lose your freedom.
  3 If you go straight to university or college, you don't get out of the habit of studying but you may never have another opportunity to have a gap year.
  4 If you learn a language in a class, you're able to learn from, interact and communicate with the other students but an individual tutor can tailor lessons to your particular needs.
  5 If you have one long holiday every year, you can really relax and you can also travel further if you want to but it means that you use up all your holiday for the year in one go.
- When students have finished, ask pairs to make groups of 4 and to look at and discuss each pair's word map. Tell students to make suggestions for improvements.

c) Writing: practice
- Before students start to write their report, draw attention to the Remember! Box. Go through the tips with the class and remind students to keep the purpose of their report in mind as they write. Tell them to keep referring to their word map and to make sure that their report keeps to the most important points.
- You could ask students to write their report in class in pairs or individually. Or students could write their report for homework.
- When students bring the report to class, ask students to proofread each other's work in pairs and to suggest corrections. Students then write the final version of their report.
- Display the reports in the classroom for other students to read.

(11) The silver screen

Grammar / structures	*All, whole, every*; verb tenses for stories and jokes; reporting verbs
Topic / vocabulary	Films and cinema; adjectives to describe scenes / atmosphere
Wavelength pages	**Conversations** *Well, actually I . . .*: permission, requests and refusing requests; polite intonation and stress
Take to class	Props for Exercise 15b)

Coursebook page 92

When the lights go down

1 Warmer
- The questions deliberately avoid asking about students' tastes and preferences as far as films are concerned as these are discussed later.
- In groups. Students take it in turns to answer.
- Feedback with the class and listen to a selection of students' answers and comments.

2 a) Vocabulary: presentation
- Ask students to discuss the meaning of the different categories of films in pairs and to use their dictionaries to help with unfamiliar words.
- In groups. Try to get a mix of students who do and don't know a lot about films in each group.

b) Vocabulary: practice
- Students can work alone, using their dictionaries if necessary. Then check their answers in pairs before the class feedback.
- **Language note:** point out that we usually say *I like fantasy* when referring to the kind of film but we can say *I like fantasy films*. Also we can say *romantic films* as well as *romances*.

> **Key** The kinds of film that need the word *film* after them are: war, science fiction, animated, crime, action, adventure, horror.

c) 🔵🔵 65 (Recording script Coursebook page 156)
Listening: for detail
- Play the recording. Students note down the information. If necessary, play the recording again.
- Elicit the answers and write them on the board.

> **Key** **1** Likes: romantic comedies, something funny. Doesn't like: action films. **2** Likes: crime (films), thrillers, horror films sometimes. Doesn't like: musicals and (American-type) comedies. He only sees them with his wife.

Optional extras
After 2c) Listening: for detail
- Play the recording again. Students note the language the speakers use to express their positive and negative preferences.
- Students confer in pairs. Play the recording again. Students check their answers.
- Elicit answers and write them on the board. Comment on *We'll give those / them a miss*.

> **Key** **1 Positive:** my favourite (kind . . .), I like . . . **Negative:** I (really) can't stand . . . , we'll give those a miss **2 Positive:** I like . . . , if I'm in the mood . . . , really likes **Negative:** I don't really enjoy . . . , not something that I would (go out and see on my own)

d) Speaking: practice
- In groups. Students talk about their own tastes.
- Feedback and summarise on the board the broad similarities and differences between students.

3 Vocabulary: presentation
- Check meaning, pronunciation and stress before students fill in spaces 1–8.
- Feedback with the class.

> **Key** **Possible answers:** **1 Talking about films:** It's based on . . . , It was directed by . . . , It was dubbed into . . . , It's about . . . , It's set in . . . **2 Things you buy:** popcorn, soundtrack, ice cream, merchandise **3 Kinds of studios / films:** low budget, blockbuster, independent **4 People:** audience, star, actor / actress, extra, film critic, producer, usher, director **5 Before the film:** ad / advert, trailer **6 In the film:** special effects, stunt, soundtrack, subtitles, car chase, scene, plot **7 Things in the cinema:** back row, front row, screen, seat, aisle, foyer **8 Things you read:** review, script, screenplay, subtitles, credits

Coursebook page 93

4 a) 66 (Recording script Coursebook page 157)
Listening: for detail

- Play the recording. Students tick the words / phrases. Play the recording again for students to check their answers.
- Feedback with the class.

> **Key** **1** blockbuster, review, special effects, soundtrack, credits **2** It's based on . . . , It's set in . . . , It's about . . . , scene **3** screen, front row, subtitles, popcorn

b) 66 (Recording script Coursebook page 157)
Listening: for gist

- Play the recording again.
- Feedback and elicit the answers from the class.

> **Key** **actress and director** = 2 **2 people during a film** = 3 **2 people after a film** = 1

5 a) Writing: practice

- Students read Recording script 66. Students can use the conversations as models.
- In pairs. Students choose the language from the Word Box and write their conversations, leaving the actual words out and putting gaps instead.
- Give students a maximum number of lines and a time limit to help them focus on the activity and stop them getting too ambitious. Monitor and help as necessary.

b) Gap fill / Speaking: practice

- Pairs exchange conversations and fill in the missing words / phrases.
- To check answers, each pair either memorises their conversation and acts it out or reads it out expressively. The pair who wrote the conversation listens and says if the words / phrases the other pair guessed are correct.

All, whole, every

6 a) 67 (Recording script Coursebook page 157)
Listening: for gist

- Play the recording once. Ask students to confer in pairs. If they disagree, play the recording again.
- Feedback with the class.

> **Key** Jake is answering question 3.

b) 67 (Recording script Coursebook page 157)
Listening: gap fill

- Play the recording for students to fill in the gaps. Elicit the missing words from the class.
- After checking understanding, ask the students to discuss the questions in pairs before they read the Language Box.
- In the feedback help students to formulate the answers given in the Key, then ask them to read the Language Box.
- The Language Box doesn't cover all the subtleties connected with the use of *all, whole* and *every*. It deals with the main differences only and gives guidelines for Intermediate level students. *The whole of* and *each* aren't covered here.
- Go through the Language Box with the class and use the information and examples to highlight the differences in the use of *all* and *whole*, and *all* and *every*.
- **Language note:** point out that *whole* is like an adjective which means more or less *entire* or *complete*. *Whole* can also be used with numbers, e.g. *He drank 3 whole bottles of milk.* Highlight that the word *time* has got 2 different meanings. In the phrase *every time* it is countable and means *occasion*. In the phrase *all the time* it is abstract time, which is uncountable. The students may find that in their own language these 2 phrases translate with 2 completely different words which will clarify their different meanings. Point out that we usually say *all day / night / evening / year* although it isn't incorrect to say *all the day / night / evening / year*.

> **Key** **Gap fill 1** every **2** all **3** whole **4** All
> **Questions** *All, whole* and *every* are all used with singular nouns (sentences 1, 2 and 3) but in different ways. *All* is used with plural nouns (sentence 4) and uncountable nouns (sentence 2).

c) Grammar: practice

- Set this exercise for homework.
- Students then compare completed answers in pairs and agree on common answers.
- Feedback and elicit the reason why each answer is correct.

> **Key** **1** all **2** whole **3** all **4** Every **5** All **6** Every time **7** all the time **8** all

Scene by scene

7 a) Reading: for gist

- Set the scene by telling students to look at the posters. Ask students if they've ever seen any of these films.
- Read the instructions with the students. Check *memorable*. Students skim through the 5 texts and match them to the correct film poster.
- Students compare answers in pairs. Then elicit answers from the whole class.
- Refer students to the different kinds of film in the Word Box in Exercise 2a). Students discuss the question *What kind of film do you think each one is?* in pairs. When they finish, feedback with the whole class to see if students agree. If not, ask disagreeing pairs to justify their own answers.

> **Key** **1** = D **2** = A **3** = C **4** = B **5** = E
> **Possible answers:** **A** *High Noon* = western, drama **B** *The Godfather* = drama, crime film
> **C** *The Birds* = thriller, horror film
> **D** *The Wizard of Oz* = fantasy, musical
> **E** *Titanic* = drama, adventure film, romance

b) Reading: for gist

- Point out to students that the titles a–e are fictional and jokey.
- After students agree answers in pairs, feedback with the class. Point out that b) *A new world over the rainbow* refers to the song "Over The Rainbow" sung by Judy Garland in *The Wizard of Oz.*

> **Key** **a)** = 4 **b)** = 1 **c)** = 2 **d)** = 5 **e)** = 3

c) Vocabulary: practice

- Check pronunciation and stress of the adjectives in the Word Box with the class.
- Students do the activity without dictionaries at first. Then ask them to check their answers using their dictionaries.
- Feedback and elicit answers from the various groups. Try to get all the groups to agree.

> **Key** **Possible answers:** **1** exciting, frightening
> **2** dramatic, moving, tense **3** tense, frightening
> **4** shocking, dramatic, gory **5** romantic, dramatic, moving

The plot thickens

8 Grammar: presentation

- Students work individually. When they finish, ask them to confirm their answers in pairs. Feedback with the class.
- Go through the Language Box with the students.
- Refer students to the Grammar reference on page 113 for information on tenses in narrative.

> **Key** **1** Dorothy <u>watches</u> (Present Simple) as her house <u>rises</u> (Present Simple) high into the air.
> **2** Sheriff Kane <u>will have to stand</u> (the Future with *will* + infinitive) alone. **3** Melanie <u>is sitting</u> (Present Continuous) with her back to the school playground. **4** Woltz gradually <u>wakes up</u> (Present Simple). **5** Rose <u>has told</u> (Present Perfect Simple) Jack that she <u>cannot</u> (Present Simple) <u>go on</u> (infinitive) <u>seeing</u> (gerund) him.

After 8 Speaking: practice

- For homework, ask students to think of a joke to tell the class in English. Remind them to avoid racist, sexist or offensive jokes.
- The jokes can be told in groups as a warmer at the start of the next lesson. In a monolingual class students may be able to compare jokes that are well-known in their country or amongst their peers. In multilingual classes this may be a chance to compare different kinds of humour in different countries and to discuss how different cultures look at life. You need to warn students that humour doesn't necessarily cross cultural borders so that they're not too disappointed if other students don't appreciate their joke.

9 a) 68 Listening: for gist

- Ask students to read the instructions and then close their books.
- Play the recording.
- Feedback and elicit answers from the class. Play the recording again if students don't agree.

> **Key** Text 3 *The Birds.*

b) 🔵🔵 68 **Listening: gap fill**
- Ask students to read the script and try to fill in the gaps. Tell them not to worry if they leave a blank or aren't sure about the answer.
- Play the recording for students to confirm / correct their answers. Feedback with the class.
- Students read the Language Box. Make sure they're clear about the information. Give more examples of how *some* is used, e.g. *I was waiting for the bus when **some** guy just came up to me.*
- **Language note:** make it clear that the strategies in the Language Box and exercise are used in all kinds of storytelling in all tenses and are features of informal, spoken, conversational storytelling which aren't usually used for writing.
- Point out other strategies used in storytelling. We use *such (a / an)* and *so* to make adjectives, adverbs and nouns stronger and to add interest, e.g. *It's **such** a great film. The fight scene is **so** spectacular. I've never seen **such** amazing special effects.* See Unit 5, page 42. We use fillers (*um . . . , you know . . .* , etc.) to give ourselves time to think. See Unit 5, Conversations, page 47.

> **Key** 1 some 2 anyway 3 some
> 4 Well 5 some 6 anyway

10 a) Speaking: preparation
- Check students understand the instructions.
- Preparation for this exercise could be set for homework as students may need time to remember or choose a particular film scene to discuss. The discussion could then take place the following day in class. If they can't think of a film scene, they could describe a scene from a TV programme, play, book or advertisement. Any narrative will do.
- If the activity is done on the same day in class, start off the discussion with your own chosen film moment. If you set this for homework, give students a clear idea of what to do by describing your film moment when you set the homework.

b) Speaking: practice
- Students describe their scene to their group. If they have to precede their description with a plot summary, make sure they don't tell the whole story from beginning to end but keep to the necessary details to give the scene a context.
- Monitor the students. Then feedback. Highlight the use of present tenses for narrative and of *some, anyway, but, such, so*, etc.

11 Writing: practice
- Students read the instructions in pairs and discuss the activity. Then bring the class together to check all students are clear about the task.
- Refer to the Word Boxes in Exercises 2a), 3 and 7c) and elicit where different kinds of language would go in the review. Refer to the Language Box in Exercise 8 to remind students of the use of present and future tenses when they're describing the basic plot of the film.
- If students need more support, elicit further ideas and examples of language needed for the review and write them on the board. You could also elicit / supply a possible first line for each paragraph of the review.
- Give students a word limit of approximately 80–100 words.
- When students have finished their review, ask them to swap reviews with another student. Students then comment on the contents and make suggested language corrections. Ask students to write a second draft and display these for students to read.

> **After 11 Photocopiable activities**
> - See 11 *Fix it!*, page T130.

Coursebook page 96

The Lost House
12 a) Warmer
- Ask students to focus on the photos. Elicit / establish that they're all from horror films.
- You could ask students if they've seen any of the films. If students are interested you could tell them which film each photo comes from. Clockwise from top to bottom: *House on Haunted Hill* (1986); *Friday the Thirteenth Part III* (1982); *The Mummy* (1932) with Boris Karloff; *The Shining* (1980) with Jack Nicholson; *The Phantom of the Rue Morgue* (1954).
- Encourage those students who actively dislike horror films to participate in the discussion. Ask *Would you watch any of the films on these pages? Wouldn't you even watch the old classic black and white films?*
- Choose one of the photos and go through the questions with the class.
- In pairs. Students discuss the questions and speculate about the other 4 photos. Feedback.

b) 🔊 69 (Recording script Coursebook page 157)
Listening: for detail / prediction
- Tell students that their answers can't always be precise but that they should take into account what they hear. Ask them to note down their ideas.
- Play the recording. Students compare notes.
- Play the recording again and feedback with the whole class on possible answers.
- **Language note:** ask students if the speakers are British or American. Elicit that they're American and highlight typical Americanisms of that time e.g. *darn it, gee, honey.*

> **Key** **1** They could be girlfriend and boyfriend, husband and wife or newlyweds. **2** They're at a big, dark, old house because they got lost.
> **3** Answers will vary.

c) 🔊 70 Listening: for detail
- Students read the text quickly before they listen. Then play the recording. Students follow the text.
- In pairs. Students answer the questions. Point out that they'll have to guess the answer to question 4.
- Feedback with the class.
- **Language note:** focus briefly on the use of *will* to express willingness / unwillingness (as opposed to its future use) in: *I **will** not take one more step, Bud!* and *Just come in out of the rain, **will** you?* Point out the play on words in *dead tired* which means *very tired* but also evokes the literal meaning of *dead* in the context of a horror film.

> **Key** **1** First Bud holds up his lighter, then he lights a candle. **2** First because the door slams, then because Glutz appears out of the shadows.
> **3** In their car. **4** Answers will vary.

After 12c) Speaking: practice
- In groups of 3. Students act out the scene.
- You could prepare the students for this activity in a number of ways. You could allocate the parts and ask students to study their lines for homework but don't ask students to learn them, just to practise saying them. You could play the recording and ask students to repeat. Students could read the scene in groups a number of times. Encourage students to use gesture, melodrama, facial expression and intonation.

Coursebook page 97

Reporting verbs
13 a) 🔊 71 (Recording script Coursebook page 157)
Listening: for detail
- Play the recording twice. Students write answers individually. In pairs. Students compare answers.
- Play the recording a third time. Feedback.

> **Key** She's at the police station because Bud has disappeared. Bud was probably attacked, killed or kidnapped by someone or something that lives in the cellar.

b) 🔊 71 (Recording script Coursebook page 157)
Listening: gap fill
- Pairs try to fill in the gaps before they listen.
- Play the recording. Students swap partners and check their answers in different pairs.
- Play the recording again. Then feedback.

> **Key** **1** to take **2** to go **3** for getting
> **4** me to hold **5** us not to go **6** not to go
> **7** to get **8** us **9** us to go **10** us not to come

c) Matching / Grammar: presentation
- Students could work individually in class or do the activity for homework.
- With books closed. Feedback by reading the sentences from the film script and eliciting the reported sentences. Prompt with the appropriate reporting verb if necessary. Then reverse the process by reading the reported sentences and eliciting the sentences from the film script.
- Highlight the different patterns in the Language Box and elicit sentences to illustrate their use.
- **Language note:** point out that the pattern for *apologise* (verb + preposition + gerund) is very common, e.g. *He insisted on paying, He's thinking of leaving his job, She's talking about getting a new car.*

> **Key** **1** "I will not take one more step."
> **2** "Oh . . . but . . . OK . . . I'm in." **3** "I'm sorry I got lost." **4** "You hold the candle . . ." **5** "Don't . . . go into the cellar, sir." **6** "OK, I won't, really."
> **7** "Shall I get your luggage from the car?"
> **8** "Or would you like a glass of warm milk?"
> **9** "Go . . . upstairs, madam . . . sir . . ."
> **10** "And don't come back down!"

14 Grammar: practice

- Go through the instructions and the example.
- Students work individually and report the sentences in writing. They then check answers in pairs. Monitor and give help as necessary.
- When students finish, feedback with the class.

> **Key   Possible answers: 2 Bud** offered to go and see what the noise was.   **3 Betsy** warned / told / asked Bud not to leave the room. / **Betsy** didn't want Bud to leave the room.   **4 The mad old woman** wanted / asked Betsy to open the door. She promised / offered to tell Betsy where her husband / Bud was.   **5 Glutz** warned / told Betsy not to let the mad old woman in.   **6 Glutz** apologised for letting the mad old woman out of the cellar.   **7 Betsy** wanted / asked Glutz to tell her where Bud was.

After 14 Grammar: practice

- Write the example and sentences 1–8 on the board or on an OHT. Explain that the sentences are from some more old films.
  Example: "<u>Now everybody must be very careful.</u> He's a dangerous man."
  He / She wanted / told everybody to be very careful.
  1 "<u>I will love you forever.</u> Nothing can change that, my darling."
  2 "<u>Do you want me to kill Rico?</u> I'll do it for the right price."
  3 "<u>Don't open the door</u>, you fool! It'll escape and kill us all!"
  4 "<u>I can't take you with me!</u> The jungle is no place for a woman!"
  5 "Sergeant – <u>telephone headquarters.</u> We need reinforcements!"
  6 "Here – <u>take my car and $2000</u> – just leave this family alone!"
  7 "Tina – <u>could you look at this screen?</u> There seems to be some kind of flying object out there."
  8 "<u>OK, Sheriff. I'll help you.</u> We'll find those bandits together."
- Discuss with the class what kind of film the example and sentences 1–8 are from and who is speaking. Then go through the example.
- Students report the underlined parts of sentences 1–8 using a verb from the Language Box in Exercise 13c). Feedback.

> **Key   1** He / She promised to love him / her forever.   **2** He / She offered to kill Rico.   **3** He / She warned / told them not to open the door.   **4** He refused to take her with him.   **5** He / She told the sergeant to telephone headquarters.
> **6** He / She offered him / her a car and $2000.   **7** He / She asked Tina to look at the screen.   **8** He / She agreed to help the sheriff.

15 a) Speaking: preparation / Writing: practice

- Build up the atmosphere and encourage students to go as over the top as they like.
- Tell them to write the script in direct speech and to make some brief script notes about where the people are, how they feel and what they do. Questions 1–5 and the 7 lines of script provide a framework. Students can also use the film script on page 96 as a model for the dialogue and for length. The finished product should take a maximum of 2–3 minutes to read / act out.
- Give students 20–30 minutes to write the scene. Monitor and help as necessary.
- Each group then practises reading their scenes and plans where they'll stand and what they'll do. How much time you allow for this will depend on your class and how much you're developing this activity, but a minimum of about 10 minutes will probably be needed.

b) Speaking: practice

- Bring some props, e.g. hats, a candle, a torch, a jacket for Glutz to wear, a white sheet, a cassette with spooky music, objects to make sound effects, etc.
- Before students act out their scene remind them of the importance of facial expression, intonation, etc. Turn off the lights and use the overhead projector / candle / torch for light. Put on spooky music. The performing group can ask the class to make sound effects like howling wind, a wolf, an owl or tap the desks for driving rain.
- Groups act out their scenes for the class. With very large classes 2 groups act out their scenes for each other. If space is a problem students don't have to stand up but ask them to concentrate on atmosphere and expression.
- This is an ideal opportunity to film or record your students, for feedback and students' motivation.

Conversations *Well, actually, I . . .*

Grammar / structures	Permission, requests and refusing requests; degrees of formality and politeness
Functions	Asking for permission, making and refusing requests politely
Pronunciation	Polite intonation and stress

Coursebook page 98

The right thing to say

1 Warmer

- In pairs. Students look at their information.
- Feedback. Ask students to note down the phrases.

> **Key** 1 = d)   2 = e)   3 = c)   4 = b)   5 = a)
> 6 = h)   7 = j)   8 = i)   9 = f)   10 = g)

2 a) ⦿⦿ 72 (Recording script Coursebook page 157)
Listening: for detail

- Play the recording. Students compare answers in pairs. Play it again if necessary. Feedback.

> **Key** Answers will vary. **Possible answers:**
> **1** stranger to stranger   **2** employee to boss
> **3** probably friend to friend   **4** probably friend
> to friend   **5** probably family member to family
> member   They're all making requests or asking
> for permission. See Recording script 72.

b) ⦿⦿ 72 (Recording script Coursebook page 157)
Listening: gap fill

- Students try to fill in the gaps before listening.
- Play the recording twice. Students fill in the gaps and decide how polite / formal the questions are.
- Feedback with the class.

> **Key** **1 Would you mind** (polite)   **2 Do you mind
> if** (polite)   **3 Is it OK if** (less formal)   **4 Could I**
> (less formal but not as informal as *Can I* . . .
> possibly because the CD is new so he's being
> more polite)   **5 Can you please** (less formal but
> slightly more polite as it's a restated request)

c) ⦿⦿ 72 (Recording script Coursebook page 157)
Listening: for detail

- Make sure students understand that they listen to and write down the answers to questions 1–5 in the 5 conversations.
- Play the recording once or twice as necessary. Elicit the responses and write them on the board.

- Students read the Language Box. Highlight that when we answer questions with the word *mind* we use the word *No* to mean a positive response (i.e. *Yes*), because the word *No* links back to the word *mind*, i.e. *Do you **mind** if I leave early? No, (I **don't mind**,) go ahead.* Point out that we don't usually answer *I don't mind*, we usually use the answers given in the Language Box.
- **Language note:** explain that *Would you mind if I left a bit early?* is a more polite version of *Do you mind if I leave a bit early?* Point out that the first question is a Second Conditional and has that same feeling of unreality which makes it more tentative and polite.

> **Key** **1** No, not at all.   **2** No, of course not.
> That's fine.   **3** Sure – go ahead.   **4** Yeah, sure.
> **5** Yeah. Yeah, OK.

Pronunciation: stress and intonation

3 a) ⦿⦿ 73 Listening: for stress and intonation

- Students read the sentences aloud in pairs and practise the stress and intonation.
- Play the recording for students to underline the stressed words / syllables.

b) ⦿⦿ 73 Listening: to check /
Pronunciation: practice

- Write the sentences on the board. Play the recording again for students to listen and check.
- Feedback by asking students to underline the stressed words / syllables.
- Go through the Language Box with the class. Model a sentence with flat intonation, then model the sentence again with wide intonation to show how the wider contrast increases the politeness of the request.
- Students practise reading the requests in Exercise 1b). Feedback on their stress and intonation.

> **Key** **1** Would you <u>mind</u> taking our <u>picture</u>?
> **2** Do you <u>mind</u> if I leave a bit <u>early</u> on Friday?
> **3** Is it O<u>K</u> if I use your <u>phone</u>?   **4** Could I <u>borrow</u>
> it?   **5** Can you <u>please</u> answer the <u>phone</u>?

4 a) 🔊74 (Recording script Coursebook page 157)
Listening: for detail and gist
- Stress that *strange* refers to the way the people talk, not what they're talking about.
- Play the recording once. Students confer in pairs. Then play it again. Feedback and point out that if you're overpolite you can sound sarcastic.

> **Key** The man wants the music turned down. The woman doesn't want to turn it down. The conversation is ridiculously overpolite.

b) Reading / Speaking: practice
- Feedback with the whole class.

> **Key** The speakers are rude and are using informal language. Polite and formal language between strangers would be appropriate.

c) Speaking: practice
- Pairs rewrite the conversation. Monitor. Select pairs to act out their conversations. Feedback.

Coursebook page 99

Freddy on the Riviera

5 a) Preparation
- In pairs. Students discuss the questions. Elicit suggestions. Write them on the board.

b) 🔊75 (Recording script Coursebook page 158)
Listening: to check
- Students listen to the conversation.
- Feedback and compare students' suggestions with what Freddy says and wants. Point out that Freddy is a freeloader.

> **Key** He's trying the woman's soup. He's making a lot of very polite requests. He wants some soup, wine, food and a cigar.

c) Gap fill
- Monitor pairs but don't confirm answers.

d) 🔊75 (Recording script Coursebook page 158)
Listening: to check
- Play the recording. Students check answers.
- Feedback. Go through the Language Box and highlight the different ways of refusing requests politely. They should be said with polite intonation.

> **Key** She feels embarrassed. She wants to refuse Freddy's requests but she is polite and so refuses very politely. **1** actually **2** afraid **3** Sorry

Pronunciation: stress and intonation

6 a) 🔊76 **Pronunciation: presentation**
- Students read the sentences aloud in pairs and practise the stress and intonation.
- Play the recording for students to underline the stressed words / syllables.

b) 🔊76 **Listening: to check /**
Pronunciation: practice
- Write the sentences on the board. Play the recording again for students to listen and check.
- Feedback by asking students to underline the stressed words / syllables.
- Ask students to practise refusing the requests politely by saying the responses 1–3 from Exercise 5c). Listen to a selection of students and feedback on their stress and intonation.

> **Key** **1** Well, <u>act</u>ually I was <u>just</u> about to <u>drink</u> it. **2** Well, I'm <u>afraid</u> I don't <u>eat</u> <u>meat</u>. **3** <u>Sorry</u>, they're my <u>hus</u>band's.

Sorry, I was just about to . . .

7 a) Writing: preparation / practice
- In groups of 4: Pair A and Pair B. Encourage students to have fun with the ridiculous situations but remind them to use the correct intonation when they refuse the requests and to use *Well, actually I . . .* , *Sorry I . . .* , and *Well, I'm afraid I . . .*
- Elicit ideas from the class for requests and excuses to refuse the requests.
- Set a time limit for groups to prepare and write their conversations. Monitor and help with language and ideas as they work.

b) Speaking: practice
- Ask pairs to take it in turns to act out their conversations while the other pair in the group listens and ticks the phrase from the Language Boxes in Exercise 2c) and 5d).
- Students could then take it in turns to act out their conversations in new groups of 4.
- Monitor the conversations and feedback on the language, intonation and stress.

12 Taking off

Grammar / structures	Modal verbs of present and past deduction
Topic / vocabulary	Holidays and travel
Pronunciation	Stress in modal verbs of deduction
Wavelength pages	**Day to day English** *Was it worth it?*: phrases / expressions for giving opinions and recommending, adding emphasis and giving contrasting opinions
	Reading for pleasure 4: *Merry Christmas*
	Do you remember? Units 10–12

Coursebook page 100

Come fly with me

1 a) Vocabulary: practice
- Check the pronunciation and stress of the words / phrases in the Word Box.
- In groups. Students match the words / phrases to the photos. Point out that some words / phrases can go with more than one photo. Ask students to do the exercise without using their dictionaries. Tell them to pool knowledge among the group and guess and deduce the meaning of phrases based on their knowledge of the individual words.
- Once students have matched the words / phrases to the photos, they can check their answers using their dictionaries. You could help with the more problematic expressions, e.g. *off the beaten track* (a remote and little visited place), *getting away from it all* (an expression used especially in advertisements meaning having a relaxing holiday), *chilling out* (relaxing, taking things as they come), *doing Europe* (seeing lots of places round Europe).
- Feedback by eliciting the answers from the various groups. Ask students to justify their answers. Try to get all the groups to agree on the most suitable phrases for photos 1–5.

> **Key   Possible answers: 1** a holiday romance, seeing the sights, taking it easy, doing Europe
> **2** breathtaking scenery, backpacking, exploring, off the beaten track, getting away from it all
> **3** seeing the sights, package holiday, it's for tourists, doing Europe   **4** getting away from it all, chilling out, package holiday, it's for tourists, taking it easy   **5** all the comforts of home, getting away from it all, first-class travel, chilling out, taking it easy

b) Speaking: practice
- Students express the reasons why they like or dislike particular kinds of holiday in as much detail as they can. Encourage them also to relate the photos 1–5 to holidays they've had.
- In pairs. Students talk about their holiday preferences and the photos that remind them of holidays / trips they've had.
- Feedback and listen to a selection of preferences, views and accounts of holidays. See if any patterns emerge about students' holiday habits. Are there any kinds of holiday which are more / less popular than others with your students? Are the reasons students put forward for taking or rejecting particular kinds of holidays the same or different? Do students choose holidays on the basis of cost or on the basis of preference? Do students like to go on holiday with their friends? family? in a small group? in a large group?

> **Optional extras**
> **After 1b) Speaking: practice**
> - As a follow-up, ask students to bring in their own holiday photos and / or souvenirs, maps, books, etc. Put them on one or two tables and ask the students to mill and chat, e.g. *Where was this taken? Who are these people?* Tell them to try to find people who have been to the same place or who like the same holidays, etc.

Coursebook page 101

2 a) Reading: for gist
- Give students a time limit.
- Feedback and elicit the answer from the class.

> **Key   3** Advice about travelling with another person.

b) Reading: matching

- Students match the pictures to the correct line / lines of the extract. Ask them to check their answers in pairs.
- Feedback with the class.

> **Key** **a)** = lines 23–25 **b)** = lines 9–11
> **c)** = line 18 **d)** = lines 20–22

c) Vocabulary: matching

- Read the definitions and check that students understand them. Initially don't let students use their dictionaries. Tell them to look for the words / phrases in the extract to match the definitions 1–7 on the basis of context and meaning. Once they've found them, they can work with a partner and check their answers in a dictionary.
- Feedback with the class by asking students to close their books. Write the correct answers on the board in random order and elicit the definitions of the words / phrases.

> **Key** **1** based on **2** tying the knot
> **3** incompatible **4** underestimate
> **5** fallback plan **6** compromise
> **7** whining

Coursebook page 102

Travel troubles

3 a) Warmer

- Highlight the picture and the situation.
- In groups. Ask students to discuss the questions.
- Feedback with the class by listening to a selection of students' comments but don't go into the theme in too much depth or you'll pre-empt Exercises 3b)–3d).

b) 👀 77 (Recording script Coursebook page 158)
Listening: for detail

- Read the instructions and check understanding of the questions. Ask students to note down the answers as they listen.
- Play the recording for students to take down notes. Ask students to discuss their answers with a partner and to expand or change them. Monitor a selection of students' work. If you find that most students' responses aren't complete, play the recording again.
- Feedback by eliciting the answers from the class.

> **Key** **1** Children have problems on family holidays because parents take children to really boring places; they want to introduce their children to everybody; they make their children play with kids they don't want to play with; they make their children do things they don't want to do. **2** Parents have problems on family holidays because holidays can be stressful. Children want to do the same thing every day, e.g. go to the beach. When children get there they always want things, e.g. an ice cream.

c) Speaking: practice

- Introduce the activity by discussing the idea of "the family holiday from hell", i.e. a holiday in which everything goes wrong and everyone has a terrible time. Ask students if they have personally experienced a holiday or part of a holiday which has gone badly wrong.
- Set up the pair work by going through the examples with the whole class. Encourage students to be anarchic and not just to give sensible advice. This can be a great revenge activity for teenage students, for parents who've had a difficult time with their children or for any age group with memories of problems with parents, children or siblings! Students make 2 lists of dos and don'ts: one for parents and one for children.
- Feedback by making a summary of ideas in 2 lists on the board.

d) Writing: practice

- Put students in groups of 4 and go through the nature and structure of the writing activity. Tell students to discuss ideas, content and language in their groups but to write their own articles. Make sure their articles keep to the theme of "The art of family travel" and contain the 4 paragraphs indicated. Remind them that they're writing for a website, so they can think about illustrations, sound effects, links to other websites, e.g. holiday websites, chatrooms.
- Monitor and help with ideas and language. When students have finished their article, display their work for the other students to read.
- If you've got access to the Internet, you could ask groups to search the web for a suitable travel website. They could then publish their ideas on the website.

That can't be right!

4 a) 👓 78 (Recording script Coursebook page 158)
Listening: for gist

- Elicit that Sarah is at a hotel reception desk talking to a hotel receptionist.
- Play the recording and elicit the problem. Ask students if they've ever experienced any problems when they've arrived to check in at a hotel where they've booked a room. Ask for brief details.

> **Key** The room she thought her company had booked for her is occupied and her name isn't on the list of bookings for the hotel.

b) 👓 78 (Recording script Coursebook page 158)
Listening: gap fill

- Ask students to fill in the gaps as they listen rather than trying to predict the missing words in the gaps before they hear the recording.
- Play the recording twice, the first time for students to fill in the gaps, the second time for students to identify who said each sentence.
- Feedback by asking students to swap answers in pairs. Only feedback with the whole class if there are problems.

> **Key** 1 S can't   2 R may   3 S must
> 4 S must   5 R might   6 R could

c) Matching
- Ask students to do the matching task in pairs.
- Feedback with the class.

> **Key** a) I think this is possible. = sentences 2, 5 and 6. b) I'm sure this is true. = sentences 3 and 4. c) This is impossible. = sentence 1.

> **Coursebook page 103**

d) Grammar: presentation / Gap fill
- Students read the Language Box and fill in the gaps individually. They then check their answers in pairs.
- Feedback with the class and go through the Language Box with the students. Highlight the form and use of *must, can't, might, could* and *may* (all + infinitive) to make guesses, speculations and logical deductions about the present based on available evidence.
- Ask students to give additional examples of modals. Highlight that we don't usually use the contracted form of *might not / may not.*

- **Language note:** contrast the meaning of *He might / may not be there* (= *perhaps he isn't there*) and *He couldn't be there* (= *it's impossible for him to be there*).
- Refer students to the Grammar reference on page 119 for information on modal verbs of present deduction.

> **Key**
> When we're sure that something is true, we use **must** + infinitive:
> Steve failed the exam. He **must** feel awful.
> When we think something is possibly true, we use **might**, **could**, or **may** + infinitive:
> I don't know where they are. They **might / could / may** be upstairs.
> When we're sure that something is impossible or not true, we use **can't** + infinitive:
> You **can't** be hungry! You've just had lunch!

Pronunciation: stress in modal verbs of deduction

5 a) 👓 79 Listening: for stress
- Ask students to read the sentences from Exercise 4b) aloud and to think about the stress of modal verbs but tell them not to underline the stressed words / syllables at this point.
- Play the recording for students to listen and underline the stressed words / syllables.

b) 👓 79 Listening: to check /
Pronunciation: practice
- Write the sentences on the board. Play the recording again for students to listen and check their answers.
- Feedback by asking students to underline the stressed words / syllables on the board. Then play the recording again for students to listen and repeat.
- Go through the Language Box with the whole class. Highlight the fact that we stress the modal verb of present deduction and the important new information.
- Ask students to practise reading the sentences from Exercise 4b) aloud again in pairs.

> **Key** 1 The room <u>can't</u> be <u>occupied</u>!   2 You <u>may</u> be in <u>another</u> room.   3 I <u>must</u> be on the <u>list</u>!
> 4 You <u>must</u> be looking at the <u>wrong day</u>.   5 You <u>might</u> be thinking of the <u>Queen's</u> Hotel.   6 The booking <u>could</u> be under your <u>husband's</u> name.

6 Grammar: practice

- This exercise can be done individually in class or for homework. Make sure students understand they have to use one of the modals in each sentence and make the sentence mean the same as the prompt.
- When students have written the sentences, ask them to compare their answers in pairs.
- Feedback by eliciting the correct sentences and writing them on the board. Then ask students to give you the original prompt sentence without looking at their books, e.g.:
  YOU: 1 They can't be watching TV.
  STUDENT: I'm sure they aren't watching TV.

> **Key**   1 They **can't be watching TV.**   2 She **must be lying.**   3 Joan **might / could be ill.**   4 They **can't be married.**   5 He **might not be telling the truth.**   6 This **painting can't be by Picasso.**   7 It **might / could be closed.**   8 They **must be angry about the delays.**

Don't leave home without it!

7 a) Warmer

- In pairs. Students write lists and then compare their lists in groups of 4.
- Feedback and elicit any interesting items.

b) Speaking: practice

- Organise students into equal numbers of A and B pairs. Students then read their instructions and sentences. Check they understand.
- Before students work in pairs, give an additional example to the class to make the activity clear. Write a gapped sentence on the board and ask the class to guess the missing travel item, e.g. *Get ready for your new holiday souvenirs by putting your clothes in a medium-sized ___ and putting that inside a large empty one.* Elicit the answer (*suitcase*) from the class.
- Tell students that each pair has got the answers to the other pair's questions so they can steer each other a bit towards the correct answer during the guessing phase. You could give them language for this, e.g. *You're close . . . , Well, not quite . . . , Almost . . . , Yes, it's a kind of . . .*
- Tell each pair to read out the complete sentence with the missing object / noun filled in when they take it in turns to try and guess what the missing object / noun is.

- Groups discuss the advice given on pages 143 and 145 and compare it with the lists students made in Exercise 7a).
- Feedback with the class and ask students to recall as many of the 10 pieces of holiday advice as they can without looking at their books.

> **Coursebook page 104**

What went wrong?

8 a) Listening: preparation

- To set the scene, ask students what happened when Sarah Carmichael arrived at her hotel. Elicit that there wasn't a room reserved for her.
- Ask students to read the sentences in brackets and to decide whose ideas they are, Sarah's or the receptionist's.
- Students can compare answers but don't correct or confirm them at this point or you'll pre-empt Exercise 8b).

b) 👀 80 (Recording script Coursebook page 158)
Listening: to check

- Play the recording once. Students listen and check their predicted answers.

> **Key**   1 = S   2 = S   3 = R
> 4 = S   5 = R   6 = R   7 = S

c) 👀 80 (Recording script Coursebook page 158)
Gap fill / Listening: to check

- Ask students to work in pairs and read the ideas in brackets in Exercise 8a). Then tell students to fill in what they think were Sarah's and the receptionist's exact words.
- Play the recording for students to check and agree on their answers.
- Feedback and elicit the answers from the class. If there are mistakes, play the recording again.

> **Key**   1 "You **must have made** a mistake."
> 2 "You **might have written** the reservation on a different day."   3 "I **can't have made** a mistake about the reservation."   4 "I **can't have dreamt** it all!"   5 "Your travel agent **might have booked** you into another hotel."   6 "You **might have cancelled** your reservation."   7 "My company **must have changed** the hotel at the last minute."

d) Grammar: presentation

- Elicit from the class that Sarah and the receptionist are talking about the past.
- Ask students to read the Language Box. Then go through the information with them. Highlight the form and use of *must, might, could, may* and *can't* (all + *have* + past participle) to make guesses, speculations and logical deductions based on available evidence about the past.
- **Language note:** explain that we use *must* + *have* + past participle when we're sure that something happened in the past. Elicit additional examples. Highlight the fact that the 3 modals, *might, could* and *may* (all + *have* + past participle) can be used when we think something possibly happened or was possibly true in the past. Point out that *can't* + *have* + past participle is used when we're sure something didn't happen or was completely impossible in the past. Draw students' attention to the fact that *couldn't* + *have* + past participle and *can't* + *have* + past participle can have the same meaning.
- Refer students to the Grammar reference on page 119 for information on modal verbs of past deduction.

> **Key** They're talking about the past.

9 Grammar: practice

- This exercise can be done individually in class or for homework. The students have got 2 tasks: to decide if the gapped sentences are about the present or the past and to insert the correct form of the verbs in brackets and the modals *must, might / could* or *can't* in the gaps in the sentences. Tell the students to take into account the contextual information given in the rest of the sentence before they fill in the gap.
- When students have filled in the gaps, ask them to compare their answers with a partner and to agree on a final common version.
- Feedback by writing the gapped sentences on the board or on an OHT. Elicit the correct forms of the verbs in brackets and the modals *must, might / could* or *can't*. Write them in the gaps. Ask students to use the context in the rest of the sentences to explain why the answers are correct. If necessary refer them to the Language Box in Exercise 8d) to help them to phrase the explanations correctly.

> **Key** 1 A: Where's Rod gone? B: I'm not sure, but he **might have gone** into the village. He said he wanted to have a look round. 2 A: I'm afraid Mr Butler has checked out, madam. B: But he **can't have checked out**! He's my husband!
> 3 A: What's all that noise coming from room 12? B: Oh, the drama group **must be using** it again.
> 4 Terry's skiing has really improved since last year! He **must have had** lessons before the holiday. 5 You'd better phone the hotel. It's the holiday season. There **might not be** any rooms.
> 6 They **can't be** brothers! They're completely different!

Pronunciation: stress in modal verbs of deduction in the past

10 a) 👁👁 81 Listening: for stress

- The aim of this exercise is for students to practise stress in modal verbs of past deduction.
- Ask students to read the sentences aloud and to think about the stress of modal verbs but tell them not to underline the stressed words / syllables at this point.
- Play the recording for students to listen and underline the stressed words / syllables in sentences 1–3.
- Don't feedback with the class or you'll pre-empt Exercise 10b).

b) 👁👁 81 Listening: to check / Pronunciation: practice

- Write sentences 1–3 from Exercise 10a) on the board or write them on an OHT. Play the recording again. Ask the students to listen and to check their answers.
- Feedback by asking students to underline the stressed words / syllables in the sentences on the board. Then play the recording again for students to listen and repeat. Draw attention to the fact that we stress the modal verbs of past deduction and the important new information. Point out that the important new information is often the main verb.
- Ask students to practise reading sentences 1–3 aloud again in pairs.

> **Key** 1 She <u>might</u> have <u>stolen</u> the <u>money</u>.
> 2 They <u>can't</u> have <u>known</u> about <u>Paul</u>. 3 He <u>must</u> have <u>left</u> during the <u>night</u>.

After 10b) Pronunciation: practice
- Focus students on the gapped sentences 1–6 from Exercise 9. Write the completed gapped sentences on the board or use an OHT (see Key).
- Ask students to underline the stressed words / syllables.
- Feedback with the class and ask the students to practise saying the sentences in pairs.

Key 1 I'm not <u>sure</u>, but he <u>might</u> have <u>gone</u> into the <u>village</u>. 2 But he <u>can't</u> have <u>checked</u> <u>out</u>! 3 Oh, the <u>drama</u> group <u>must</u> be <u>using</u> it a<u>gain</u>. 4 He <u>must</u> have <u>had</u> <u>lessons</u> before the <u>holiday</u>. 5 There <u>might</u> not <u>be</u> any <u>rooms</u>. 6 They <u>can't</u> be <u>brothers</u>!

Coursebook page 105

Travelling light

11 a) Grammar / Speaking: preparation
- Set the scene for this activity by asking students to describe Alex's hotel room in pairs. Tell students that they can use their dictionaries to look up unknown words. Then get them to swap partners and check and extend their descriptions with another student.
- Read through the instructions with the whole class. The prompt questions should help to guide students' deductions. Elicit one or two examples if necessary.
- In pairs. Ask the students to start their discussion. Monitor to check that they're using the evidence in the picture and that their ideas are logical.
- Encourage students to make guesses about what Alex is doing at the moment, what he obviously does regularly (i.e. what he's like) and what he has done / did in the past. Make sure that you give students enough time to prepare a reasonable number of guesses.
- This is a speaking as well as a grammatical activity. Let students say what they want but try to guide them lightly towards the target language. If students say *Maybe he went to an island* say *Yes, that's possible, he **might have gone** to an island* and ask them to repeat the sentence using the target language.

Key Possible answers:
He could be getting ready to meet the woman who wrote the note.
He might be exploring the town.
He could be having a shower.
He can't be playing tennis / have gone to the tennis club because his racket is broken.
He might have gone to the tennis club and hired a racket there.
He could be playing golf.
He must be playing his guitar because the guitar case is empty.
Someone could have stolen his guitar.
Thieves can't have stolen his guitar because they didn't steal his CD player.
He might be on the beach.
He could have run away from the brother.
He could have had a fight.
He might have gone to one of the islands.
He can't have gone to the islands because his snorkel is still in his room.
He could have gone to a club.
He must have gone out in a hurry because the television is on.
He can't have gone very far because he has left his glasses and his watch in his room.
He must have had some kind of party because there are 2 wine bottles on the floor.
Somebody must have left the high heels there.
He must ride a motorbike because he's got a crash helmet.
He might have had an accident because the crash helmet is broken.
He might have gone to hospital.

b) Speaking: practice
- When students finish their preparation, ask them to change partners and make new pairs. Turn the activity into a game. The new partners exchange guesses. Each student tries to say more sentences than the other and to present arguments to prove that their partner's guesses are illogical. If students enjoy the challenge, let them swap partners a number of times.
- Feedback and elicit which student / students had the highest number of logical guesses.

After 11b) Writing: practice
- Ask students to write their guesses about Alex for homework.

Grammar / structures	Phrases / expressions for recommending and giving opinions
Functions	Ways of giving and contrasting opinions and points of view
Pronunciation	Stress and intonation when contrasting opinions

Coursebook page 106

Havana highlights

1 a) 🆗 82 (Recording script Coursebook page 158)
Listening: for gist
- Play the recording. In pairs. Students check their answers. Then play the recording again.
- Feedback. Focus on the photo of the Hotel Nacional. Ask students if they've ever been to Cuba.

> **Key** **1** Hotel Nacional: positive **2** Havana Café: negative **3** The crocodile farm: negative

b) 🆗 82 (Recording script Coursebook page 158)
Listening: for detail
- Check *a load of rubbish, a tourist trap, a rip-off* and *a letdown*.
- Play the recording twice. Students fill in the boxes.
- Feedback by eliciting the answers from the class.

> **Key** **1** = F **4** = C **5** = H **6** = F **8** = H **12** = H

c) Vocabulary: presentation
- Monitor and help pairs with any problems.
- Feedback. Point out that we can say *You've got to see / stay . . .* or *You have to see / stay . . .*

> **Key** **1** = negative **2** = positive **3** = negative
> **4** = negative **5** = positive **6** It's worth it. = positive   It isn't worth it. = negative
> **7** = negative **8** = positive **9** = negative
> **10** = negative **11** = positive **12** It's worth seeing / going to . . . = positive   It isn't worth seeing / going to . . . = negative

2 a) 🆗 83 (Recording script Coursebook page 158)
Listening: for gist
- Students listen to the recording.
- Feedback with the class.

> **Key** They're talking about Cuba. Derek doesn't agree with Guy.

b) 🆗 83 (Recording script Coursebook page 158)
Listening: gap fill /
Pronunciation: presentation
- Ask students to try to fill in the gaps.
- Play the recording. Students check their answers in pairs. Then play the recording again.
- Feedback with the class and highlight that we stress *that* for emphasis.
- Go through the Language Box with the class. Make sure that students understand how to disagree with an extreme opinion adjective by using *isn't / aren't* + *that* + a less extreme form of the opinion adjective and by stressing *that* in the contrasting opinion.
- **Language note:** remind students of the 2 possible correct forms of the negative contractions of *is not*: *It isn't **that** bad* and *It's not **that** bad.*

> **Key** **DEREK:** Oh, it **isn't that bad**. **GUY:** Oh, come on! It **isn't that good**. **GUY:** Oh, they **aren't that good-looking**. *That* is stressed the most.

c) Pronunciation: practice
- In pairs. Students practise the exchanges. Remind them to use facial expression, gesture and to stress *that* for emphasis.
- Monitor students and feedback.

3 a) Speaking: preparation
- In pairs. Remind students to use the phrases in Exercise 1b) and to use *isn't / aren't* + *that* + a less extreme form of the same adjective when giving contrasting opinions.
- Monitor pairs as they prepare and check their use of stress and intonation.

b) Speaking: practice
- Before students make groups of 4, emphasise that the 2 students reporting their holiday experience must contrast their opinions and use the appropriate stress and intonation. Encourage them to have a natural conversation rather than just list their opinions.
- Monitor the conversations. Feedback.

Wavelength page (side tab)

Reading for pleasure
④ Merry Christmas

Vocabulary *according to, aggressive, beat* (v), *beyond, breath* (n), *cascade* (n), *comfort* (v), *emotion, firework, get through to someone, ghost, go dead, go for something, hang up one's stocking, hesitate, hug* (n), *identity, inspiration, last-minute, look out over, on duty, over the moon, pause* (n / v), *pray, properly, receiver, redundant, response, sarcastic, sob* (n), *survive, take over, tick* (v), *training course, volunteer, yacht*

Coursebook page 107

Before reading

1 Presentation
- Before students open their books, pre-teach / check *volunteer = someone who does something without being paid* to set the scene for the story.
- Elicit suggestions for different kinds of volunteers. Ask students if they've done any voluntary work.
- Ask students to open their books. Check students understand the rubric. In groups of 4. Students discuss what kind of people might use this service.
- Feedback. You could point out the work of the Samaritans and other helplines in Britain and many other countries throughout the world.

2 ⓞⓞ 84 (Recording script Coursebook page 107)
Reading and listening: for detail
- Focus students on the picture. Then pre-teach vocabulary as necessary.
- Students read and listen to the recording. They could work in pairs before the class feedback.
- Feedback on questions 1–3. Elicit the clues in the picture that helped students to answer question 1 (Sydney Harbour Bridge and Christmas trees / decorations). Discuss the answer to question 4. Elicit ideas and write them on the board.

> **Key** 1 On Christmas Eve in Sydney, Australia.
> 2 Because she'd never been on duty alone before.   3 She let it ring 4 times before she picked it up.   4 Because the caller was probably desperate and very upset, worried or frightened.

3 Reading: for gist and detail
- Pre-teach vocabulary. Explain "Jingle Bells" (a Christmas song) and the traditions of Santa Claus (hanging up a stocking and presents under the Christmas tree). Students read the story and answer the questions for homework.

> **Key** 1 Because she felt stronger with a different identity.   2 Because Joss didn't like eating by herself.   3 For about 3 weeks.
> 4 15. 16 in January.   5 At some friends' place.
> 6 Joss talked about looking older than her age when she had her make-up on and her hair right.   7 Because the woman asked about how she thought her parents were feeling and Joss didn't want to talk about her parents.   8 Her six-year-old little sister, Mags.   9 Her father.
> 10 She talked about her own life.   11 She'd had a fight with her father.   12 To say that she hoped the woman's son would come home soon and to wish her Merry Christmas.

After reading

4 Speaking: discussion
- Feedback on the answers to Exercise 3.
- You could ask more questions.
  1 Why do you think the woman works as a volunteer for Hotline?
  2 What qualities do you think a person needs to do this kind of voluntary work? Do you think the woman has got these qualities?
  3 Where do you think James is? What do you think he's doing?

5 Writing and speaking: practice
- In groups of 4. Students write the scene between Joss, her parents and Mags when Joss finally arrives home. Students act out their scene.

6 Personalisation
- Discuss with the class what the woman meant by her statement at the end of the story: "Either we love or we die . . . but to survive, we also have to keep hoping . . ."
- If you've got a multilingual class, ask students about Christmas traditions in their countries.

Grammar / structures / vocabulary 1 Consolidation of vocabulary, the Passive and negative questions
2 Modal verbs of present and past deduction
3 Grammar / structures / vocabulary from Units 10–12

Wavelength page

Coursebook page 108

1 Disgrace!

a) Speaking: preparation

- Make sure the students understand *in disgrace = a situation where people strongly disapprove of you because you've done something that they consider wrong.* You could also teach *in the public eye.*
- Remind students of Andrew Chalmers in Unit 10. Ask students to think of international / national public figures in disgrace at the moment or recent / historical public figures who have been in disgrace.
- Make sure students are clear that they have to invent a story about a disgraced person and plan the interview on Judy Spike's TV show.
- Go through the questions with the class and if students need extra support, invent a disgraced character and his / her fictional story before groups begin to work together.
- Emphasise the importance of negative questions in this interview. Judy Spike will be suspicious and unbelieving so she will use them a lot. Think also of possible replies to her questions, where the interviewees will use the Passive to avoid personal responsibility, e.g. *I was never told about the money.*
- Tell students to make sure Judy asks questions about the husband's or wife's feelings as well, e.g. *So, how did you feel when you discovered . . . Why have you stayed with your wife / husband? Don't you ever feel . . . ?*
- In groups of 3. Students prepare the interview. Monitor and help with ideas and language.

b) Speaking: practice

- Groups practise their interviews and then act them out for the class. The class is the jury and decides whether the disgraced people are innocent or guilty.
- Make notes during the interviews paying particular attention to negative questions. You could also video students' interviews or record them as radio programmes. Feedback.

2 *You could be telling the truth . . .*

a) Writing: preparation / practice

- Lead in to the activity by giving the class 3 sentences about yourself now and in the past, one of which is false and two of which are true. Use the Present Simple, Present Continuous and a past tense. Ask the class to say which sentences they think are true, which they think are false and why. Don't tell students how many sentences are true and how many are false. Students may not begin by using modal verbs of deduction. Create the need for modals of deduction and then alter what students say if necessary to bring modals in, e.g.:

STUDENT: I think maybe that's true.

YOU: So it might be true. Why?

STUDENT: Well, you've travelled a lot. Maybe you lived in France.

YOU: So, I might have lived in France.

- Make it clear that part of the aim of the activity is for students to use modals of deduction when making guesses about the sentences.
- Check the instructions with the students. Draw students' attention to the fact that they don't have to write the same number of sentences about each student but half of the total number of sentences must be true and half must be false.
- Before students get into groups for the writing, encourage them to come up with interesting sentences about themselves. Tell them to spend time discussing their ideas before they write and really try to find information from each other's past and present lives that will be of some surprise or interest. If the event or information is unusual, the other group are more likely to think that it can't be true! This doesn't mean they all have to be fascinating people, but encourage them to give information that the other students in the class probably don't know. This could be a fun opportunity to find out some interesting facts about each other, particularly as students are coming to the end of the course.
- In groups. Students write sentences. Monitor and help with vocabulary and grammar.

b) Reading / Speaking: practice

- Groups swap sentences with another group and discuss the ones they receive.
- Monitor groups and help them to understand the sentences. Encourage students at the same time to use modals during their discussion, e.g. *Well this sentence must be true because 3 of the other sentences are definitely false . . . He might have bought 3 expensive pairs of shoes in one afternoon because he always likes to be well-dressed.*

c) Speaking: practice

- Bring the sets of paired groups back together again when they've finished reading and discussing the other group's sentences and have decided if they're true or false.
- Go through the instructions and example in Exercise 2c) to make sure that students understand what to do.
- Ask groups to tell each other their conclusions about the other group's sentences and to say why they think they're true or false. The second group listens and confirms or corrects the first group's conclusions.
- Feedback with the whole class and then elicit interesting and true information that students have found out about each other.

Coursebook page 109

3 A letter to the editor

Grammar: practice

- This exercise revises grammar, structures and vocabulary from Units 10–12: the Passive; negative questions; modal verbs for laws, rules and social behaviour; verb + *-ing* and verb + infinitive; *all, whole* and *every*; reporting verbs; modal verbs of present and past deduction.
- Revise the structures or vocabulary from Units 10–12 which you consider might cause students problems before they do the activity. Alternatively delay review activities on the structures until students have completed the exercise as this will help to identify problem areas.
- To set the scene for the activity, ask students to look at the title and the instructions. Ask students to try and predict what the letter will say and what tone the writer will adopt.
- Students could do the activity for homework or individually in class before checking their answers in pairs.

- In the feedback elicit answers from the whole class. Go into more detail with areas which seem to cause problems to a lot of students. You could refer individual students to exercises from Units 10–12 which deal with the structures that are still causing difficulty.

> **Key**   **1** was sentenced   **2** has been released
> **3** committing   **4** are given   **5** might
> **6** 're / are arrested   **7** a whole   **8** all
> **9** had been interviewed   **10** scene   **11** can't
> **12** every   **13** Stealing   **14** illegal   **15** against
> **16** can't   **17** arrested   **18** it   **19** comforts
> **20** have enjoyed   **21** fiddling   **22** behaving
> **23** to be   **24** must   **25** to stay

Optional extras
After 3 Writing: practice

- Ask students to write a letter to the editor of their local newspaper about crime in their city / town / village.
- Tell the students to focus on problems caused by criminals in their area and how best to stop them.
- Ask students to brainstorm ideas in pairs. Give students a time limit of 5 minutes.
- Elicit ideas from the class and write them on the board.
- Ask students to write their letters individually in class or for homework.
- When students finish or bring their work back to class, ask them to swap letters with another student. Tell them to help each other with correction, ideas and comments.
- Students then write a second draft which you can display in the classroom for students to read.

After 3 Photocopiable activities
- See 12 Quiz night, page T132.

> Encourage students to learn the new words from Units 10–12 on Coursebook pages 128–129 and do Puzzle 4 on Coursebook page 121 before you give them Progress test Units 10–12 on page T145.

Photocopiable activities

① Who is the real Lord Slimey?

Activity	Pair / whole class / group work: speaking; reading
Aim	Information gap activity
Time	45 minutes
Grammar / structures	Present Perfect Simple; Past Simple; *used to* + infinitive
Vocabulary	Pre-teach: *appearance, aristocrat, body-building, handmade, health clinic, muscle, publicity, request, resort, suite*
	Revise: adjectives of personality, *charity, entertain, local, mansion, rent out*
Before class	Photocopy and cut up page T111: half the class will need one copy of the Student A suspects card each; the other half will need one copy of the Student B suspects card each.

In class

1 Pre-teach and revise vocabulary as necessary. Then read out this background information:

   In 1994, Lord Peter Slimey, a famous English aristocrat, stole £3,000,000 and disappeared completely. Some people thought he went to live abroad, others thought he changed his appearance and stayed in England. For many years there were no further clues and most people believed Lord Slimey had died. However, a newspaper recently received secret information that Lord Slimey is still alive and 4 possible suspects have been identified.

2 In 2 groups: A and B. Students are police officers. Give the As a copy of the Student A suspects card and the Bs Student B suspects card. Explain the headings / vocabulary to each group as necessary.

3 In AB pairs / whole class mingle. Students ask and answer questions giving information in complete sentences in their own words and fill in their suspects cards. Tell students not to show each other their cards.

4 In new groups of 4. Students check the information on their suspects cards and start discussing which suspect they think is Lord Slimey.

5 Explain that Scotland Yard has just received more information about Lord Slimey. Write clues a–j one at a time on the board. Students discuss the information before you write up the next clue. When you've written up the final clue, groups decide which suspect they think is Lord Slimey.

   a) Was shy and unsociable, not very self-confident.
   b) Had a back injury so could do only a limited number of sports.
   c) Used to get poor reports from school.
   d) Clever at making things with his hands.
   e) Was always very smartly dressed.
   f) Was afraid of flying.
   g) Thought England was the best country in the world.
   h) Was extremely mean.
   i) Had bad scar on right forearm.
   j) Parents both died when he was a child. No up-to-date information about brothers and sisters.

6 Feedback. Ask students why Lord Slimey must be Suspect 3 and why they eliminated Suspects 1, 2 and 4.

> **Key** **a)** Probably not Suspect 2 (assertive, self-confident). **b)** Probably not Suspect 1 (enjoys all water sports) or Suspect 2 (brother received postcard from ski resort). **c)** Probably not Suspect 4 (intelligent). **d)** Could be Suspect 1 (gave sister handmade box) or Suspect 4 (makes things out of wood). **e)** Probably not Suspect 1 (often wears sports clothes). **f)** Probably not Suspect 2 (used to travel all over world) or Suspect 4 (has Paris flat, Florida house, London hotel suite and visits all regularly). Could be Suspect 3 (always drives himself or is driven). **g)** Probably not Suspect 4 (favourite country = France). **h)** Probably not Suspect 1 (gives a lot of money to charities). **i)** Probably not Suspect 2 (wears clothes that show muscles). **j)** Probably not Suspect 1 (very close to large family).

> **Optional extra**
> In groups of 4. Students write a newspaper report with the title "What happened to Lord Slimey?" giving the background to the case, describing Lord Slimey and saying how he was identified.

Student B

	Suspect 1	Suspect 2	Suspect 3	Suspect 4
Appearance		Very keen on body-building. Wears clothes that show muscles.		Always wears a hat. Embarrassed about his bald head.
Personality	Gives a lot of money to charities. Very hard-working.		Avoids all publicity. Seems insecure about his appearance.	
Free-time activities	Enjoys all water sports: sailing, swimming, wind-surfing.		Likes being near the sea.	
Home		Homes in many different countries. Most rented out to friends.		Has Paris flat, Florida house near golf course, London hotel suite. Visits all regularly.
Travel			Only ever travelled in Europe. Always drives himself or is driven when travels.	Has never been to the Far East. Favourite country = France.
Family		Goes to small party in London every Christmas. Believed to be at sister's house.		Brought up in a children's home.
Friends and acquaintances	No friends. Has never been in love. Trusts no-one.	Very popular. Many friends in the criminal world.		
Last seen / heard of	Sister received handmade box for her birthday last Friday.	Brother received postcard from ski resort in Alps last month.		

Student A

	Suspect 1	Suspect 2	Suspect 3	Suspect 4
Appearance	Often wears sports clothes.		Always wears long-sleeved shirts, even in hot weather.	
Personality		Assertive, self-confident. Worked for local radio.		Intelligent, unfriendly. Impatient with stupid people.
Free-time activities		Writes good novels about criminal world.		Spends a lot of time alone. Makes things out of wood.
Home	Lives in mansion in south of England. No other homes.		Used to have a home in south of France. Sold it several years ago.	
Travel	Has never been out of England.	Used to travel all over world. Bad accident in China in his twenties.	No known information.	
Family	Very close to large family.			
Friends and acquaintances			Very few friends. Never invites people out or to his home.	Depends on a few close friends. Never goes out with them, entertains them at home.
Last seen / heard of			Attended London health clinic 2 months ago. His driver helped him get into / out of car.	Sent rude letter to Museum of England last week refusing request for money.

 **City sights**

Activity	Pair work: speaking; writing
Aim	Revise: nouns and adjectives describing cities
Time	15 minutes
Vocabulary	Pre-teach / revise: *compound noun, definition*
Before class	Photocopy and cut up page T113: half the class will need a copy of Student A's crossword each; the other half will need a copy of Student B's crossword each.

In class

1   Pre-teach *definition* by writing *1 park, 2 river, 3 taxi* and *4 market* on the board. Students match the correct noun to the definition *You can use this for transport, relax or catch a fish here.* Elicit *2 river*.

2   Give the As one copy of Student A's crossword each. Give the Bs one copy of Student B's crossword each. Tell students not to show each other their crosswords. Point out that each student has got the same crossword but with different words filled in and that all the words are either nouns or adjectives to do with cities. Explain that some of the words are compound nouns, e.g. *car park*.

3   Do an example with the class. Tell a student to ask about one across.
    Example: STUDENT: What's one across?
                        YOU: It's a building where you can buy things.
    If a Student A suggests *store* ask a Student B to point out that their answer to two down begins with a *P*. Elicit the answer *shop*. Ask the students to fill in the word in their crosswords.

4   In 2 groups: A and B. Students check they understand the words in their crosswords and the definitions.

5   In AB pairs. The As sit opposite the Bs. Students take it in turns to read out the definitions for the words and fill in their crosswords. If a student can't guess a word he / she marks it on his / her crossword.

6   When students have filled in as much as they can of their puzzles, ask them to compare crosswords, checking the words and their spellings.

7   Feedback with the class by asking students for definitions for some of the words.

Optional extra

In AB pairs. Write these headings on the board:
a) 3 adjectives to describe a city
b) 4 building words
c) 5 pollution words
d) 6 street furniture words
Students copy the headings on a piece of paper. Tell them to write down from memory words from the crossword under the headings. The first pair to finish wins. Feedback with the class.

Key to Optional extra   **a)** boring, cosmopolitan, expensive   **b)** block of flats, cathedral, exit, lift, rooftop, shop, skyscraper, store   **c)** dust, exhaust fumes, litter, noise, smog, smoke   **d)** bench, fountain, lamp-post, neon sign, phone box, postbox, railing, road sign, statue, traffic lights

Student A

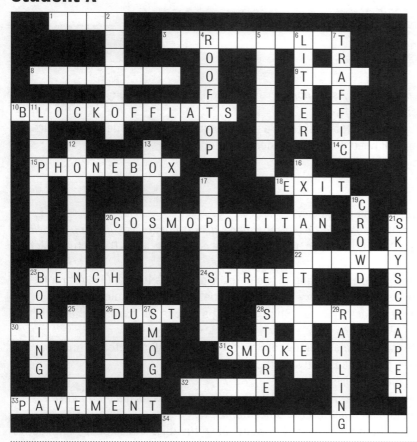

DEFINITIONS FOR STUDENT A TO READ TO STUDENT B

Across

10 a large building with many flats
15 a small structure where you can make a telephone call
18 the way out of a place
20 consisting of people from many different parts of the world
23 a long seat made of wood or stone for 2 or more people
24 a road in a town or village with buildings on one or both sides
26 very small bits of dirt you can see like a powder in the air
31 the white, grey or black gas produced when something burns
33 a place covered with stone at the side of a street for people to walk on

Down

4 the highest point of a building
6 small things that have been thrown away, usually in the street
7 the vehicles travelling on a road
19 a large number of people
21 a very tall modern city building
23 not interesting
27 a mixture of fog, gases and chemicals found in the air in some industrial cities
28 the American word for *shop*
29 metal bars joined together to divide 2 areas of land

Student B

DEFINITIONS FOR STUDENT B TO READ TO STUDENT A

Across

3 the American word for *car park*
8 a decoration often in the street that pumps water into the air
9 a public electric vehicle that runs on metal lines in the road
14 the American word for *taxi*
22 the American word for the *Underground*
28 an open space in a city, often with 4 sides
30 a machine in buildings that carries people up and down between floors
32 a sound, often unpleasant
34 a set of coloured lights for controlling cars

Down

2 a box you put letters in that you want to send
5 a glass tube that lights up, advertising something
11 a tall pole with a light on top in the street
12 the American word for *town centre*
13 a piece of metal in the street with words or drawings on it that gives people information or directions
16 the waste gases produced when a car engine is working
17 costing a lot of money
20 a very large church
25 something that looks like a person or animal made of stone or metal

Spot the difference!

Activity	Pair work: speaking; writing
Aim	Spot the difference: describing places
Time	15 minutes
Grammar / structures	*It's got . . . ; there is / are; he / she looks;* Present Continuous; relative clauses
Vocabulary	Revise: Unit 3 vocabulary
Before class	Photocopy and cut up page T115: half the class will need a copy of Student A's picture each; the other half will need a copy of Student B's picture each.

In class

1 Pre-teach and revise vocabulary and structures as necessary.

2 Write on the board and check the meaning of *people, clothes, atmosphere, decor, noise level, lighting, activities.*

3 In AB pairs. Give the As one copy of Student A's picture each. Give the Bs one copy of Student B's picture each. Tell them not to show each other their pictures.

4 Tell students they're going to describe their picture according to the categories on the board. Give examples.

    Examples: **A:** In picture A there's a waitress who looks very happy. Does she look happy in picture B?

             B: No, she doesn't. In picture B she looks furious. She's wearing a blouse, an apron and a skirt. Is she wearing the same in picture A?

    Elicit which categories (*people, clothes*) these examples belong to. Give the students 10 minutes to find as many differences as they can. (There are 15 more differences between the 2 pictures.)

5 Feedback with the class. The pair with the most differences wins.

6 Write on the board *In picture A the waitress looks very happy, but / whereas she looks furious in picture B.* Point out the use of *but / whereas.* You could also teach *On the other hand.*

7 In the same pairs. Ask the students to look at both pictures and to write down the differences using contrastive language. Make a note of any errors in the sentences or take in the sentences for feedback in a future lesson.

Key

STUDENT A	STUDENT B
1 waiter with 4 cocktails	waiter with champagne bottle, 4 glasses
2 waitress with wine bottle, 2 glasses	waitress with 2 glasses
3 smart woman with jacket	casual woman with T-shirt
4 waiter in jacket, shirt and trousers	waiter in shirt and trousers
5 woman with scarf	woman without scarf
6 not smoky	smoky
7 not many people	more people / more crowded
8 waterfall	fountain
9 vase of flowers on one table	ashtray on one table
10 not so noisy / quiet music	noisy / loud music
11 bright lights	dimly-lit
12 camera on one table	mobile phone on one table
13 woman talking on mobile phone	woman taking a photo
14 couple talking / laughing / smiling	couple arguing
15 no-one dancing	people dancing

Optional extra

In pairs. Ask the students to think of a theme for a wedding, party or special night in a location of their choice. Tell them to think about the people, clothes, atmosphere, decor, noise level, lighting and activities. Ask them to draw and label a diagram or write a description under the headings *people, clothes,* etc.

Student A

Student B

Photocopiable ✂

The rise and fall of Mimi Mee

Activity	Pair work: reading
Aim	Practice of collocations, compound nouns and linkers from Unit 4
Time	25 minutes
Vocabulary	Pre-teach: *behaviour, dynamic, in charge of*
	Revise: *at first, award, Buckingham Palace, colleague, Queen*
Before class	Photocopy and cut up page T117: each pair of students will need one set of cards, mixed up.
	If you have time, each pair of students will need one set of comprehension questions.
	Optional extra: photocopy and make a gap fill of page T117 with *succeeded _____ , accounts _____ ,* etc. Each student will need a copy of the gap fill.

In class

1 Pre-teach *collocation* and *compound noun*. Write on the board *1 consist _____ , 2 have a lot _____ common* and *3 get on _____ someone*. Students fill in the gaps. Elicit *1 of, 2 in* and *3 with*. Explain that words we expect to go together are called collocations. Then draw some traffic lights, a postbox and a lamp-post on the board labelled *4 traffic _____ , 5 post_____* and *6 lamp-_____* . Ask students to fill in the gaps. Elicit *4 lights, 5 box* and *6 post*. Explain that these are compound nouns and are made up of 2 words. Point out that compound nouns can be written as 2 words (*traffic lights*), one word (*postbox*) or a hyphenated word (*lamp-post*). Remind students to look at the *Longman WordWise Dictionary* if they aren't sure about the spelling of a word. Explain that the story they're going to work on has got collocations and compound nouns from Unit 4.

2 Pre-teach and revise vocabulary as necessary. Explain that the story the students are going to work on is about someone who was very ambitious and successful at work, but also very unpopular with her colleagues.

3 In pairs. Give each pair a set of cards which has been mixed up. Ask students to put the first 4 cards of the story, cards 1, 2, 3 and 4, in the correct order. Point out the compound noun *childhood* which connects cards 1 and 2, the collocation *succeeded in* which connects cards 2 and 3 and the compound noun *accounts department* which connects cards 3 and 4. Explain that the grey card is the last card of the story.

4 Ask the students to put the cards in the correct order. Tell them to think about collocations and compound nouns. Also encourage them to think about how the story is organised, with a chronological order and the use of linkers. Don't point out the meaning of the letter code which spells out the message *Very good work – you've got it right.*

5 Ask quick finishers to check with another pair. When the class has finished, check that students have put the cards in the correct order by pointing out the letter code.

6 If you've got time, give each pair a set of comprehension questions. In pairs. Students read the story again and answer the questions. Feedback with the class.

> **Key to comprehension questions 1** 2 **2** The first. **3** Yes. **4** She wanted a less traditional job, to earn more money and to be more creative. **5** In an advertising agency. **6** More independence and longer holidays. **7** An idea for an advertisement for a new television series. **8** Dealing with colleagues and taking criticism. **9** They tricked her into thinking that the Queen wanted to give her an award. **10** Answers will vary.

> **Optional extra**
> Give each student a copy of a gap fill of the whole story (see **Before class**). In pairs. Students fill in the gaps. Feedback with the class.

1	2	3	4
Mimi Mee came from a very unhappy background and had a difficult child	hood. She left school as soon as she could and she finally succeeded	in getting an extremely boring job in a local company in the accounts	department. It was better than being unemployed. The job was not well-
v paid, the boss was unpleasant and the employees worked under a lot of	**e** pressure all the time. But Mimi was hard-working and ambitious. She had a natural	**r** talent for working with numbers and started to work her way up the career	**y** ladder. Her boss began to depend on her. She worked long hours and she always looked
g smart. She was confident in stressful situations and she was very good at thinking	**o** on her feet. But after a while, she started to feel unhappy	**o** about her lifestyle. She wanted to have a less traditional job and to earn	**d** more money. She turned down the offer of a rise in that company because she wanted to be more
w creative. In the newspaper, she saw an advertisement for a job in an advertising	**o** agency. It sounded really interesting and dynamic. There wasn't so much job	**r** security but she could be independent, work the hours she wanted and make	**k** her own decisions. She could also have longer holidays. She decided to fill
y in the application form. The interview went well and she got the job. At	**o** first, she was very impressive in her new job. She was good	**u** at managing projects and she had a brilliant idea for an advertisement for a new television	**v** series, which was very successful. The technique she used in the advertisement was a break
e through in advertising. Her boss put her in charge of a team and gave her	**g** a huge bonus. Unfortunately she was impatient with her colleagues, hopeless at dealing	**o** with the members of her team and when things went wrong, she never learned to take	**t** criticism. Then one day she received a letter from Buckingham Palace saying "Congratulations! You have
i won an award from the Queen for your talented and intelligent TV master	**t** piece." The letter described her as a "genius" and asked her if she was able	**r** to receive the award on 20th August. She told everyone about it and immediately she wrote	**i** an article for the local newspaper about her success. However, when she wrote
g to accept the invitation, the Palace replied that, according	**h** to their records, her name wasn't on the list. She finally discovered that the letter was	**t** from her colleagues. They wanted to play a joke on her and show	her that they were fed up with her ambitious and insensitive behaviour – and it worked!

Comprehension questions

1 How many companies did Mimi work for?
2 Which company did she like the least?
3 Did she do her first job well?
4 What were the 3 reasons she decided to leave?
5 Where was her second job?

6 What were the 2 main advantages of her new job?
7 What was her main achievement?
8 What 2 aspects of the job was she not so good at?
9 How did her colleagues play a joke on her?
10 Do you feel sorry for her?

⑤ *Right or wrong?*

Activity	Group work: speaking
Aim	Board game with correct / incorrect sentences
Time	40 minutes
Grammar / structures	Subject / object questions; modifying adjectives; *so, such*; Present Perfect Continuous
Vocabulary	Pre-teach: *crime wave, make waves, on the crest of a wave, tidal wave, waver, wavy*
	Revise: *heat wave, on the same wavelength, wave* (n / v)
Before class	Photocopy page T119: each group of 3 or 5 students will need a copy of the game board, 2 counters, a dice. Photocopy and cut up page T118: each group of 3 or 5 students will need a copy of the instructions and a Key for Student C (the referee).

In class

1 Write the word *wave* on the board. Elicit different meanings of *wave*. Remind students of the Reader *Heat wave and other stories*. Elicit other words and phrases with *wave* in them and build up a *wave* word map.

2 Divide the class into ABC or AABBC groups where AA and BB pairs play as a single person. Give each group a copy of the game board, the instructions, 2 counters, a dice and the Cs a copy of the Key each.

Instructions

● A and B are the players. C is the referee with the Key which lists and explains the incorrect sentences.

● As and Bs put their counters on the Start. Student A throws the dice, then Student B. The student with the highest number begins, throws the dice and moves forwards that number of spaces. If the student lands on:

   a) a Wavelength square, the student follows the instruction.

   b) an empty square, the student stays where he / she is.

   c) a ✓ or ✗ square, the student has one minute to decide whether the sentence is correct or not and to correct it if necessary. The mistakes can be in grammar, vocabulary, word order or spelling. If the student is correct, he / she stays on the square and the other player has a turn. If the decision is wrong, the student goes back to the first available empty square and the other player has a turn.

● The winner / winning pair is the first to reach the Finish (students don't have to get the exact number).

Key   **Correct sentences:** 2, 4, 10, 14, 19, 33, 39   **Incorrect sentences:**

6 The statue of David is a famous ~~sculptor~~ sculpture. (*sculptor* = a person who makes sculptures)

8 It's ~~so~~ such a large house. (we make singular nouns stronger with *such a*)

12 Her flat is slightly ~~big~~ bigger than mine. (comparative = adjective + *-er* + *than*)

17 They're playing my favourite classical music at the Mozart ~~gig~~ concert on Friday. (*gig* = a concert of pop music)

22 A BMW isn't quite ~~faster than~~ as fast as a Ferrari. (*not quite as* + adjective + *as*)

25 How much did ~~earn Rebecca~~ Rebecca earn? (object question)

27 What ~~did give~~ gave you the idea? (subject question)

30 I like ~~listening~~ listening to pop music when I'm working. (*listen to something*)

34 She's ~~talked~~ been talking since two o'clock! (Present Perfect Continuous for continuing activity)

37 He's kinder ~~that~~ than his sister. (comparative = adjective + *-er* + *than*)

41 It's ~~easyer~~ easier than you think. (comparative adjective of 2-syllable adjectives with *-y* at the end = *-y* → *-i* + *-er*)

43 How many times have I ~~been telling~~ told you to leave?! (Present Perfect Simple for completed results)

45 This mobile phone is ~~such~~ so expensive. (we make adjectives stronger with *so*)

48 What's the name of the ~~composer~~ author of that book? (*composer* = a writer of music)

Optional extra

In pairs. Students choose 6 different *wave* words or phrases and write a story of 50–60 words using all 6. Pairs write the 6 words / phrases in random order on a piece of paper. In groups of 4, pairs swap pieces of paper and take it in turns to read their story aloud, leaving out the words / phrases. The other pair listens and chooses the correct word / phrase to fill in the gaps.

     Photocopiable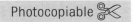

1	2	3	4	5	6	7
Start	Sarah is more beautiful than Marie. ✓ ✗	Your new wavy hairstyle looks fantastic! Go forwards 2 spaces.	Who sold the car? ✓ ✗		The statue of David is a famous sculptor. ✓ ✗	You aren't on the same wavelength. Miss a turn.
14	13	12	11	10	9	8
Work is much more important to you than our relationship. ✓ ✗		Her flat is slightly big than mine. ✓ ✗	You feel insecure in waves. Go back 2 spaces.	He's much more attractive with short hair. ✓ ✗		It's so a large house. ✓ ✗
15	16	17	18	19	20	21
	You wave aside your partner's worries. Go forwards 2 spaces.	They're playing my favourite classical music at the Mozart gig on Friday. ✓ ✗		How long have you known that? ✓ ✗	There's a crime wave in your town. Go back 2 spaces.	
28	27	26	25	24	23	22
A tidal wave destroys your home. Go back 2 spaces.	What did give you the idea? ✓ ✗		How much did earn Rebecca? ✓ ✗		The director waves you onto the stage. Have an extra turn.	A BMW isn't quite faster than a Ferrari. ✓ ✗
29	30	31	32	33	34	35
	I like listening pop music when I'm working. ✓ ✗		Your popularity has never wavered. Go forwards 3 spaces.	The dancers gave an amazing performance. ✓ ✗	She's talked since two o'clock! ✓ ✗	
42	41	40	39	38	37	36
	It's easier than you think. ✓ ✗	You're on the crest of a wave! Go forwards 2 spaces.	Did you see that fantastic film on TV last night? ✓ ✗		He's kinder that his sister. ✓ ✗	The new boss is making waves. Go back 1 space.
43	44	45	46	47	48	49
How many times have I been telling you to leave?! ✓ ✗	There's a heat wave. Miss a turn.	This mobile phone is such expensive. ✓ ✗		You're feeling waves of loneliness. Go back 1 space.	What's the name of the composer of that book? ✓ ✗	**Finish**

6 *Leave it with us!*

Activity	Group work: speaking
Aim	Design presentation revising vocabulary from Units 1, 2, 4 and 6
Time	30 minutes
Grammar / structures	Superlative adjectives; Second Conditional; infinitive of purpose and *by* + verb + *-ing*
Vocabulary	Pre-teach: *benefit, setting, upside-down, useless*
	Revise: adjectives / phrases for describing people (Unit 1), city vocabulary (Unit 2), skills, ability and aspects of jobs (Unit 4), clothes and parts of the body (Unit 6)
Before class	Photocopy page T121: each student will need a copy of the whole page.

In class

1 Pre-teach and revise vocabulary as necessary.

2 Tell the students that they're all consultants who work for a company called "Leave it with us!". In the in-tray today they've got information about 4 different jobs from 4 different clients.

3 Give each student a copy of page T121. Tell them to read the information. Explain that all 4 jobs are urgent and they've only got time to work on one.

4 Ask students to choose which job they would like to work on and organise themselves into groups of 3 or 4. Encourage groups to work on different designs.

5 Give students 20 minutes to prepare a presentation of their ideas with drawings / diagrams for their clients (the rest of the class).

6 When students have finished, ask groups to take it in turns to give their presentations to their clients. To avoid lengthy presentations with larger classes, ask 2 groups who've chosen a different design to work together and to take it in turns to make their presentations.

7 Display students' work and ask the class to vote for the best idea for each design.

> **Optional extra**
> Students choose one of descriptions 1–3:
> 1 your perfect person, including details of his / her personality and / or appearance
> 2 your perfect city or town
> 3 your perfect job
> Ask them to write the description for homework and to illustrate it with drawings if they want to.

Design 1
JOB AD

You've been asked to design a job advertisement on the Internet for the manager of the first theme park in space. Write a job description, including details of the kind of person who is needed for the job and the benefits that the person will get.

Think how you can attract the right kind of person to the job. Look at the Word lists for Units 1 and 4.

You want your design to win the contract:
➤ describe the person's qualities and skills
➤ think about the job's duties, benefits, conditions
➤ think how you'll design the ad and use diagrams / photos to attract the right person
➤ give reasons for the decisions you've made

Design 3
MONSTER

You've been asked to design the appearance of a monster for a horror film. Every night at midnight the handsome star of the film changes into a terrifying monster who can fly, climb anything, eat anything and see everything.

Think how you can use make-up or special effects to change the features of his face and body. Look at the Word list for Unit 6.

You want your design to win the contract:
➤ make the ideas fresh and exciting
➤ be ready to describe the monster in detail
➤ give reasons for the choices you've made
➤ if possible, use drawings to explain your ideas

Design 2
OUTFITS

You've been asked to design the clothes and setting for a famous female pop star's latest pop video, "Heat". The video can be shot anywhere in the world and it will feature the pop star as well as 2 male dancers.

Think how you can use clothes and the setting to illustrate the title of the song. Look at the Word list for Unit 6.

You want your design to win the contract:
➤ make the ideas fresh and exciting
➤ be ready to describe the outfits and setting
➤ give reasons for the choices you've made
➤ if possible, use drawings to explain your ideas

Design 4
STREET SCENE

You've been asked to design a street called "Upside-down Street" for a children's magazine competition. The children have to find 10 more useless objects in the picture apart from the upside-down postbox. Don't make it too easy for them!

Design "Upside-down Street" with 10 more useless objects. Look at the Word list for Unit 2.

You want your design to win the contract:
➤ make the ideas fresh and exciting
➤ be ready to describe the street and the useless objects
➤ give reasons for the choices you've made
➤ if possible, use drawings to explain your ideas

⑦ *How did you get into this mess?!*

Activity	Group work: speaking; writing
Aim	Narrative writing to revise past tenses and linkers
Time	30 minutes
Grammar / structures	Past Simple; Past Perfect Simple; reported speech (sentences, questions); *because* and *so*
Vocabulary	Pre-teach: *basket, desert, earring, fancy-dress outfit, picnic, rabbit, rescue* (v)
	Revise: *because* and *so*, *helicopter*, *rope*, *strawberry*, *suitcase*
Before class	Photocopy page T123: each group will need a copy of the page of cartoons.

In class

1 Write these questions on the board:
  What's the strangest situation you've ever found yourself in?
  Where were you?
  Who else was involved?
  Had you planned to be there?
  Why? / Why not?
  What went wrong?
  Whose idea / fault was it?
  What did the people involved say?
  How did you feel afterwards?

2 In pairs. Give students 5 minutes to tell each other their stories.

3 Explain that there's a newspaper competition to write the best explanation for a cartoon.

4 In groups of 2 or 3. Give one copy of page T123 to each group. Draw attention to the title "How did you get into this mess?!".

5 Pre-teach and revise vocabulary as necessary. Explain that all the people in the cartoons are in their current situation because of something that someone else either asked or told them to do.

6 Ask each group to choose a cartoon and to write a story which answers the questions on the board and explains how the situation in the cartoon happened. Tell them to write the story from the point of view of the person or one of the people in the cartoon. Remind them to use *I* or *we* and to include reported speech.

7 Give groups 20 minutes to write their stories. Go round the class and give help as necessary.

8 When the groups have finished, ask them to put their stories round the class. Number the stories.

9 Ask the students to go round the class and read each story. Tell them to match each story to a cartoon (a–d). Feedback with the class.

10 Ask the students to vote for one story for each cartoon. Then read out the winning story for each cartoon.

11 Feedback with the class on any errors you've noted.

> **Optional extra**
> In pairs. The competition has been so successful that the newspaper wants the artist to draw more cartoons. Ask the students to think of one more cartoon to illustrate the question "However did you get into this mess?!". Tell them to write a description of the cartoon to give to the artist.

Photocopiable

The Terry Stinger Show

Activity	Pair / group work: reading; speaking. Whole class work: speaking; listening.
Aim	Chat show role-play to practise predictions, regrets and wishes
Time	30–60 minutes
Grammar / structures	*Will / going to* + infinitive; Second and Third Conditional; *wish* + Past Simple
Vocabulary	*arrange, concentrate, contract* (n), *hire, part-time, support* (v), *ultimatum, van*
Before class	Photocopy and cut up page T125: 4 pairs of students will need a guest card each; 4 students will need an expert card each.

In class

1 Tell the students that they're going to take part in a TV chat show, *The Terry Stinger Show*. Explain that the show is the kind of TV programme where members of the public talk about their problems and fight about them. Experts are then invited to give their help and advice and the host of the show asks the audience to make comments before the guests say what they're going to do to change their lives.

2 Pre-teach and revise vocabulary as necessary.

3 Take the part of the show host, Terry Stinger, yourself. Ask for volunteers or choose:

a) 8 students to be guests and divide the students into Guest pairs A, B, C and D.

b) 4 students to be experts and allocate the roles of Experts 1, 2, 3 and 4.

c) the rest of the class to be the audience.

With a small class, have 4 guests (Guest pairs A and B) and 2 experts (Experts 1 and 2). You don't need to have an audience.

4 Give students the relevant role cards and ask them to read the information on the cards.

5 Write these questions on the board:

How should a couple divide up the work involved in running a home?

How much freedom should you have to be yourself in a relationship, e.g. to enjoy hobbies or act as you please?

How much freedom should you have as a sixteen-year-old to make decisions about your own life?

6 Explain that these questions deal with the problems the guests on the show are experiencing. Give students 10 minutes to prepare and monitor and give help as necessary.

a) In their pairs: ask the guests to think of how they will present their problems.

b) In a group of 4: ask the experts to discuss the questions and form their own opinions.

c) In a group, ask the audience to discuss the questions and form their own opinions.

7 Facing the audience, the guests sit in the centre and the experts sit at the side. Each pair of guests sits together. Remind students that the host is in charge of the show and ask the audience to listen carefully to the guests and the experts. If possible, make a video or audio recording of the show. Use the recording to note errors for feedback at a later date.

8 For each problem, ask the guests to give their side of the story. Then invite the experts to ask questions and give opinions. Chris Little will speak first about Dee and Jody, Dr Robin Weaver about Paul and Annie, Dr Jay Saunders about Rob and Lola and Sandy Mackay about Clara and her parent. When the main expert has spoken, ask the other experts and the audience for their questions and opinions. Then ask the guests to say what they're going to do next.

> **Optional extra**
> Tell the students that they work as "agony aunts / uncles" for a magazine or newspaper.
> Ask them to choose one of the problems and write a letter to the pair giving their advice.

Guest pair A

Dee: Although your friend, Jody, works part-time, her husband has always refused to help her with cooking, cleaning and shopping, saying they're "women's work". Your friend was unhappy and exhausted, so a month ago you persuaded her to offer her husband an ultimatum: "Help me in the house or we're finished!" He left her the next day and went back to live with his mother. You think she's much better off without him. You hope the experts will give her some advice about how to start her new life.

Jody: Your husband has never done anything in the house, even though you work part-time yourself. When you complained to your friend, Dee, she said, "Tell him to help you more or you're going to leave him." You told him and the next day he went back to live with his mother. That was a month ago and you're missing him terribly. You wanted him to change but you still love him. You know Dee has never really liked your husband. She went out with him once before he met you but he never asked her out again. You hope the experts will tell you how you can get him to come back home.

Guest pair B

Paul: You've been going out with your girlfriend, Annie, for two years. You plan to marry next year but at the moment you just can't understand her. You had told her several weeks ago that you couldn't help her to move flats last Saturday because you had tickets for a football match in Paris, but she still arranged to move on that day. You only go to football matches about once or twice a month and this was a very special game. You hope the experts will help her to see that football is part of your life and that she must accept it if she wants to share her life with you.

Annie: You've been very happy with your boyfriend, Paul, for two years but now you don't know if you want to get married to him next February. The most important thing in his life is football and nothing must ever stop him from going to a match or watching it on TV. Last weekend you had arranged to move flats and paid a lot of money to hire a van. Paul had promised to help you but at the last moment he got a ticket for a match in Paris. You had to change your moving date and you lost your money on the van. You hope the experts will make him see how selfish he is.

Guest pair C

Rob: You've come onto the programme because you don't know what to do. Your wife, Lola, smokes all the time. The house smells, she smells, it costs a fortune and you know it's making her ill. She's always got a terrible cough. Last week you had a really important business dinner. Not only was Lola the only one smoking but she didn't even wait for people to finish eating. Of course, you lost the business contract. You're angry about this and also worried about her health. You hope the experts will tell her that it's time to stop smoking.

Lola: Your husband, Rob, used to be fun and out-going but suddenly he has become really boring. Until recently, he didn't mind you smoking, but now he says that he hates it. He says that he lost an important business contract last week because you smoked at a dinner with his clients but you think that he didn't get the contract because he was asking for too much money. You believe that everyone has a right to do what they like. You've come onto the programme because you hope that the experts will agree with you and keep Rob quiet.

Guest pair D

Clara: You're sixteen years old and you're really interested in fashion. You're sure that you want to be a model when you leave school. All your friends say that you're very pretty. Last month you and a schoolfriend applied for an interview with an agency in London. You had to take a form signed by your mother or father to the interview. Both your mother and your father refused to sign the form. Your friend went and got a modelling job. Why can't your parents see that modelling is your future? You hope the experts will make them see how important it is to support you in the career you've chosen.

Clara's parent: Your daughter, Clara, is an extremely pretty girl and wants to be a model. You've read about the health problems models have and you don't think this is the future for your daughter. She's got important exams soon and you think she should be concentrating on them. Last week, without asking you, she arranged to go to a modelling interview. The evening before, she wanted you to sign a form giving her permission to take modelling jobs. You refused but she says she will be a model whatever you say. You hope the experts will make Clara see that modelling isn't a suitable career for her.

Expert 1

Chris Little: You're a marriage guidance expert. You'll give advice first on Dee and Jody's problem. Be prepared to give opinions on all the problems.

Expert 2

Dr Robin Weaver: You're a psychologist. You'll give advice first on Paul and Annie's problem. Be prepared to give opinions on all the problems.

Expert 3

Dr Jay Saunders: You're a medical expert. You'll give advice first on Rob and Lola's problem. Be prepared to give opinions on all the problems.

Expert 4

Sandy Mackay: You're a youth counsellor. You'll give advice first on Clara and her parent's problem. Be prepared to give opinions on all the problems.

What's the missing word?

Activity	Individual / pair work: listening
	Optional extra: listening; speaking
Aim	Gapped story: vocabulary revision
Time	20 minutes
Grammar / structures	Collocations; *should / shouldn't have done*; uses of *get*; *always* + *-ing*; giving reasons and contrasting
Vocabulary	Pre-teach: *instead*
	Revise: wedding and family relationship vocabulary
Before class	Photocopy and cut up page T127: each student will need a set of the cut-up and shuffled word cards. Prepare a Key by filling in the gaps in the story. Photocopy and cut up the page to provide a Key for each pair of students or make an OHT.
	Optional extra: photocopy and cut up the Key you've prepared. Half the class will need a copy of the first paragraph each; the other half will need a copy of the second paragraph each.

In class

If your students are confident about reading aloud, this activity could be done in pairs.

1 Pre-teach or revise vocabulary as necessary.
2 Explain that you're going to read out a gapped story 3 times. Tell them to listen the first time. Read the gapped story slowly, saying *peep* where there's a word missing.
3 Give each student the word cards. Ask the students to read the words and spread them out on their table.
4 Read the story again, pausing at each oblique (/). Ask the students to put the word cards for each gap in the correct order on their tables.
5 Read the story again for the students to check their work.
6 Either: in pairs, give each pair a copy of the Key and ask them to check their answers. Or: read the story again, pausing at the gaps to let students call out the words.
7 Feedback with the class.

> **Key**
> 1 been   2 always   3 sick   4 bride   5 best   6 though   7 ceremony   8 made   9 leave
> 10 bridesmaid   11 treated   12 that   13 aback   14 because   15 decorations   16 stained
> 17 get   18 through   19 should   20 barely

> **Optional extra**
> In AB pairs. Give Student A the Key for the first paragraph of the story and Student B the Key for the second paragraph of the story (see **Before class**). Ask Student A to choose 5 different words to gap in the first paragraph of the story and to make new word cards using these words. Ask Student B to do the same for the second paragraph. Tell the students to give the new word cards to their partners. Students then take it in turns to read out their paragraphs while their partners fill in the gaps.

 **Susie's story**

Susie had never . . . .[1] married. / She was . . . .[2] saying how much she enjoyed her independence, / but everyone knew that she was . . . .[3] of being by herself. / Then one day, she was invited to a wedding. / The . . . .[4] was an old schoolfriend / and she asked Susie to be her matron of honour on her special day. / The groom had asked an old schoolfriend of his, Marcus, to be the . . . .[5] man, / even . . . .[6] Marcus had moved to the USA in his early twenties / and he and the groom hadn't seen each other for years. / At the wedding reception after the . . . .[7], / Marcus . . . .[8] a very funny speech. / Susie laughed and laughed and afterwards Marcus wouldn't . . . .[9] her side. / He told everyone that Susie was the most beautiful . . . .[10] he had ever seen / and he . . . .[11] her like a queen. /

Marcus organised several business trips to England after the wedding / so . . . .[12] he and Susie could see each other a lot. / After four months, Marcus asked Susie to marry him. / Susie was completely taken . . . .[13]. She burst into tears and said yes. / Susie arranged the wedding herself . . . .[14] Marcus was so busy. / She spent thousands of pounds on a photographer, / the party afterwards, flowers and . . . .[15] to make everything look beautiful, / as well as a two-week honeymoon in Barbados. / On the day of the wedding, Susie arrived at the church on time. / The sun shone through the . . . .[16] glass windows and Susie looked wonderful. / But half an hour later, Susie was beginning to . . . .[17] worried. / Marcus still hadn't appeared. / Susie eventually found out that Marcus was already married / and spoke to his wife on the phone. / Marcus' wife explained . . . .[18] clenched teeth / that this was the third time Marcus had done this in the last two years. / Naturally, Susie was extremely upset and felt that she . . . .[19] have realised what Marcus was really like. / However, ...[20] six months later, Susie married the photographer instead!

though	**leave**	**sick**	**that**	**through**
best	**made**	**ceremony**	**aback**	**been**
always	**bridesmaid**	**bride**	**should**	**decorations**
barely	**stained**	**treated**	**because**	**get**

Who can go free?

Activity	Group work: speaking; reading
Aim	Group decision-making; revision of crime vocabulary
Time	30 minutes
Grammar / structures	The Passive; negative questions
Vocabulary	Pre-teach: *commit a crime / an offence, hack* (v), *hacker, hang around with, jail* (v), *limit, overdose* (n), *parole* (n / v), *parole board, regular* (n), *serve a sentence, set free, transfer* (v), *violence, violent*
	Revise: crimes and types of criminals, *prison, prisoner*
Before class	Photocopy page T129: each student will need one copy of the information about all the criminals.

In class

1 Pre-teach and revise vocabulary as necessary.

2 Explain to students that they're going to be members of a parole board. 6 prisoners have asked to be set free before the end of their sentence. The members of the parole board are having a meeting to choose one prisoner who will be set free on parole.

3 Give each student a copy of the information about the criminals. Ask the students to read through the information. Check for understanding.

4 Write these headings across the top of the board:
Name
Crime
Age
Length of sentence
How much of sentence completed
Fairness of sentence
Reasons for / against parole
Ask the students to make a table in their notebooks using the headings on the board.

5 In groups of 4–6. Give the students 20 minutes to fill in the table for each prisoner, discuss and finally decide which of the 6 prisoners they're willing to set free. Tell the students that the decision has to be a majority, not a unanimous one.

6 If a group finishes early, ask students to discuss whether an alternative punishment to prison would have been more appropriate for any of the prisoners.

7 Ask each group to choose a spokesperson. Each spokesperson then tells the rest of the class the group's decision and justifies it, even if it's against their own personal opinion.

8 Feedback with the class and compare each group's decision.

> **Optional extra**
> Students choose one of the criminals. Ask them to write the letter sent by the criminal to the parole board before the meeting takes place. Tell them to:
> a) argue their own case for being set free
> b) justify why they committed the crime
> c) say why they would benefit from an early release

Molly the murderer
Age: 63

Molly was jailed for 10 years after she gave an overdose of sleeping pills to her husband. Her husband had been very ill for over a year and had been given only 3 months to live. He wrote a letter saying that he had asked Molly to put an end to his life. She's got 2 more years of her sentence to serve.

Harry the hacker
Age: 30

Harry has always been interested in computers. For fun, he hacked his way into the computer system of a large international bank and destroyed their records. As a result, hundreds of people lost their jobs and many customers lost their money. He was jailed for 20 years. He has served 5 years of his sentence.

Reg the regular
Age: 72

Reg has been in and out of prison for most of his life. At the moment he has served 6 years of an 8-year sentence for taking part in a bank robbery in which no-one was hurt. He has never committed a violent crime. The prison doctor says that Reg has got an illness which is being made worse by the stress of prison life.

Belinda the burglar
Age: 19

Belinda was doing well at college until she started to hang around with the wrong crowd. She's in prison for 5 years for several crimes, including burglary with violence. She and her friends were surprised by the house owner, panicked and attacked him. He hasn't been able to work since. She has 4 years left to serve.

Thelma the thief
Age: 40

Thelma is a single mother and she worked in the accounts department of a London company. Her daughter wanted to go to an expensive ballet school in London and she couldn't afford it. She transferred money from the company into her own bank account. She got 5 years. She has served half of her sentence.

Dave the drunk
Age: 24

Dave had too much to drink one Saturday night. He drove his car onto a pavement and killed 2 people who were waiting at a bus stop. When tested for alcohol, he was 3 times over the legal limit. This was the first time he had ever committed any offence. He has already served 6 years of a 7-year sentence.

(11) *Fix it!*

Activity	Pair work: reading
Aim	Word puzzle to revise spelling and word formation of vocabulary from Units 1–11
Time	15 minutes
Vocabulary	Revise: *syllable*
Before class	Photocopy and cut up page T131: each pair of students will need one set of cards, mixed up. Make an OHT of page T131 for class feedback. Prepare and photocopy a list of definitions from page T130 for each student or provide an OHT.

In class

1 Write on large separate pieces of paper: *pa su un al cu u oc tion*. Stick them on the board. Explain that these are the separate syllables of 2 words mixed up. Students rearrange the papers and make the words *occupation* and *unusual*.

2 In pairs. Give each pair a set of cards, mixed up. Explain that they're going to do a puzzle. Hold up a blank landscape piece of paper to show students the shape of the finished puzzle. Point out that:
- the puzzle is made up of 2, 3 and 4-syllable words
- the grey piece makes up the left-hand edge of the puzzle
- a grey letter shows the beginning of a word
- a full stop shows the end of a word.

3 Tell students to try and predict the formation of the words. Explain that they can ask you for help but that they'll incur a one-minute penalty for each word you give them. Give students 15 minutes to do the puzzle.

4 The winners are the pair who complete the puzzle in the shortest time when the minute penalties have been added on. Ask quick finishers to check with another pair. Feedback with the class using an OHT.

5 Students write out the 37 words from the puzzle. Provide each student with a copy of definitions a–o or use an OHT. Students work individually to match the definitions to words from the puzzle. Feedback.

Definitions
a) the opposite of *success* (n)
b) extremely tired (adj)
c) the people who watch or listen to a performance, e.g. a play or concert (n)
d) sure that you can do something well or depend on something (adj)
e) the effect on your teeth of eating too many sweets (n)
f) unhappy because something unpleasant has happened (adj)
g) involving a lot of violence and blood (adj)
h) the opposite of *noisy* (adj)
i) 2 people who are married or who have a romantic relationship (n)
j) not controlled by another organisation (adj)
k) happening or behaving in the way you expect (adj)
l) someone who writes music (n)
m) facts, statements or signs that make you believe that something exists or is true (n)
n) the crime of illegally copying something, e.g. a document or painting (n)
o) annoying (adj)

> **Key to definitions** **a)** failure **b)** exhausted **c)** audience **d)** confident **e)** decay **f)** upset **g)** gory **h)** quiet **i)** couple **j)** independent **k)** predictable **l)** composer **m)** evidence **n)** forgery **o)** irritating

> **Optional extra**
> In 2 teams. Students choose 5 other words from the puzzle. Teams take it in turns to mime and guess the words.

     Photocopiable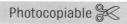

fail | ure. | **a** p | pear ance. | **e** v | i | dence. | **r** i | dic | **u** lous. | **a** t | tach.

un | so | cia ble. | **a** t | mo spher | ic. | **c** rit | i | cis m.

com | e | dy. | **m** is | for tune. | **p** o | et | **g** or | y. | **c** rit | i | **u** p | set.

an | i | ma ted. | **s** at | is | fac tion. | **m** ar | riage. | **i** n | tel | li | gent.

im | pres sive. | **g** en | e | rous. | **c** ou | ple. | **i** r | ri | ta ting. | **s** tu | pid.

com | pos | er. | **e** x | haust ed. | **q** ui | et. | **p** re | dic | ta ble. | **s** elf | ish.

sim | ple. | **a** u | di | ence. | **i** n | de pen dent. | **r** ec | og | nise. | **d** e | cay.

ne | ces | sa ry. | **c** on | fi | dent. | **c** er | e | mo | ny. | **f** or | ge | ry.

⑫ *Quiz night*

Activity	Group work: listening; speaking; writing
Aim	To revise grammar / structures / vocabulary from Units 1–12
Time	30–45 minutes
Before class	Each team will need one joker from a pack of cards and 6 pieces of paper. You could provide a small prize for the winning team.

In class

1 Explain to students that it's very popular for people to organise quiz nights in England. Teams of friends answer questions and the team with the highest score wins a prize.

2 Students work in teams of 4–8 depending on the size of your class and choose a name for their team. Write the team names up on the board. Give each team 6 pieces of paper, one for each round, and ask teams to nominate one student to write down each team's answers.

3 Explain that there are 6 rounds in the quiz. Write the names of the rounds on the board: *1 Problem prepositions, 2 Complex collocations, 3 Challenging conversations, 4 Stressful synonyms / antonyms, 5 Rotten rules* and *6 Difficult differences*. Check / elicit the meaning of *synonyms, antonyms, collocations*. Point out that each round has 10 questions.

4 Give each team a joker. Explain that each team can play their joker by giving it to you before a round begins. The team's score for that round will then be doubled. Point out that each team can only use their joker once.

5 Take the part of the quizmaster. Announce the start of the first round, *Problem prepositions*. Ask if any team wants to play their joker for this round and take in any jokers. Ask each team to write the team's name and the name of the round at the top of one piece of paper. Read out the instructions for round 1 on page T133. Then read out each sentence twice saying *peep* for each missing word. Give time for the students in each team to discuss, agree on and write down their answers.

6 At the end of round 1, teams swap answer sheets. Feedback. Teams mark the other team's answers, giving one mark for each correct answer. Elicit the scores and write them up by each team's name on the board.

7 Follow the same procedure for rounds 2–6. In round 3, as well as saying *peep* for each missing word in sentences 1–5, tell students how many words are missing in each sentence. Note that the final round, *6 Difficult differences*, is more demanding and that the feedback will involve some discussion.

Key **1 Problem prepositions: 1** on **2** at **3** under **4** about **5** off **6** in **7** with **8** in **9** with **10** for / to **2 Complex collocations: 1** make / take **2** earn / make **3** high **4** best **5** scene **6** forge **7** effects **8** sleeved **9** travel **10** ladder **3 Challenging conversations: 1** Hold **2** This is / It is / My name's **3** Come / Go **4** I see / know what you **5** do you **6** When we've met someone for the first time and are saying goodbye. **7** When we say goodbye. **8** Give an opinion. **9** Trying to persuade you. **10** Using fillers / hesitating / thinking of what to say next. **4 Stressful synonyms / antonyms: 1** elevator **2** sidewalk **3** cab **4** exhausted **5** chatty **6** freezing **7** illegal **8** failure **9** plain **10** tight **5 Rotten rules: 1** seeing **2** I lived **3** had red hair **4** opened the window **5** No. **6** infinitive without *to* **7** Present Simple **8** got **9** (She) can't have . . . **10** I want you to sit down. **6 Difficult differences: 1a)** When we ask a positive question, we're asking for information. **1b)** When we ask a negative question we're checking that what we're saying is correct. **2a)** We usually use *whole* with singular nouns. **2b)** We use *all* with uncountable nouns and plural countable nouns. **3a)** We use the Past Continuous and Past Simple to describe events that happened in the past. **3b)** We often use present tenses to increase the drama when we describe the plot of a book or film or tell jokes. **4a)** is a suggestion. **4b)** is advice. **5a)** describes a fact about a person's habits. **5b)** describes a habit which happens a lot and is irritating. **6a)** is less polite than 6b). **6b)** is more polite than 6a). **7a)** We use *could* to talk about general past ability. **7b)** We use *was able* to talk about success on one occasion. **8a)** An anniversary is a date that is special because it's exactly a year or a number of years after an important event. **8b)** A celebration is a party, meal, dance, etc. when you celebrate something special or good. **9a)** *although* + subject + verb **9b)** *despite* + noun, + gerund or + *the fact that* + clause **10a)** We use the Active when we're interested in who did something. **10b)** We use the Passive when the action is the important idea, not who did it or when we don't know who did the action.

1 Problem prepositions

Write down the missing preposition in sentences 1–10.
1 It depends . . . . you.
2 I'm hopeless . . . . singing.
3 I don't like working . . . . pressure.
4 How . . . . going for a meal?
5 I like holidays . . . . the beaten track.
6 When did you two fall . . . . love?
7 I'm really fed up . . . . him.
8 Are you interested . . . . films?
9 I'm really busy so can you deal . . . . this?
10 How many people is he responsible . . . . ?

2 Complex collocations

Write down the missing word in sentences 1–10.
1 He's got to . . . . a final decision by the end of next week.
2 She's going to . . . . a large amount of money in her new job.
3 She likes to be taller than her sisters so she always wears . . . . heels.
4 My oldest friend made a great speech when he was my . . . . man at my wedding.
5 The police took a lot of photos at the . . . . of the crime.
6 She tried to . . . . his signature so that she could get money out of his bank account.
7 In that science fiction film they had the most fantastic special . . . .
8 I like to get my arms brown in the summer so I wear short-. . . . . shirts.
9 Don't take a great big suitcase with you on holiday – it's much better to . . . . light.
10 He's really working hard to try and climb the career . . . . quickly.

3 Challenging conversations

Write down the missing word / words in sentences 1–5.
1 When you ask someone to wait a moment on the phone you say . . . . *on.* (1 word)
2 When you introduce yourself on the phone you say . . . . *Trevor Trink.* (2 words)
3 When you want to persuade someone you say . . . . *on!* (1 word)
4 When you agree with someone you say . . . . *mean.* (4 words)
5 When you ask a tag question you say *You don't come from here,* . . . . *?* (2 words)

Answer questions 6–10.
6 When do we say *Nice meeting you?*
7 When do we say *Cheerio?*
8 If I begin a sentence with *If you ask me . . .* am I going to disagree, give an opinion or repeat an opinion?
9 If I say *What have you got to lose?* am I agreeing with you, trying to persuade you or refusing to do something?
10 What are we doing when we say *Er . . . um . . . ?*

4 Stressful synonyms / antonyms

Write down the correct word.
1 American English for *lift.*
2 American English for *pavement.*
3 American English for *taxi.*
4 The word beginning with *e* which means *extremely tired.*
5 The word beginning with *ch* which means *talkative.*
6 The opposite of *boiling.*
7 The opposite of *legal.*
8 The opposite of *success.*
9 The opposite of *patterned.*
10 The opposite of *baggy.*

5 Rotten rules

Finish the sentences in 1–4.
1 Using the verb *see*, finish the sentence *I look forward to* . . . . *you.*
2 Change the question *Where do you live?* into reported speech by finishing the sentence *She asked me where . . .*
3 You want red hair. Finish the sentence *I wish I . . .*
4 You want to open the window. Finish the polite request *Would you mind if I . . . ?*

Answer questions 5–10.
5 Is the polite reply to question 4 *Yes* or *No?*
6 Which part of the verb comes after *I'd rather . . . ?*
7 Which tense comes after *if* in the sentence beginning *I'll tell him if I . . . ?*
8 Which other word can you use in place of *was* in the sentence *I was hit on the head?*
9 We say *She must have . . .* when we're sure that something happened in the past. What do we say when we're sure that something didn't happen in the past?
10 Which sentence is correct: *I want that you sit down* or *I want you to sit down?*

6 Difficult differences

Explain the difference between a) and b) in 1–10.
1 a) Is that John's car? b) Isn't that John's car?
2 a) the whole b) all the
3 a) Kate was walking down the street when she met a man with a parrot on his head.
  b) Kate is walking down the street when she meets a man with a parrot on his head.
4 a) Have you tried phoning them?
  b) You should phone them.
5 a) He always phones late at night.
  b) He's always phoning late at night.
6 a) Can I use your phone?
  b) Do you mind if I use your phone?
7 a) I could swim. b) I was able to swim.
8 a) an anniversary b) a celebration
9 a) The grammar after *although.*
  b) The grammar after *despite.*
10 a) Using the Active, e.g. *A hacker destroyed the bank's records.* b) Using the Passive, e.g. *The bank's records were destroyed.*

It should have been me

Activity	Individual / pair work: reading; listening; speaking
Aim	Gapped song to practise sentence structure, parts of speech, predicting meaning
Time	15–20 minutes
Grammar / structures	*Should / shouldn't have done;* Past Simple; Present Continuous
Vocabulary	Pre-teach: *faithful, objection, part* (v), *preacher*
Before class	Photocopy and cut up page T135: half the class will need a copy of Student A's song each; the other half will need a copy of Student B's song each. Set up Recording 85.

In class

1 Write the word *wedding* on the board. In groups of 4. Give students 3 minutes to list as many words as possible to do with weddings. Build up a word map on the board of students' suggestions.

2 Explain that students are going to hear a song about a wedding. Pre-teach vocabulary and revise *aisle*.

3 In 2 groups: A and B. If students need to work together, divide the groups into AA and BB pairs. If not, students work alone. Give the As a copy of Student A's song each and the Bs a copy of Student B's song each.

4 Check students understand the instructions. Go through the 4 examples and highlight the past tenses *saw, passed*. Students then fill in the gaps.

5 Divide the class into AB pairs. Students check and complete the song together.

6 When students have finished, ask these questions and elicit the answers in brackets: *Where did the event described in the song take place? (In a church.) What was happening there? (The singer's ex-boyfriend was getting married.) How did she feel? (Upset.) Why did she feel like this? (Because he had promised they would never part.) What did she do in the middle of the event? (She shouted out "It should have been me!")* Point out the title of the song. Ask the students to suggest other titles.

7 ∞ 85 Play the recording. Students listen and check. Then play it again for them to sing along.

Key (Students A's answers = 1–20; Student B's answers = a–t)

I saw my love walking[1] down the aisle
And as[2] he passed me by[a],
He turned[b] to me and gave[3] me a smile.
Then the preacher, then the preacher,
The preacher joined[c] their hands[4]
And all the people, the people began[5] to stand[d]
When[6] I shouted[e], "You know that it should have been me
Instead[7] of her walking[f] with you,
You know that it should have been me, oh baby,
Getting[g] ready to marry[8] you, darling, darling, darling."

You made[9] a promise[h] that we'd never[i] part[10],
Then you turned around[11] and you broke[j] my little heart[12],
Now you're standing[13] there saying "I do [k],"
Holding[14] hands with[l] somebody new.
You know that it should have been me,
Instead of her standing[15] by[m] you,
You know that it should have been me,

It should have been me
Getting[n] ready to say[16], "I do[o]."

Then the preacher, oh yeah, the preacher asked[p]
"Let there be silence[17], please.
If any objections to[q] this wedding
Speak[r] now or forever, forever hold your peace."
Then I shouted[18], "It should have been me,
You know that it should have been me,
You know that it should have been me,
Baby, how could[s] you do[19] this to me?
Darling, darling, darling, it should have been me,
Don't you know that it should have been me?
You know that it should have been me,
It should have been me.
I've been faithful[t] to[20] you, baby, baby, baby.
It should have been me."

Optional extra

In 2 groups: A (grooms) and B (jilted girlfriends). Students prepare to accuse, blame and express regrets. Tell them to think about where the relationship went wrong, how they feel and how they're going to get their revenge! Remind them to use *should / shouldn't have done, wish / if only* + Past Perfect Simple. In AB pairs. Students confront their former partner and act out a conversation.

Student A

Fill in the gaps with the correct form of the verbs and with the other words in the Word Box.

> **Verbs** see ✓ do part say stand (x 2) begin hold shout make marry give walk
>
> aisle ✓ when around instead hands as silence heart to

IT SHOULD HAVE BEEN ME

I _saw_ my love . . . . (1) down the _aisle_
And . . . . (2) he passed me by,
He turned to me and . . . . (3) me a smile.
Then the preacher, then the preacher,
The preacher joined their . . . . (4)
And all the people, the people . . . . (5) to stand
. . . . (6) I shouted, "You know that it should have been me
. . . . (7) of her walking with you,
You know that it should have been me, oh baby,
Getting ready to . . . . (8) you, darling, darling, darling."

You . . . . (9) a promise that we'd never . . . . (10),
Then you turned . . . . (11) and you broke my little
. . . . (12),
Now you're . . . . (13) there saying "I do,"
. . . . (14) hands with somebody new.
You know that it should have been me,
Instead of her . . . . (15) by you,
You know that it should have been me,

It should have been me
Getting ready to . . . . (16), "I do."
Then the preacher, oh yeah, the preacher asked
"Let there be . . . . (17), please.
If any objections to this wedding
Speak now or forever, forever hold your peace."
Then I . . . . (18), "It should have been me,
You know that it should have been me,
You know that it should have been me,
Baby, how could you . . . . (19) this to me?
Darling, darling, darling, it should have been me,
Don't you know that it should have been me?
You know that it should have been me,
It should have been me.
I've been faithful . . . . (20) you, baby, baby, baby.
It should have been me."

Student B

Fill in the gaps with the correct form of the verbs and with the other words in the Word Box.

> **Verbs** pass ✓ walk ask can get (x 2) stand join speak break turn shout do (x 2)
>
> love ✓ to never faithful promise by (x 2) with

IT SHOULD HAVE BEEN ME

I saw my _love_ walking down the aisle
And as he _passed_ me . . . . (a),
He . . . . (b) to me and gave me a smile.
Then the preacher, then the preacher,
The preacher . . . . (c) their hands
And all the people, the people began to . . . . (d)
When I . . . . (e), "You know that it should have been me
Instead of her . . . . (f) with you,
You know that it should have been me, oh baby,
. . . . (g) ready to marry you, darling, darling, darling."

You made a . . . . (h) that we'd . . . . (i) part,
Then you turned around and you . . . . (j) my little heart,
Now you're standing there saying "I . . . . (k),"
Holding hands . . . . (l) somebody new.
You know that it should have been me,
Instead of her standing . . . . (m) you,
You know that it should have been me,

It should have been me
. . . . (n) ready to say, "I . . . . (o)."

Then the preacher, oh yeah, the preacher . . . . (p)
"Let there be silence, please.
If any objections . . . . (q) this wedding
. . . . (r) now or forever, forever hold your peace."
Then I shouted, "It should have been me,
You know that it should have been me,
You know that it should have been me,
Baby, how . . . . (s) you do this to me?
Darling, darling, darling, it should have been me,
Don't you know that it should have been me?
You know that it should have been me,
It should have been me.
I've been . . . . (t) to you, baby, baby, baby.
It should have been me."

1 ●● 86 Mandy and Sarah are walking along the street when Mandy sees a man she knows. Read sentences 1–10 and then listen to the conversation. Fill in the boxes with *T* (true) or *F* (false).

1 ☐ Rebecca is going out with Steve Jones.
2 ☐ Sarah is interested in Steve.
3 ☐ Mandy works with Steve.
4 ☐ Steve plays tennis at Mandy's club.
5 ☐ Mandy is a member of the tennis team.
6 ☐ Mandy liked the atmosphere in the new club in town.
7 ☐ Sarah's sister and Mandy had different opinions about the new club.
8 ☐ Sarah would prefer not to go to the pub.
9 ☐ They're going to go into town by bus.
10 ☐ Sarah's father works in London all the time.

(10 marks)

2 Listen to the sentences. Listen again and write them down. Then listen again and check.

1 . . . .
. . . .
. . . .
. . . .

2 . . . .
. . . .
. . . .
. . . .

3 . . . .
. . . .
. . . .

4 . . . .
. . . .
. . . .

5 . . . .
. . . .
. . . .

(30 marks)

3 Read sentences 1–10 and underline the correct word / words in brackets.

Example: If you (will go / go) past a postbox, will you post this letter for me, please?

1 She (drove / was driving) home from work when her mobile phone rang.

2 There aren't (much / many) sidewalks in Los Angeles because people drive everywhere.

3 (Did you go / Have you been) here before or is this your first visit?

4 One hundred years ago the smog in London (was / has been) terrible.

5 Shall we have a picnic on Saturday unless it (doesn't rain / rains)?

6 I come from Ireland but I (live / 'm living) in Australia at the moment.

7 There (is / are) a lot of pollution in the city on a busy day.

8 I've decided where I ('ll go / 'm going) for my next holiday.

9 I've got the tickets and we ('ll leave / 're leaving) at six a.m. next Sunday.

10 I (don't like / 'm not liking) this nightclub. It's too noisy.

(10 marks)

4 Read sentences 1–5. Fill in the gaps with *which*, *who*, *whose* or *where*.

1 The man . . . . lives in the house on the corner of the square is an old friend of my father's.

2 This is the place . . . . I had my accident.

3 I took a photograph of the balcony in Verona . . . . is in the film of *Romeo and Juliet*.

4 His watch, ... is always going wrong, was really expensive.

5 Have you met my friend . . . . father's a professional wrestler?

(5 marks)

5 Ben was enjoying a quiet drink in a pub when an old schoolfriend, Adam, sat down at his table and started talking. Match Adam's questions / statements to Ben's replies (a–k). Fill in the boxes with a–k. Then write Adam's questions / statements 2–11.

Adam's questions / statements

1 ☐ *f* How / you? ✓
   How are you? ....

2 ☐ Ever / visit / Iceland?
   ....

3 ☐ When / finish / your university / course?
   ....

4 ☐ Go / eat / that sandwich?
   ....

5 ☐ How about / go / cinema this evening?
   ....

6 ☐ Shall / play / tennis / weekend?
   ....

7 ☐ My sister / marry / millionaire / next Saturday.
   ....

8 ☐ My parents / live / California / three years in the 1990s.
   ....

9 ☐ Like / Madonna's music?
   ....

10 ☐ He / crazy, / he?
   ....

11 ☐ What / do / when / hurt / your head?

(15 marks)

Ben's replies

a) I'd rather not. I've got a headache.

b) Yes, I am.

c) Really?

d) Just walking along the pavement.

e) No, I haven't.

f) Fine, thanks. ✓

g) I used to but I don't any longer.

h) In the summer of 2001.

i) OK. If it doesn't rain.

j) Absolutely.

k) Did they?

Photocopiable

6 Underline the stressed syllables / words.

Examples: int<u>e</u>lligent, <u>phone</u> box

1	fountain	6	self-confident
2	road sign	7	techniques
3	cathedral	8	improve
4	miserable	9	manage
5	interesting	10	fashionable

(5 marks)

7 Which phrases in the Word Box go with *for*, *ago, since* or *on*? Some can go with more than one. Fill in the table.

> 10th January   three weeks   we got married
> a few days   1997   Tuesday

for	since
. . . .	. . . .
. . . .	. . . .
. . . .	. . . .
. . . .	. . . .
ago	**on**
. . . .	. . . .
. . . .	. . . .
. . . .	. . . .
. . . .	. . . .

(5 marks)

8 Read the sentences. Then fill in the gaps with the correct word in the Word Box.

> keep   tidy   deal   start   depend
> get   fall   meet   wind   work

1 You can . . . . on Charlie. If he promises to do something, he will.
2 Can you please . . . . your room? It looks terrible!
3 Well, he's an actor but he's been out of . . . . since last year.
4 Don't get so upset. It's much better if you can . . . . calm.
5 Her car has broken down but I've told her not to worry. I can . . . . with it.
6 I think she's strange. I really don't . . . . on with her.
7 She's on holiday in Cyprus at the moment. She hopes to meet someone new and . . . . in love!
8 Hello Mrs Walker. My name's Samantha. Pleased to . . . . you.
9 She's had a terrible week at work so she's lying in the bath and trying to . . . . down.
10 It's very difficult to . . . . a conversation with her. I never know what to say.

(10 marks)

9 Tick one of the titles 1–3 and write about 100 words on the subject you've chosen.

1 ☐ My favourite restaurant
2 ☐ One thing or person that changed my life
3 ☐ The best place for a night out in town

. . . .

. . . .

. . . .

. . . .

. . . .

. . . .

. . . .

. . . .

. . . .

(10 marks)

1 📼87 **Look at the table and then listen to Emily, Josh and Helen. They're all unhappy with their present jobs. You'll hear each person twice. Fill in the table.**

	1 Emily	2 Josh	3 Helen
Present job			
Good at			
Problem with the job			
Perks of the present job			
Future plans			

(15 marks)

2 **Listen to the sentences. Listen again and write them down. Then listen again and check.**

1 . . . .
. . . .
. . . .
. . . .

2 . . . .
. . . .
. . . .

3 . . . .
. . . .
. . . .

4 . . . .
. . . .
. . . .

5 . . . .
. . . .
. . . .

(30 marks)

3 **Read the letter and fill in the gaps. There's one word missing in each gap.**

> Sernanders vag 48
> Uppsala
>
> Kungensteater
> Stortorget
> 270 21 Lillebro
>
> 14th March
>
> . . . . (1) Sir,
>
> I am writing in response to your . . . . (2) for a theatre manager in the *Dagbladet* newspaper of 10th March.
>
> At the moment, I am working . . . . (3) a theatre manager in the Old Theatre in Uppsala. My . . . . (4) involve organising the programme and employing and paying the . . . . (5) who come from all over Europe and have performed throughout the world.
>
> Although I am happy in my . . . . (6) position, I am looking for a post with more responsibility. I am good at . . . . (7) with people and at working . . . . (8) pressure.
>
> I . . . . (9) an up-to-date CV and the names and addresses of two referees.
>
> I look forward to . . . . (10) from you.
>
> Yours faithfully,
>
> Gunnel Nilsson

(10 marks)

4 Five of the sentences are correct and five aren't. Put a tick (✓) or cross (✗) in the boxes. Correct the sentences that are wrong.

Example: ☒ Why don't you phoning him?
Why don't you phone him?

1 ☐ The tin's empty! How many biscuits have you been eating this morning?

2 ☐ He succeeded in getting the job in the USA.

3 ☐ These shoes are more comfortable than those boots.

4 ☐ I wish I lived in a really big house and not in this tiny flat.

5 ☐ If I am taller, I'd ask her to go out with me.

6 ☐ Who composed that music?

7 ☐ It's ten o'clock! What are you doing for the last three hours?

8 ☐ He's such a clever playwright. I love his work.

9 ☐ He opened a gallery for exhibit his friends' sculptures.

10 ☐ After trying for many years he could get a job at the opera house.

(10 marks)

5 What are Dawn and Robin wearing? Read the examples. Then fill in the gaps to give a detailed description of each item of clothing (1–5).

a leather jacket

3 a . . . . hat

4 a . . . . jumper

1 a . . . . scarf

a sleeveless top

5 . . . . trousers

2 a . . . . skirt

(5 marks)

6 Read what one film critic said about the five entries competing for the best film award at the Harton Film Festival. Order the films from the best (1) to the worst (5).

There are three films at the Harton Film Festival that are really impressive and two which are entertaining but nothing special.

My three top choices are *Heat Wave*, *The Genius* and *Skin Deep*. I think that the director of *The Genius* isn't quite as talented as the director of *Heat Wave* whose film is slightly less interesting than *Skin Deep*. Far less successful is the ordinary *Famous and Free* which is still much more colourful than *Murder in the Gallery*.

1 . . . .

2 . . . .

3 . . . .

4 . . . .

5 . . . .

(5 marks)

7 Read the sentences. Fill in the gaps with the correct word / words.

1 I love his work. He writes such good stories. I think he's a wonderful . . . .
a) poet b) publisher c) composer d) author

2 I've found something in his papers that looks . . . . it's important.
a) if b) as if c) sort of d) as

3 You can always contact her by . . . . this number.
a) phone b) phoning c) to phone d) phoned

4 If you're late, you'd better . . . . in quietly.
a) coming b) to come c) come d) have come

5 . . . . in that small plane made me feel really ill.
a) To fly b) Fly c) Flew d) Flying

6 He's not coming. He drank too much at the party last night and he's got a . . . .
a) hiccups b) hangover c) decay d) sore throat

7 I'm not really very interested . . . . black and white films.
a) in b) to c) for d) with

8 If you . . . . live so far away, we could meet more often.
a) wouldn't b) not c) don't d) didn't

9 He may be really rich now but he comes from a very poor . . . .
a) childhood b) lifestyle c) background d) influence

10 She's not good at . . . . criticism.
a) taking b) having c) earning d) making

(10 marks)

8 Fill in the word map with the words in the Word Box. Fill in the boxes with five jobs. Fill in the gaps with one thing connected with each job.

actor ✓ performance ✓ masterpiece
advertising executive joke skyscraper
librarian agency shelf architect artist
stand-up comic

performance
. . . .

actor

PEOPLE

(5 marks)

---

9 Tick one of the titles 1–3 and write about 100 words on the subject you've chosen.

1 ☐ Why I would love / hate to be a famous person
2 ☐ My favourite painting, sculpture or building
3 ☐ Fashion today

. . . .
. . . .
. . . .
. . . .
. . . .
. . . .
. . . .
. . . .
. . . .

(10 marks)

1 ◗◗88 **Read sentences 1–10. Then listen to Melanie's conversation with her boss, Roger. Fill in the boxes with *T* (true) or *F* (false).**

1 ☐ Melanie and Roger have a formal relationship.

2 ☐ Melanie definitely won't need any help from Roger.

3 ☐ Roger isn't sure when Melanie is travelling to the exhibition.

4 ☐ Melanie is embarrassed about not going by car.

5 ☐ Roger understands why Melanie doesn't want to go by car.

6 ☐ Melanie criticises Roger for not knowing that Wayne has taken the brochures.

7 ☐ Melanie and Roger didn't want Mark to have a holiday.

8 ☐ Mark went to Germany before he went to Paris.

9 ☐ Roger knows Mark has a health problem.

10 ☐ Melanie couldn't afford to go to Majorca.

(10 marks)

2 **Listen to the sentences. Listen again and write them down. Then listen again and check.**

1 . . . .
. . . .
. . . .
. . . .

2 . . . .
. . . .
. . . .
. . . .

3 . . . .
. . . .
. . . .
. . . .

4 . . . .
. . . .
. . . .

5 . . . .
. . . .
. . . .
. . . .

(30 marks)

3 **Read the definitions 1–10 of wedding words. Fill in the gaps using the mixed up words in the Word Box.**

> derib ✓ redsnoocati heepsecs ottas
> mercyone varlitees tusges vinseryrana
> moberdirog strepnes pucole

Example: the woman who is getting married

. bride.

1 the two people who are getting married

. . . .

2 the people who are invited to the wedding

. . . .

3 the things the people who come to the wedding give to the man and woman for their new home

. . . .

4 the man who is getting married

. . . .

5 the serious part of the wedding when the man and woman are married, before the party

. . . .

6 members of the family

. . . .

7 flowers, balloons and ribbons which make the room where the party takes place look pretty

. . . .

8 the talks given at the party by the man who's got married, the woman's father and the best man

. . . .

9 the moment when people lift their glasses and drink to a happy future for the man and woman

. . . .

10 the same day the man and woman got married that they remember every year after the wedding

. . . .

(10 marks)

  Photocopiable

4 Fill in the gaps with reported sentences and questions.

1 "Are you hungry?"
She asked me . . . .

. . . .

2 "I'll come back tomorrow."
He said . . . .

. . . .

3 "I'm getting married," Mary said to her mother.
Mary told . . . .

. . . .

4 The teacher said to his pupils, "You must all pass your exams."
The teacher told . . . .

. . . .

5 "Where do you live?"
She asked me . . . .

. . . .

(5 marks)

5 Fill in the gaps with the correct linker in the Word Box.

because of   so   even though   in order to
otherwise   despite   so that   in case
in spite of the fact   because

1 He worked very hard . . . .
he could buy that expensive car.
2 . . . . that he has a
mobile phone, it's really difficult to contact him.
3 He missed the bus . . . .
he was late for work again!
4 . . . . he's rich and
handsome, she doesn't want to marry him.
5 Don't forget to take an umbrella with you
. . . . it rains.
6 . . . . working in a bank,
she's absolutely hopeless at dealing with money!
7 They didn't go and play golf on Saturday
. . . . the bad weather.
8 Give me back the money you stole from me
. . . . I'll call the police.
9 . . . . avoid the traffic, he got
up at four in the morning.
10 He couldn't call me . . . . he'd
forgotten his mobile phone.

(10 marks)

6 Fill in the gaps in the conversation with the correct verb / preposition in the Word Box.

Verbs   ring   turned   hung   look   took
get (x 2)   cut   went

Prepositions   through   down   up (x 4)
off (x 3)   with   back

RUPERT: What's the matter? Are you having a bad day?
JACK: Yes, I am. I'm fed . . . . (1)
. . . . (2) everything.
RUPERT: What's happened?
JACK: Well, first of all my mobile phone
. . . . (3) . . . . (4)
in the middle of an important meeting.
Then I was in the middle of writing an
important report and someone came into
the office and . . . . (5) my
computer . . . . (6) so I lost all my
work. Then I tried to . . . . (7)
Millie . . . . (8) at work but the
phone lines were busy so I couldn't
. . . . (9) . . . . (10) to
her and when I finally succeeded, I got
. . . . (11) . . . . (12) by
our stupid receptionist. The line went dead.
RUPERT: I know. She's new. So how are things going
with you and Millie these days?
JACK: Don't ask me. When I finally managed to
contact her company, the receptionist said
she was busy and . . . . (13)
. . . . (14) a message for her. She
said she'd ask Millie to . . . . (15)
. . . . (16) to me when she had
time but she didn't. In the end I rang again
and spoke to Millie. When I told her I
couldn't go out with her tonight but asked
her what she would like to do tomorrow
she . . . . (17) . . . . (18)
She didn't even say goodbye.
RUPERT: So what are you doing tomorrow night?
JACK: Nothing now it seems.
RUPERT: Come on! Here's the phone book.
. . . . (19) . . . . (20) the
number of the cinema. Let's go and see
that new comedy.
JACK: Good idea! It'll be a laugh!

(10 marks)

7 Fill in the gaps with the correct form of the verbs in brackets.

1 A: Can I speak to Melissa Harvey, please?
   B: Certainly. Who . . . ., please? (call)

2 A: I'm afraid Mr Potter is in a meeting at the moment. Can I take a message?
   B: Yes, please. Can you tell him that Jack Duggan . . . . (ring)

3 I wish I . . . . this job in London – I hate it. (not accept)

4 I ask him over and over again to come home on time but he . . . . to say that he'll be late. (always phone)

5 If you ask me, he . . . . an accident soon – he drives far too fast. (have)

6 This hat cost a lot and looks horrible. I shouldn't . . . . it. (buy)

7 He looked tanned and relaxed when I saw him. He . . . . back from Florida the Friday before. (come)

8 I . . . . to meet you if you'd sent me an e-mail. (not forget)

9 George, there's a cyclist ahead. Look out! You . . . . into him! (going to crash)

10 I know she's very interested in his paintings so she may well . . . . to the exhibition. (go)

(10 marks)

8 Fiona and Henry Tremaine have just got married. Read what five local women said about the chance of the marriage lasting. Order the comments and fill in the boxes with 1 (most certain it will last) to 5 (least certain it will last).

☐ ANNIE:
She's very pretty but I doubt if it'll last. Good looks don't last for ever you know.

☐ DORIS:
They'll probably be OK. They've known each other for a long time so they know each other's faults.

☐ BETTY:
Well, I'm sure it won't. She's far too rebellious to make a good wife.

☐ ELIZA:
Although I knew my Alf for ten years before I married him it didn't help me. Still, they might be OK.

☐ CONNIE:
But they're really good together. I think she's definitely chosen the right man for her.

(5 marks)

9 Tick one of the titles 1–3 and write about 100 words on the subject you've chosen.

1 ☐ A letter to a friend about a family wedding you went to
2 ☐ A letter to a friend about a disaster that happened to you
3 ☐ A magazine article about technology in the home ten years from now

. . . .
. . . .
. . . .
. . . .
. . . .
. . . .
. . . .
. . . .
. . . .

(10 marks)

1 **⊙⊙**89 **Read the statements. Then listen to Andrea and Tom's conversation. Tick the correct answers.**

Example: Yesterday Tom:
a) ☐ went out with Andrea
b) ☑ wanted to go out with Andrea
c) ☐ didn't want to go out with Andrea

1 Andrea's opinion of the new cinema is:
a) ☐ it's a waste of time going there
b) ☐ it's worth a visit
c) ☐ it's a let down

2 The film that Andrea went to see yesterday was:
a) ☐ an animated film
b) ☐ a horror film
c) ☐ an action film

3 Andrea thought that the film was:
a) ☐ predictable
b) ☐ gory
c) ☐ funny

4 The main character in the film has been:
a) ☐ released from prison
b) ☐ sentenced to prison
c) ☐ put in prison

5 The star of the TV series was:
a) ☐ Harrison Anderson
b) ☐ Craig Bridges
c) ☐ Craig Brown

6 Tom thinks that the film star:
a) ☐ didn't marry Julia Richards
b) ☐ married Julia Richards
c) ☐ divorced Julia Richards

7 The film took a long time to start because of:
a) ☐ trailers
b) ☐ advertisements
c) ☐ credits

8 The film was:
a) ☐ English with German subtitles
b) ☐ German with English subtitles
c) ☐ German with an English soundtrack

9 Andrea found the people in the cinema:
a) ☐ irritating
b) ☐ entertaining
c) ☐ shocking

10 The people throwing popcorn:
a) ☐ might have bought it at the cinema
b) ☐ can't have bought it at the cinema
c) ☐ didn't have to buy it at the cinema

(10 marks)

2 **Listen to the sentences. Listen again and write them down. Then listen again and check.**

1 ....
....
....
....

2 ....
....
....

3 ....
....
....

4 ....
....

5 ....
....
....

(30 marks)

3 **Read definitions 1–11. Match words / phrases in the two parts of the Word Box. Then fill in the gaps with the whole phrase.**

first ✓ against tying special
the scene of go travelling breaking
taking it queue forging
class ✓ effects the speed limit
the crime light a signature easy
the knot the law ahead jumping

1 of very good quality first-class

2 where a bad thing is done ....

3 a phrase giving permission ....

4 going without much luggage ....

5 driving faster than is allowed ....

6 getting married ....

7 not legal ....

8 relaxing ....

9 not waiting for your turn ....

10 illegally copying someone's name ....

11 pictures and sounds in a film ....

(10 marks)

Photocopiable

4 **Read the sentences and fill in the gaps with the correct word in the Word Box.**

> illegal   annoying   charming   selfish
> anti-social   romantic   cool   impressive
> bad-mannered   violent

1 Please don't keep kicking the back of my seat while I'm driving. It's very . . . .
2 She's very . . . . She never asks if anyone would like one of her sweets.
3 I wish my husband was as . . . . as Maria's. He buys her flowers every weekend.
4 I don't know why he's so . . . . He never comes to parties or goes out with friends.
5 I hate these . . . . films. Why do they have to have so much fighting in them?
6 Take your ID with you everywhere because it's . . . . to travel in that country without it.
7 Did you see the James Bond lookalike in his dark glasses? He thinks he's so . . . .
8 That woman is so . . . . I've never heard her say please or thank you.
9 What a . . . . girl. She's so polite and always smiling.
10 He passed all his exams with A grades. That's very . . . . !

(5 marks)

5 **Five of the sentences are correct and five aren't. Put a tick (✓) or cross (✗) in the boxes. Correct the sentences that are wrong.**

Example: ☒ It's bad manners point at people.
It's bad manners to point at people.

1 ☐ Look – the stuntman's got a broken leg! He can have had an accident.

. . . .

2 ☐ He spends his whole money on videos.

. . . .

3 ☐ She's in hospital because she got knocked down yesterday.

. . . .

4 ☐ A: Aren't you supposed to be at school?
B: Yes, I am but don't tell my mum!

. . . .

5 ☐ He apologised not coming sooner.

. . . .

6 ☐ During the college riot last week every student was arrested.

. . . .

7 ☐ Is it all right if I am borrowing your newspaper?

. . . .

8 ☐ Would you mind if I open the window?

. . . .

9 ☐ That new Chinese film has been dubbed into English.

. . . .

10 ☐ He promised her a lot of money for doing just one scene in the film.

. . . .

(10 marks)

6 **Write correct sentences.**

Example: She / wasn't / said / bad / it / load / that / rubbish / it / a / was / but / of.
She said it was a load of rubbish but it wasn't that bad.

1 It's / trap / a / I / bother / there / tourist / so / going / wouldn't.
It's . . . .
. . . .

2 I'm / sorry / you / but / I / your / bother / to / could / phone / use?
I'm . . . .
. . . .

3 The / audience / in / the / isn't / sit / aisle / supposed / to.
The . . . .
. . . .

4 The / blockbuster / film's / based / a / is / on / novel / screenplay.
The. . . . .
. . . .

5 It's / breathtaking / in / a / which / scenery / musical / is / set.
It's . . . .
. . . .

(5 marks)

7 **Read what Stella, Oliver and Pat say about their holidays. Fill in the table with the correct words / phrases in the Word Box.**

> off the beaten track ✓   on a budget ✓
> package holiday by air   seeing the sights
> a rip-off   it's worth every penny   chilling out
> a holiday romance   getting away from it all
> backpacking round Europe   exploring
> it was a tourist trap

	1 Stella	2 Oliver	3 Pat
Type of holiday	off the beaten track		
Main activity			
Cost		on a budget	
Best / worst thing			

2 Oliver

Well, you know — it's what most students do, isn't it? I'd saved up a bit of extra money by working in the holidays so two friends and I made a list of all the cities that we wanted to visit and off we went. We saw all the famous places — I thought Paris was the most beautiful. We worked out how much money we'd need each day so we found the cheapest places to sleep and moved on when we felt like it. We ended up with just enough to get home but we wouldn't have managed without the friendly people we met in every country we travelled through — especially this really lovely girl I met at the Eiffel Tower. She was what made the holiday so special and she's coming to see me in London this weekend . . .

1 Stella

It was something I'd always wanted to do — go into the rain forests of Brazil — and I got the chance last year. A friend of mine saw the brochure and she invited me to go with her. It was such an adventure — we didn't know where we were going — actually I don't think the guide knew where we were going either some of the time. We kept finding all sorts of things that weren't on the map! I would never have gone if my friend hadn't asked me. Although I didn't feel frightened I suppose it was a bit dangerous really. It was quite expensive too, but I don't regret the money at all — I'm so glad I went. Some people never get the chance to make a journey like that. Maybe I won't again. It was a once in a lifetime experience — I loved being away from everything and everyone for a while.

3 Pat

I'd been so busy at work that the idea of just lying in the sun really appealed to me. I didn't want to have to do anything — just get to the airport and let someone else organise it all for me. So that's what I did. From the time I left Heathrow to the day I came back one week later, I didn't do a thing. I didn't even get my own drinks — a waiter brought them to me by the pool. Unfortunately, I wasn't told about all the extras you have to pay when you stay in a really smart hotel — they were far too expensive and really not worth it. My friend Sue had two weeks in Cyprus for the same amount of money. The other big letdown was that the reception area was crowded with souvenir shoppers during the day and the bar was full of people from other hotels who came to see the shows in the evening.

(10 marks)

Photocopiable

8 Read sentences 1a)–10a). Then finish sentences 1b)–10b) so that they mean the same. Follow the instructions for each group of sentences (1–3, 4–6 and 7–10).

Example: How about going to Paris for a long weekend in April?
Why don't we go to Paris for a long weekend in April?

Write sentences in the Passive using the correct form of the verb *be*.

1 a) Someone has broken into the top-secret government building.

b) The top-secret government building

....

2 a) The police are going to interview the witness tomorrow afternoon.

b) The witness ....

....

3 a) Somebody must stop these terrible riots immediately.

b) These terrible riots ....

....

Write sentences using *must, can't* or *might*.

4 a) I think he's coming but I'm not sure.

b) He ....

....

5 a) His car's there so I'm sure he hasn't left yet.

b) He ....

....

6 a) He was holding the knife so I'm sure he did it.

b) He ....

....

Report the sentences.

7 a) "Don't worry, I'll be there on time."

b) He promised.........................

....

8 a) "I'm sorry I'm late."

b) She apologised ....

....

9 a) "Please come to the cinema with me, Flo."

b) She wanted ....

....

10 a) "Would you like my ticket, Mike?"

b) He offered ....

....

(10 marks)

9 Tick one of the titles 1–3 and write about 100 words on the subject you've chosen.

1 ☐ A holiday venue or sightseeing attraction you'd recommend
2 ☐ A film you disliked
3 ☐ A crime or offence you've heard about or experienced

....

....

....

....

....

....

....

....

....

(10 marks)

Instructions

Timing

- Each Progress test takes about 1½ hours and has 9 exercises. Exercise 1 is a listening, Exercise 2 is a dictation and each take about 10 minutes. Exercises 3–8 take about 55 minutes. Exercise 9 is a writing activity and takes about 15 minutes.
- You could do Exercises 1 and 2 at the beginning of the test and Exercise 9 at the end or you could do these exercises at different times from the rest of the test if you want.

Before class

- Photocopy the relevant Progress test. Note that Progress test Units 10–12 has 4 pages.
- Make sure you've got the appropriate recording ready to play.

Dictations

- Check punctuation with the class, e.g. *full stop,* etc.
- Read the sentences at a normal speed with natural rhythm and weak forms. Students listen for general meaning.
- Read them again, breaking them up into phrases as shown and giving the punctuation. Students write them down.
- Read the sentences again at normal speed. Students check.

Listening tests

- The listening test recordings (oo 86–89) are at the end of Cassette 2. Tell students they'll hear the recording twice. Give students time to read the information. Play the recording. Students write answers. Play it again. Students check.

Key to Progress test Units 1–3 (100 marks)

1 oo86 For each correct answer, 1 mark. (10 marks)

1 = F   2 = T   3 = T   4 = F   5 = F   6 = F   7 = T
8 = T   9 = T   10 = F

Recording script

STEVE: Hiya, Mandy.
MANDY: Oh, hi. How was the holiday?
STEVE: Great thanks. Sorry – I'm already late! I'll tell you about it on Monday.
MANDY: OK. Bye!
SARAH: Who was that?
MANDY: Steve Jones.
SARAH: What? Not *the* Steve Jones – Rebecca's new boyfriend?
MANDY: Old boyfriend you mean.
SARAH: You're joking. Already? I thought she was madly in love with him. What happened?
MANDY: She says that they've got nothing in common. Oh you know what she's like.
SARAH: Oh yes – she's crazy. He looks absolutely wonderful to me! And how do you know him? Did Rebecca introduce him to you?
MANDY: No, he's a colleague.
SARAH: Really? I didn't know that. Have you known him a long time?
MANDY: Yeah. For about five years. He used to come to the tennis club as well.
SARAH: Oh yes, of course. The tennis club. I'd forgotten about that. You go there a lot, don't you? Do you still play in the team?
MANDY: Not any longer. I'm so busy at work and it takes too much time in the evenings and at the weekend.
SARAH: Uh-huh? . . . Anyway, speaking of clubs, what are we going to do in town tonight? I've bought a new dress and I want to wear it. Shall we go to that new club in Romford Street? You know, the one by the traffic lights?
MANDY: I went there last Saturday.
SARAH: Oh yeah? What did you think of it? Was it any good?
MANDY: Well, it's very beautiful to look at – really smart, very modern and elegant but – we didn't stay long.
SARAH: Why not?
MANDY: It was really packed and noisy and the people didn't seem very friendly.
SARAH: Noisy? My sister said that it was really cosy and relaxed. But then she went on Wednesday night so maybe it wasn't so crowded.
MANDY: Maybe not . . . So, come on Sarah, what do you think? If you don't want to go to the club . . . why don't we see a film . . . or go to the pub?
SARAH: I'd rather see a film than go to the pub if that's OK with you.
MANDY: Yeah, fine. And then maybe we could have a snack later on in the evening if we get hungry. I'll meet you at the bus stop at about seven, unless you can get your dad to lend us his car.
SARAH: Oh, no chance, I'm afraid. He's working in north London at the moment and he isn't getting home until about ten at night.
MANDY: Oh, right. Oh, poor thing. He must be really tired. Oh, well. See you later then.
SARAH: Um, see ya.

2 For each totally correct sentence, 6 marks. Take off half a mark for each incorrect spelling, missing word or word out of order. Minimum mark = 0 for each sentence. (30 marks)

1 What an absolutely / fantastic city! / There are so many / fashionable stores / and lively places to visit.
2 My colleague / has been there a lot / and he told me / that the people / were impatient and unfriendly.
3 But almost everyone we met / was chatty and out-going. / We made new acquaintances everywhere / – on the subway, / in elevators and in the street.
4 I was terrified / when we stood / at the top of the tallest building. / The skyscrapers were enormous.
5 I feel exhausted / but I want to go back soon. / I used to think / England was cosy and traditional. / Now it just seems tiny and boring.

3 For each correct answer, 1 mark. (10 marks)

1 was driving   2 many   3 Have you been
4 was   5 rains   6 'm living   7 is   8 'm going
9 're leaving   10 don't like

4 For each correct answer, 1 mark. (5 marks)

1 = who   2 = where   3 = which   4 = which
5 whose

5 For each pair of sentences matched correctly, half a mark. For each correct question (even if students didn't match it correctly), 1 mark. (15 marks)

2 = e)   3 = h)   4 = b)   5 = a)   6 = i)   7 = c)
8 = k)   9 = g)   10 = j)   11 = d)

2 Have you ever visited Iceland?
3 When did you finish your university course?
4 Are you going to eat that sandwich?
5 How about going to the cinema this evening?
6 Shall we play tennis this / next / at the weekend?
7 My sister's marrying / going to marry a millionaire next Saturday.
8 My parents lived in California for three years in the 1990s.
9 Do you like Madonna's music?
10 He's crazy, isn't he?
11 What were you doing when you hurt your head?

6 For each correct answer, half a mark. Don't insist on the correct syllable division. (5 marks)

1 <u>foun</u>tain   2 <u>road</u> sign   3 ca<u>thed</u>ral   4 <u>mis</u>erable
5 <u>in</u>teresting   6 self-<u>con</u>fident   7 tech<u>niques</u>
8 im<u>prove</u>   9 <u>man</u>age   10 <u>fash</u>ionable

7 For each correct answer, half a mark. (5 marks)

for: three weeks, a few days   **ago:** three weeks, a few days   **since:** 10th January, we got married, 1997, Tuesday   **on:** 10th January, Tuesday

8 For each correct answer, one mark. (10 marks)

1 depend   2 tidy   3 work   4 keep   5 deal   6 get
7 fall   8 meet   9 wind   10 start

9 Give marks according to your students' general ability and the use they make of the structures / vocabulary from Units 1–3. (10 marks)

Key to Progress test Units 4–6   (100 marks)

1 87 For each correct answer, 1 mark. Accept any of the possible answers given. Don't insist on correct spelling. (15 marks)

	1 Emily	**2 Josh**	**3 Helen**
Present job	librarian	musician	architect
Good at	dealing with people	being dependable / available	being creative
Problem with the job	working hours	no job security	too stressful / too much pressure / demanding clients
Perks of the job	can borrow as many books as you like for as long as you like	can hear beautiful music / free concerts	wonderful colleagues / team / annual bonuses
Future plans	applied for job in opera house library	wants to teach music in a school	doesn't know / have a holiday

Recording script

1 NEIL: Hello, Emily. I haven't seen you for a long time. How's your job going?
EMILY: Oh, hi, Neil. Not very well, I'm afraid.
NEIL: I am surprised. What's the problem? The people and the place are OK, aren't they?
EMILY: Oh, yes.

NEIL: Well, isn't the salary very good or something?
EMILY: No, it's not that.
NEIL: What then? You're so good at dealing with people. I would have thought that it was the ideal job for you.
EMILY: Well it is ideal from that point of view and I love the fact that I can borrow as many books as I like for as long as I like. You know how much I love reading. No, the problem is the time really. I have to work in the evenings and at weekends and apart from Sundays, we're open every day of the week.
NEIL: Oh, I see. So what are you going to do?
EMILY: Well, I've applied for a job in the opera house library. It's just for the use of the people who work there and it's open for normal office hours only.
NEIL: Well, let me know how you get on. I'll buy you a drink if you get it!
EMILY: Thanks, Neil. I will.
2 JOSH: I've been interested in music all my life. I started playing when I was at my first school. I think I get a lot of work because orchestra managers know that they can depend on me – I try to be available for them and don't ring them up at the last moment and say I can't play. And, of course, I get to hear some of the most beautiful music in the world for free at the concerts I'm playing in. But I'm thirty-five now with a young family and there really isn't much job security so I need to do something else as well. Which is why I'm here today. I've taught a lot of children in the past and I think that I could make the children in this school really enthusiastic about music. And I could still get to play in concerts in the long summer holidays.

3 MR SNOW: Helen! You wanted to see me.

HELEN: Yes, Mr Snow. I've decided to leave the company and I wanted to tell you first.

MR SNOW: That's bad news for us, Helen. You know how much we think of you. It'll be hard to find someone else who's as creative as you are. The new housing development you designed last year was a great success.

HELEN: That's very kind of you to say so. I'll miss working here in this wonderful team of people – and I'll miss the annual bonuses.

MR SNOW: So – can I ask – have you found a better job?

HELEN: No, it's not that. I just feel that this job gets more and more stressful. Clients are becoming more and more demanding. They want the designs for their buildings too quickly these days and they want to spend less and less money. It's putting me under too much pressure. I'm afraid of making mistakes.

MR SNOW: Yes. I know what you mean. So what are you going to do?

HELEN: I don't know yet. Have a long holiday and then think about it when I get back.

MR SNOW: OK, Helen. Well, I wish you all the best. You know we'll miss you.

HELEN: Thanks, Mr Snow. I'll miss it here, too.

2 For each totally correct sentence, ½ marks. Take off half a mark for each incorrect spelling, missing word or word out of order. Minimum mark = 0 for each sentence. (30 marks)

1 He felt he was a terrible failure / but he created some impressive work / before his death in 1995.
2 In your letter of application / you say that you could be / available for interview / at our convenience.
3 She's really hopeless / at choosing clothes. / She'd look much better / in a plain dress / rather than / those tight flared trousers / and that patterned shirt.
4 He must be talented. / He's responsible / for all the museum's exhibitions / and they're always successful.
5 Would you wear pale make-up / and shave your eyebrows / in the name of beauty / or just be yourself / and look unfashionable?

3 For each correct answer, 1 mark. (10 marks)

1 Dear 2 advertisement 3 as 4 responsibilities / duties 5 actors / performers 6 present / current 7 dealing / working 8 under 9 enclose 10 hearing

4 For each answer, half a mark for correctly identifying whether the sentence is correct or incorrect. 1 mark for correcting each incorrect sentence. (10 marks)

1 ✗ The tin's empty! How many biscuits have you eaten this morning? 2 ✓ 3 ✓ 4 ✓ 5 ✗ If I were / was taller, I'd ask her to go out with me. 6 ✓ 7 ✗ It's ten o'clock! What have you been doing for the last three hours? 8 ✓ 9 ✗ He opened a gallery to exhibit his friends' sculptures. 10 ✗ After trying for many years he was able to get / managed to get / succeeded in getting a job at the opera house.

5 For each correct answer, 1 mark. (5 marks)

1 patterned 2 tight / plain / short 3 checked 4 polo-neck 5 pin-striped / striped

6 For each correct answer, 1 mark. (5 marks)

1 Skin Deep 2 Heat Wave 3 The Genius 4 Famous and Free 5 Murder in the Gallery

7 For each correct answer, 1 mark. (10 marks)

1 = d) 2 = b) 3 = b) 4 = c) 5 = d) 6 = b)
7 = a) 8 = d) 9 = c) 10 = a)

8 For each correct answer, half a mark. (5 marks)

advertising executive (box), agency (gap); librarian (box), shelf (gap); architect (box), skyscraper (gap); artist (box), masterpiece (gap); stand-up comic (box), joke (gap)

9 Give marks according to your students' general ability and the use they make of the structures / vocabulary from Units 4–6. (10 marks)

Key to Progress test Units 7–9   (100 marks)

1 🔊88 For each correct answer, 1 mark. (10 marks)

1 = F 2 = F 3 = T 4 = T 5 = T 6 = T 7 = F
8 = F 9 = F 10 = T

Recording script

MELANIE: Melanie Williams.
ROGER: Hello, Melanie. It's Roger.
MELANIE: Oh, hang on. I'll just go to the other phone. OK?
ROGER: Sure.
MELANIE: Sorry about that.
ROGER: That's OK. I'm just calling to see if you need any help with the exhibition next week.

MELANIE: Thanks. I may well do, although things are going quite well at the moment.
ROGER: OK. No problem. I'm going there myself on Saturday evening. You're going to travel down there on Friday, aren't you?
MELANIE: That's right. I've got a friend who lives nearby so we're going to spend the evening together. I haven't seen her for years so it's a good chance to meet.
ROGER: That's nice. And how are you getting there? By car?
MELANIE: No, by air. I don't want to drive all that way by myself. I know that I'm a wimp but that motorway is just so busy, especially on Fridays.
ROGER: I see what you mean.

MELANIE: Is an air ticket going to be too expensive for the company?

ROGER: As far as I'm concerned, the most important thing is that you arrive relaxed and ready for a busy week. But, hold on! What about all those thousands of advertising brochures we need?

MELANIE: Don't you read your e-mails? Wayne took those down yesterday in the company car. You should have seen him. He couldn't see out of the windows!

ROGER: Why did Wayne take them?

MELANIE: So that I could let Mark have a holiday. He hasn't had one for about nine months, has he?

ROGER: That's true. I know he works really hard.

MELANIE: Last week he drove to Germany the morning after he'd been in Paris for the day. I don't know how he does it.

ROGER: I know. I'm always telling him to take it easier. He's not a young man any more. He'll have a heart attack if he's not careful.

MELANIE: Well, he's in Majorca now so that's OK. I wish I was there. He invited me to go too.

ROGER: So why didn't you?

MELANIE: I would have done if I'd had enough money.

ROGER: Oh, well. We're having a few days in France next month.

MELANIE: Yes, but it won't be a holiday exactly, will it?

2 For each totally correct sentence, 6 marks. Take off half a mark for each incorrect spelling, missing word or word out of order. Minimum mark = 0 for each sentence. (30 marks)

1 The professor said / that there was definitely / going to be an explosion / in the number of gadgets / we'd be able to buy.

2 If only my father / had given me more independence, / I might not have rebelled so much.

3 It's difficult to believe / that only twelve years before, / a scientist predicted / that we'd never reach the moon.

4 I'm sorry. / I didn't recognise your voice. / Hold the line. / Mr White is expecting your call.

5 There was an e-mail / from my lawyer's secretary / saying that the meeting had been cancelled. / She's so efficient.

3 For each correct answer, 1 mark. (10 marks)

1 couple 2 guests 3 presents 4 bridegroom
5 ceremony 6 relatives 7 decorations
8 speeches 9 toast 10 anniversary

4 For each correct answer, 1 mark. If only the verb in bold is correct, half a mark. (5 marks)

1 She asked me if I **was** hungry.   2 He said (that) he **would come / go** back the next day / the day after.
3 Mary told her mother (that) she **was getting** married.   4 The teacher told his pupils (that) they **had to** pass their exams.   5 She asked me where I **lived**.

5 For each correct answer, 1 mark. (10 marks)

1 so that 2 In spite of the fact 3 so 4 Even though
5 in case 6 Despite 7 because of 8 otherwise
9 In order to 10 because

6 For each correct answer, half a mark. (10 marks)

1 up 2 with 3 went 4 off 5 turned 6 off
7 ring 8 up 9 get 10 through 11 cut 12 off
13 took 14 down 15 get 16 back 17 hung
18 up 19 look 20 up

7 For each correct answer, 1 mark. (10 marks)

1 's / is calling 2 rang 3 hadn't / had not accepted
4 's / is always phoning 5 'll / will have 6 have bought 7 'd / had come 8 wouldn't / would not / might not have forgotten 9 're / are going to crash
10 go

8 For each correct answer, 1 mark. (5 marks)

Annie = 4 **Betty** = 5 **Connie** = 1 **Doris** = 2
Eliza = 3

9 Give marks according to your students' general ability and the use they make of the structures / vocabulary from Units 7–9. (10 marks)

Key to Progress test Units 10–12   (100 marks)

1 ◠◠89 For each correct answer, 1 mark. (10 marks)

1 = b) 2 = c) 3 = b) 4 = b) 5 = b) 6 = b)
7 = a) 8 = c) 9 = a) 10 = b)

Recording script

TOM: Oh, hi, Andrea. How are you? I tried to phone you last night to see if you wanted to go out for a pizza but you weren't in.

ANDREA: No, that's right. We went to the new cinema in Oldford.

TOM: Oh yeah. What's it like? I've heard it's very expensive.

ANDREA: Well, it isn't that expensive but I suppose it costs more than the other cinemas round here.

TOM: And it's a long way to go.

ANDREA: Yes, it is. But it's such an unusual building. The foyer's decorated like a scene from King Kong. You have to go just for that.

TOM: And what film did you see? Was it that one where all the coffins open in the middle of the night?

ANDREA: Oh, you mean *The Bodies?* I saw that with my friend last week. I spent most of the time under the seat! No this was called *The Wrong Man*. You never knew what was going to happen next so it was very exciting but there was a bit too much blood in it for me.

TOM: I think Kevin told me about it. Does the guy get sent to prison for his wife's murder?

ANDREA: Well, he's been found guilty and he's on the way to prison when the train he's travelling on gets wrecked and he escapes. But the thing is that he didn't do it anyway so he's trying to find the person who did before he's caught again.

TOM: Oh, wasn't there a series like that on the TV with Craig Brown in it?

ANDREA: Craig Bridges you mean? Yes, there was but the guy in the film is Harrison Anderson.

TOM: Didn't he marry Julia Richards?

ANDREA: Yeah, that's right.

TOM: So, you had a good time then.

ANDREA: Not really.

TOM: Why was that?

ANDREA: Well, first of all it took a long time to start.

TOM: Oh, I know. The ads go on for ages, don't they?

ANDREA: Oh, they were OK but the stuff about future films went on and on and on and then when it finally started it was dubbed into English from German and I always find that hard work.

TOM: Yeah, me too.

ANDREA: And then some idiots were throwing popcorn from the back row for half the evening. I felt quite fed up by the end.

TOM: Really? Didn't the ushers stop them?

ANDREA: Hmm, they didn't know it was happening. You see, you're not supposed to take food into that new cinema – there's none for sale in the foyer so I suppose they brought it from home and hid it under their coats.

TOM: Oh you see! You should have come for a pizza with me!

ANDREA: Yeah, you're right!

2 For each totally correct sentence, 6 marks. Take off half a mark for each incorrect spelling, missing word or word out of order. Minimum mark = 0 for each sentence. (30 marks)

1 This science fiction fantasy / was beautifully directed. / The script was realistic / and the stunts were excellent.

2 He *might* have told me / there was a virus / hibernating in my computer. / I can't remember. / Anyway, / it's wrecked my report.

3 Hasn't the man / who's been arrested for forgery / already been in prison / for fraud, fiddling expenses / and shoplifting?

4 Go ahead! / You can try to switch it on if you like / but it's not worth it. / The whole town's had a power cut.

5 The critics warned / that it was the usual low budget rubbish: / a romance and a car chase / with an awfully predictable script.

3 For each correct answer, 1 mark. (10 marks)

2 the scene of the crime   3 go ahead   4 travelling light   5 breaking the speed limit   6 tying the knot 7 against the law   8 taking it easy   9 queue-jumping 10 forging a signature   11 special effects

4 For each correct answer, half a mark. (5 marks)

1 annoying   2 selfish   3 romantic   4 anti-social 5 violent   6 illegal   7 cool   8 bad-mannered 9 charming   10 impressive

5 For each answer, half a mark for correctly identifying whether the sentence is correct or incorrect. 1 mark for correcting each incorrect sentence. (10 marks)

1 ✗ He **must** have had an accident.   2 ✗ He spends **all his** money on videos.   3 ✓   4 ✓   5 ✗ He apologised **for** not coming sooner.   6 ✓   7 ✗ Is it all right if I **borrow** your newspaper?   8 ✗ Would you mind if I **opened** the window?   9 ✓   10 ✓

6 For each correct answer, 1 mark. If the answer is almost correct, half a mark. (5 marks)

1 It's a tourist trap so I wouldn't bother going there. 2 I'm sorry to bother you but could I use your phone? 3 The audience isn't supposed to sit in the aisle. 4 The film's screenplay is based on a blockbuster novel.   5 It's a musical which is set in breathtaking scenery.

7 For each correct answer, 1 mark. (10 marks)

	1 Stella	2 Oliver	3 Pat
Type of holiday	off the beaten track	backpacking round Europe	package holiday by air
Main activity	exploring	seeing the sights	chilling out
Cost	it's worth every penny	on a budget	a rip-off
Best / worst thing	getting away from it all	a holiday romance	it was a tourist trap

8 For each totally correct answer, 1 mark. Half a mark if the tense of the Passive is correct in sentences 1–3; the choice of modal or the tense of the main verb is correct in sentences 4–6; the verb pattern is correct in sentences 7–10. (10 marks)

1b) The top-secret government building **has been broken** into.   **2b)** The witness **is going to be interviewed** by the police tomorrow afternoon / tomorrow afternoon by the police.   **3b)** These terrible riots must **be stopped** immediately.   **4b)** He **might** be coming.   **5b)** He **can't** have left yet (because his car's there).   **6b)** He **must** have done it (because he was holding the knife).   **7b)** He promised **to be** there / come on time.   **8b)** She apologised **for being** late. **9b)** She wanted Flo **to come / go** to the cinema (with her).   **10b)** He offered (**to give**) Mike his ticket. / He offered his ticket to Mike.

9 Give marks according to your students' general ability and the use they make of the structures / vocabulary from Units 10–12. (10 marks)

Pearson Education Limited
Edinburgh Gate
Harlow
Essex CM20 2JE
England
and Associated Companies throughout the world.

www.longman.com

First published 2001
Second impression 2004

ISBN 0 582 43868 3

Set in 11.5/13pt Bulldog

Printed in China
NPCC/02

Illustrated by Phil Healey.
Cover illustration by Tim Kahane.
The back cover photographs of the authors by Charles Yacoub.

Acknowledgements

The authors and publishers would like to thank Mike Carter and
Russell Stannard for reporting on the manuscript.

The Wavelength publishing team:

Jenny Colley (Publisher), Rose Wells (Editorial Assistant),
Jacqueline Brooks (Production Controller).

The publishers would particularly like to thank Stephen Thompson,
Jennifer Parsons, Carolyn Jones, Ruth Atkinson, Andrew Jones,
Brigit Viney and Shona Rodger for their work on this Teacher's
Resource Book.

We are grateful to the Hal Leonard Corporation for permission
to reproduce the lyrics from "It Should Have Been Me" by
Norman Whitfield and William Stevenson.